I0810627

IMAGES
of America

GRANTS-MILAN

On the Cover: According to the information received, the cover photograph was taken on the Fourth of July in the early 1970s with members of the Civil Air Patrol marching in the parade. The Royal Café, in the background, was replaced by a steakhouse that was to the left in the photograph. The retail stores to the right were added to the café, and the rest of the block was the Encanto Court, which was converted to offices by the Sakalares family. (Courtesy of the Conklin family.)

IMAGES
of America

GRANTS-MILAN

Donald Jaramillo and Paul Milan

ARCADIA
PUBLISHING

ISBN 978-0-7385-9964-9

Published by Arcadia Publishing
Charleston, South Carolina

Printed in the United States of America

Library of Congress Control Number: 2013948885

For all general information, please contact Arcadia Publishing:
Telephone 843-853-2070
Fax 843-853-0044
E-mail sales@arcadiapublishing.com
For customer service and orders:
Toll-Free 1-888-313-2665

Visit us on the Internet at www.arcadiapublishing.com

This book is dedicated to the many persons who settled the area, from the Spaniards with their mission of seeking "Glory, God, and Gold" to the immigrants from many countries seeking jobs and a better life, the migrants from many states seeking homesteads and/or jobs during the boom eras of the railroad, the huge sheep and cattle ranches, the land grants, logging and mining, farming, and the Highway 66 Mother Road mystique. This book is for those who stayed after each bust and contributed to the recovery with the slogan "Grants always comes back, there is always something in the future for the area."

Contents

ACKNOWLEDGMENTS

Images of America: *Grants-Milan* is a project that was recommended by the members of the Cibola Historical Society. This project would not be possible without the help of the *Cibola Beacon* and its editor, Don Jaramillo, who agreed to be the coeditor of the book with Paul Milan, the society historian.

Many local citizens responded to the call for photographs and their stories. Thanks to the *Cibola Beacon* and Radio KMIN for the publicity that they provided, which led to a number of images. Although some of the photographs did not make it into the publication, we would like to acknowledge their contributors.

Aurelio Apodaca brought in a large part of his collection and had one of the largest collections of postcards of local businesses, especially the motels from the 1940s to the 1970s and other businesses that don't exist today. The Mark Elkins family shared a number of ranching and rodeo pictures. The *Cibola Beacon*; the Grants State Bank; the Quad; and the Cibola Arts Council, doing business as Double 66 Gallery, shared their collections. The Aragon family shared photographs of their homestead; Sherry Robinson shared from her collection; and the Milan family contributed photographs of the Milan Ranch, the village of Milan, and the Silvestre Mirabal family. Dora Fidel sent pictures of Sen. Joe Fidel, and the *Cibola Beacon* contributed photographs of Representatives Walter and Ken Martinez. Mid-Continent Airway beacon photographs were sent in by Steve Owen; he received them from Bill Bell, and they were taken by Jack Bell, Bill's father, in 1930–1931. The photograph of Paddy Martinez was sent in his granddaughter Leona Plaineagle. Other contributors include George Rodriguez, Ted Rowley, the Redden family, the Heath family, the US Forest Service, the US Bureau of Land Management, E.B. Dawson, the Freas family, the Manuel McBride Family, the Uranium Mining Museum, Grants Rodeo Association, and the Mount Taylor Quadrathlon and La Fiesta de Colores Committees.

Introduction

The city of Grants and the village of Milan are in between two mountain ranges: the majestic Mount Taylor to the north and the Zuni Mountains to the south. Mount Taylor is the second-highest mountain in New Mexico. The lava beds, evidence of the area's volcanic eruptions, were named "El Malpais" (the Badlands) by the Spaniards.

The Grants-Milan area developed because it was easy passage from east to west and provided a natural camping area for travelers. The first European to come into this area was the Spanish explorer Francisco Vasquez Coronado, following the Spaniards' quest for "Glory, God, and Gold" and seeking the Seven Cities of Gold (Cibola) in 1540. In 1581, a Franciscan brother, Fray Augustin Rodriguez, came to the area to build missions. In 1583, Antonio de Espejo explored the area seeking two Franciscan priests that he confirmed were killed. Espejo was the first to sign his name at the great rock called "El Morro," later named the "Inscription Rock" by the Americans. Travelers recorded their names and dates as they passed through the area, including the Spanish explorer Juan de Oñate, Edward Fitzgerald Beale and P. Gilmer Breckinridge of the camel expedition, and Native American petroglyphs. In 1680, the Pueblo Indians revolted and drove the Spaniards from New Mexico; the reconquest by Don Diego de Vargas was recorded at El Morro in 1692.

The Spaniards brought sheep, cattle, pigs, chickens, and horses to the area and established towns, land grants, and missions that led to the first boom in ranching. In the 1800s, cattle drives and oxen freighters traveled to Denver and Kansas City, connecting to the Santa Fe Trail for trade. Freighters from the area also traded in Chihuahua, Mexico. After the Mexican War of Independence, Mexico ruled the area from 1821 to 1846 and established more land grants in the area, and ranching continued to thrive. The Pueblo Indians and the local Spanish towns united to keep the Navajo, Apache, Ute, and Comanche from raiding. The Mexican-American War in 1846–1848 brought the US Army, which established Fort Wingate four miles south of Grants-Milan. Protection by the US Cavalry led to the establishment of the village of San Rafael and brought prosperity to the inhabitants selling supplies to the fort, along with gambling, bars, and perhaps brothels, creating a boom for the area. The moving of Fort Wingate 60 miles west created the first bust. The inhabitants of San Rafael received a patent for the village from the US government and established themselves in farming, ranching, and logging.

Originally, the railroad was surveyed to go through the Zuni Mountains, but the 1868 survey party took a trail that was 25 miles north of El Morro. In 1882, the townsite of Grants was granted to Jesus Blea by a US patent and was named "Los Alamitos" (Little Cottonwoods). The Grant brothers maintained a railroad construction camp, and travelers on stagecoach, oxcarts, and wagons traveling west would stop overnight at the Grant camp.

The railroad became a boom for the Grants-Milan area, making it easy to travel and to market livestock, timber, fluorspar, and vegetables up to the late 1950s. Each of these commodities resulted in their own boom and bust eras. The population of the area was increased by the Homestead

Act, which brought people from all areas of the country and from other countries. There were also Mormon settlements. The building of the Bluewater dam by the Mormons provided irrigation to their settlement and the Bluewater valley, giving birth to the truck farming boom. Large farming operations from California and Arizona took advantage of a superior local carrot, naming Grants the "Carrot Capital of the World."

Highway 66 brought travelers through the area; a large number of motels, restaurants, and gas stations were built to service the travelers. Although the interstate highway was built next to Grants-Milan, most of the tourist businesses on Highway 66 disappeared, with a few motels, service stations, and restaurants moving to the interchanges.

One

SURROUNDED BY WONDERS AND HISTORY

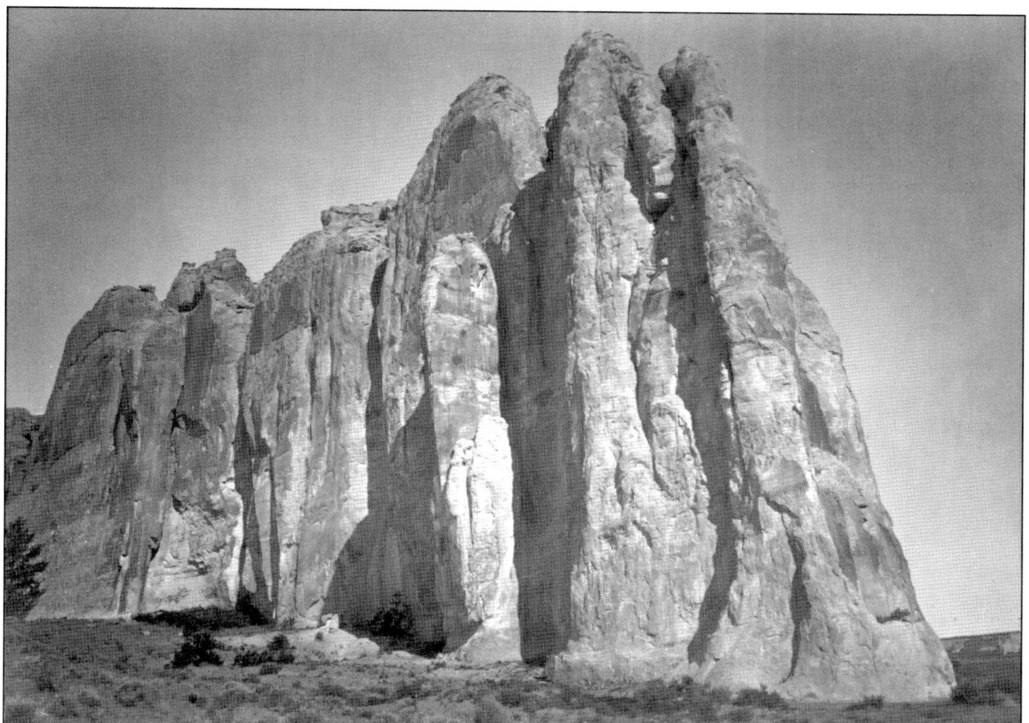

According to geologists and scholars, the portion of New Mexico now known as Cibola County shares in many of the prime interest eras of the creation of the Earth when a cataclysmic disturbance erupted some three billion years ago, hence Grants and Milan is surrounded by dormant volcanoes with the majestic Mount Taylor, second highest mountain in New Mexico, to create a magnificent landscape overlooking lava beds. In 1987, Pres. Ronald Reagan signed legislation creating El Malpais National Monument, which is home to 378,000 acres of lava rock, cinder cones, shield volcanoes, spatter cones, and trails. Pictured here is the southern side of Inscription Rock in 1873. (Photograph by Timothy O'Sullivan, courtesy of the National Park Service.)

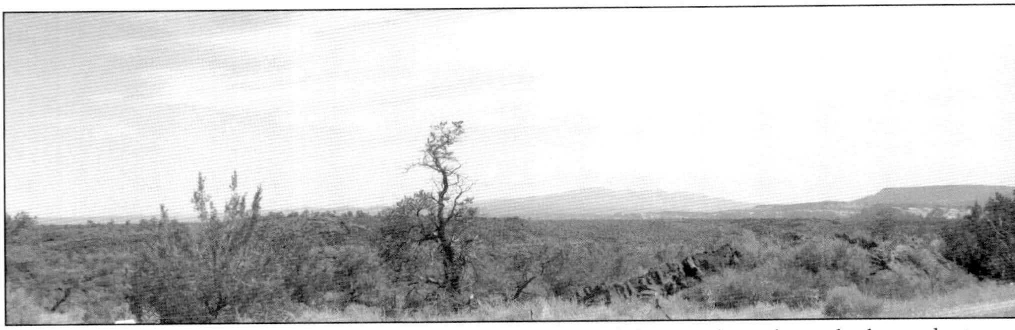

A traveler in this county would see traces of its history while traveling through the *malpais* and the petrified sea creatures and giant beasts that roamed the area millions of years ago. Within the area are the descendants of ancient peoples who continue to think and dress as did their fore-bearers and families and who trace their heritage to the Spanish conquests. Other residents fled European tyrannies, and still others escaped the Dust Bowl, came seeking treasures, or followed economic booms. Archeologists have found evidence that early man came to New Mexico 25,000 years ago. Local cultures included the Folsom, Sandia, and Anasazi, an advanced culture that lived in the area some 1,500 to 3,000 years ago and who developed a way of life and arts passed down to the Pueblo people, so named by the Spanish because they lived in villages. (Both, courtesy of the authors.)

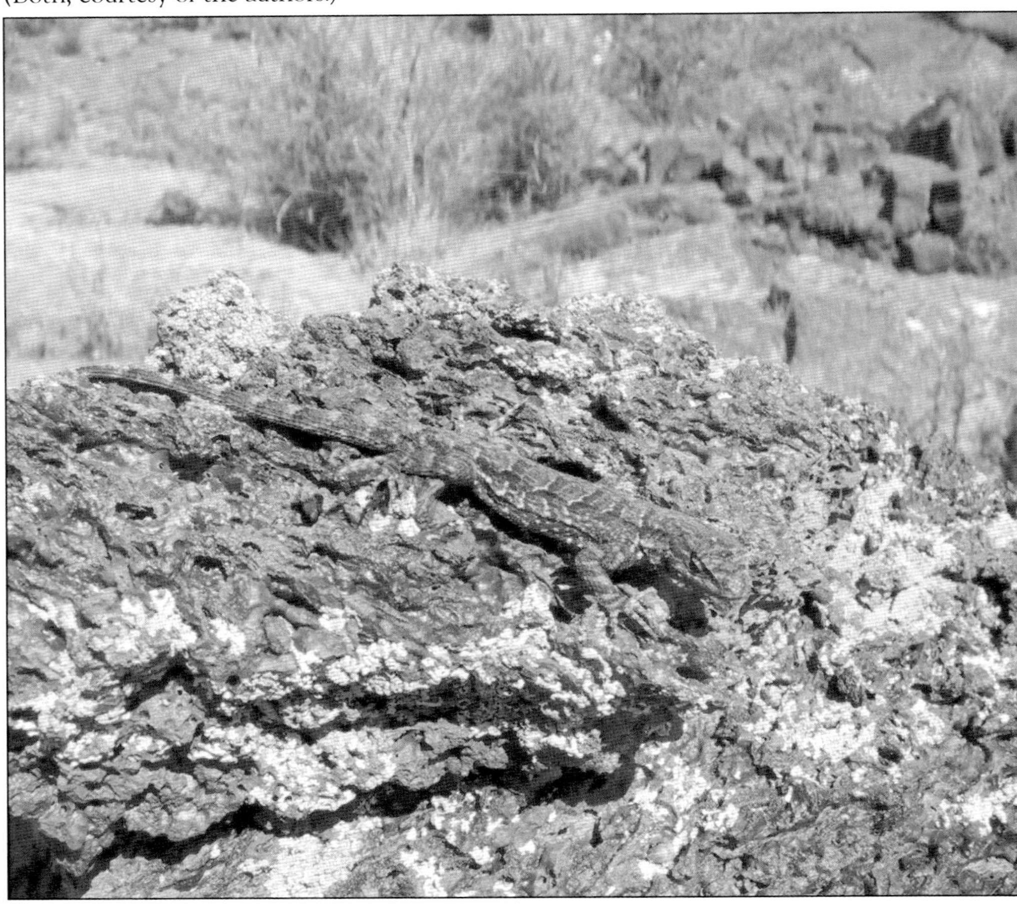

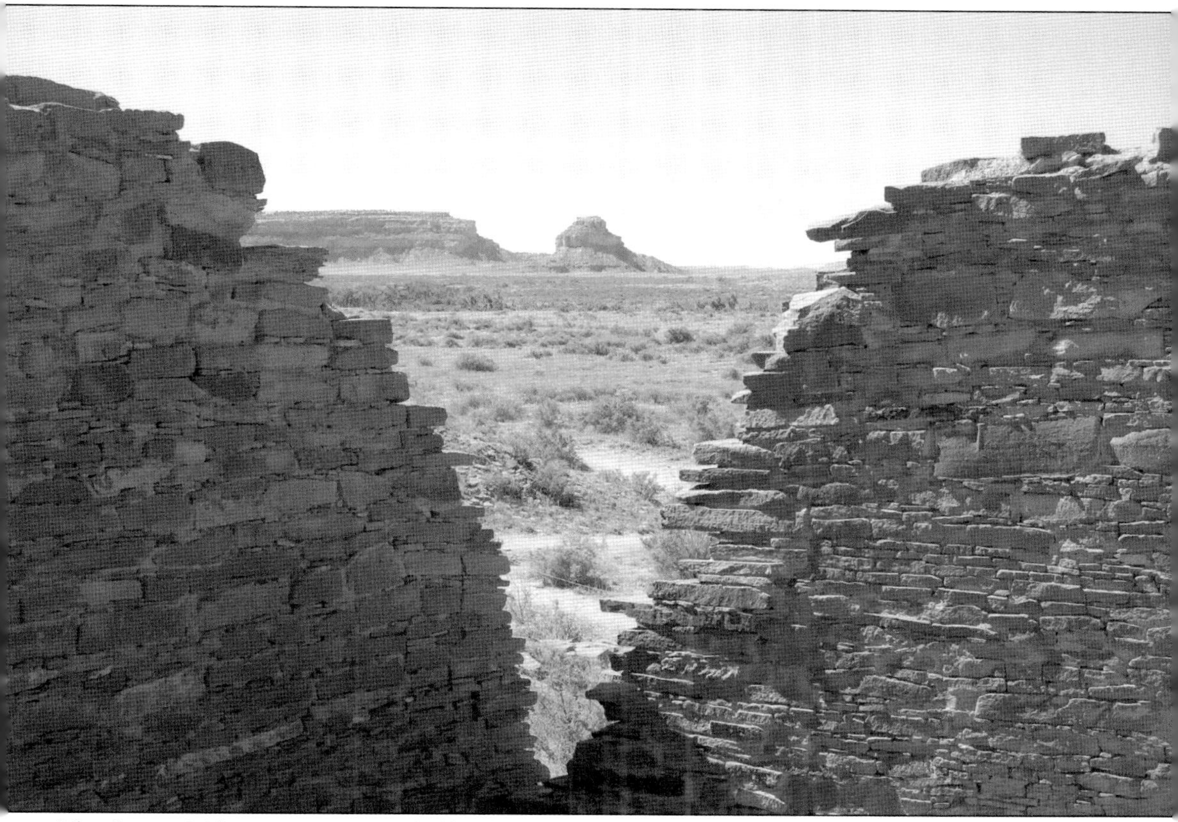

The Grants-Milan area is surrounded by the Laguna Pueblo and the Acoma Pueblo to the east and the Zuni Pueblo to the west. The Chaco Canyon ruins are also a national park. It was in this area that the Spaniards came in the 1500s, searching for the Seven Cities of Cibola. With their arrival, a different age and culture was introduced, adding another chapter to an already rich heritage. Grants, the seat of Cibola County, is defined by the Navajo and Pueblo peoples indigenous to the area. Spanish and Mexican land grants carved holdings, and US military installations such as Fort Wingate secured the area of change. The railroad established a trade route and influenced the rise and fall of economic adventures plus bringing a unique and diverse population. Pictured are the remains of an old pueblo. (Courtesy of the *Cibola Beacon*.)

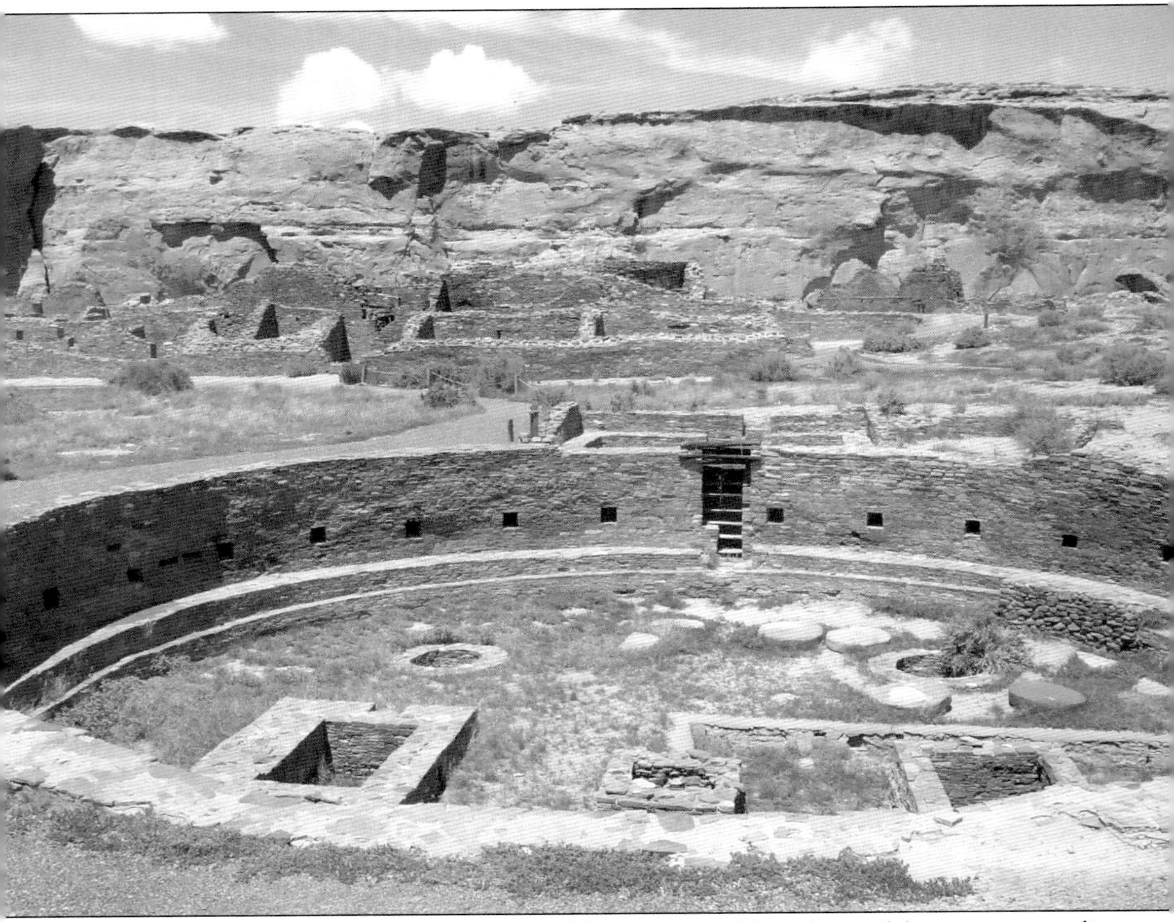

Communal dwellings built of rocks emerged from 800 to 1400, and one of the most outstanding centers in northwestern New Mexico was in Chaco Canyon. Twelve large communal dwellings of stone there represent the largest development of indigenous architecture in North America. The apartments were built from one to four stories in height. During the 1100s and 1200s, major migrations from the center took place without explanation. An accepted theory is the lack of water, and warlike tribes are also cited. Evidence shows that present-day Pueblos came from these migrations. (Courtesy of the *Cibola Beacon*.)

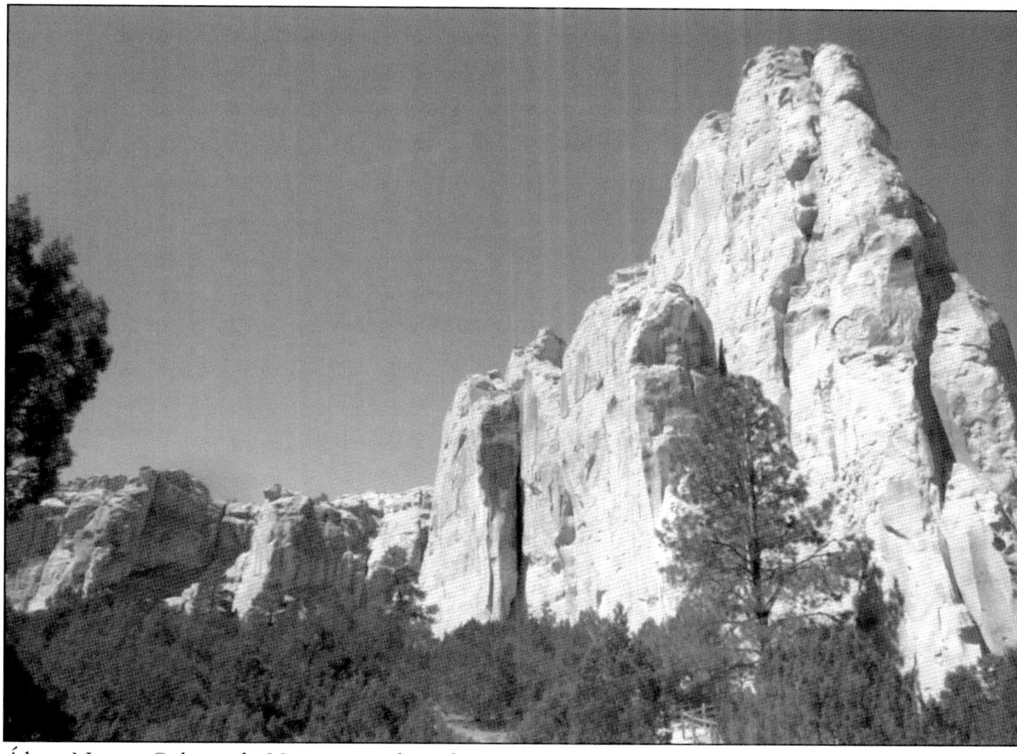

Álvar Núñez Cabeza de Vaca arrived in this area in 1536 with Esteban (the first black man to come to the Southwest), and Fray Marcos de Niza returned with Estaban in 1539, Coronado in 1540–1542, Rodriguez/Chamuscado in 1581, Espejo in 1582. Estaban was ultimately killed by the Zunis. In 1605, Don Juan de Oñate arrived and was the first traveler to inscribe his name on the famous El Morro cliff, now known as the Inscription Rock, which contains hundreds of names of travelers, including the inscriptions "Beale" and "Breckinridge," two men who carried out a camel experiment for the US Army in 1857. El Morro was designated a national monument in the early 1900s because it was evident that all of the inscriptions were of historical significance. (Both, courtesy of the National Park Service.)

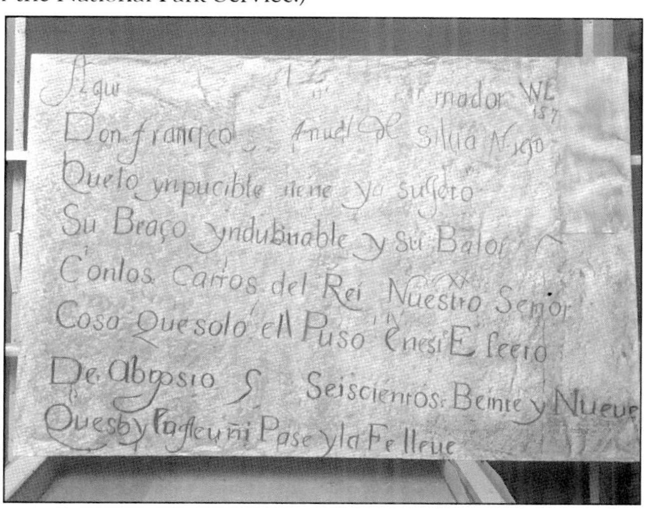

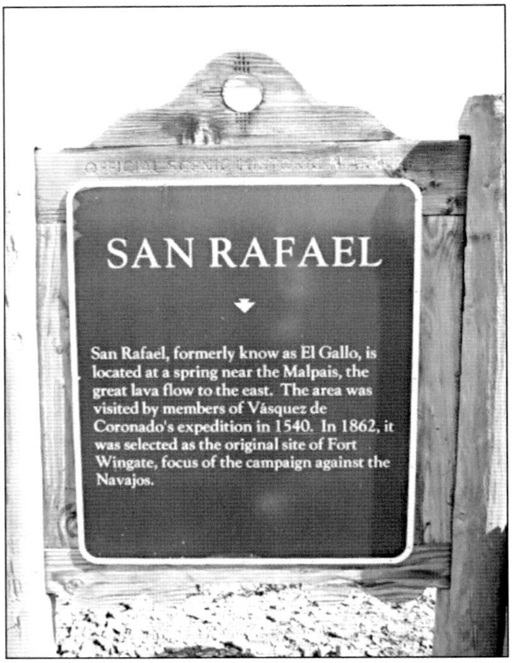

Grants and Milan are surrounded by several villages, land grants, and pueblos. The villages include San Rafael (above), San Mateo, San Fidel, and Seboyeta. The land grants include Seboyeta, Fernandez, and Cubero. The pueblos include Laguna, Acoma (below) and Zuni. The Navajo Nation is also a part of the Cibola County community. (Courtesy of the *Cibola Beacon*.)

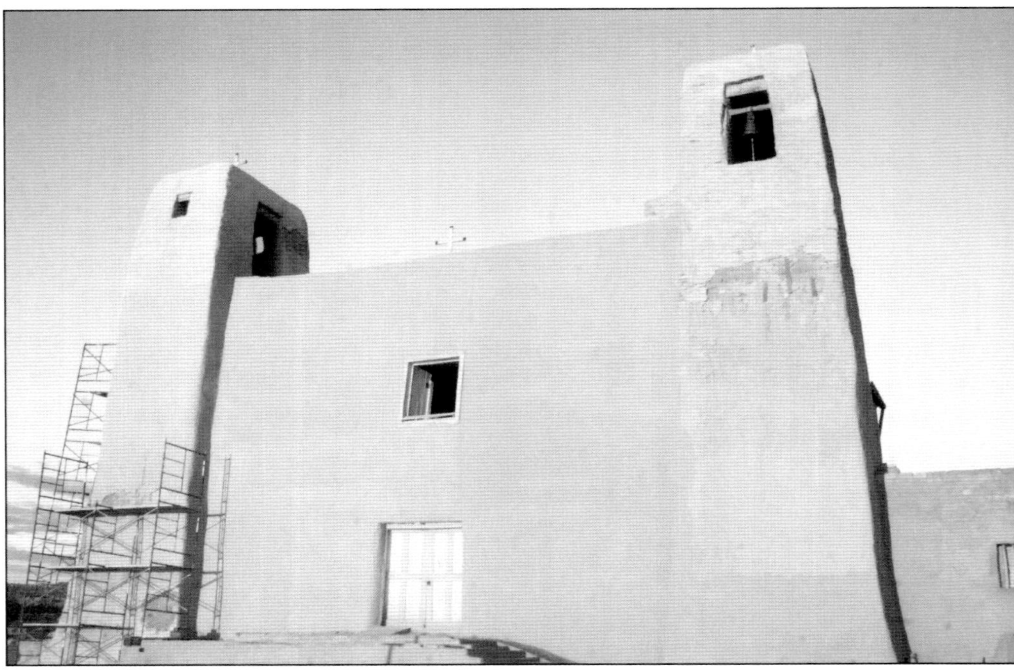

Acoma's San Esteban del Rey (St. Stephen the King) is thought to be the oldest Catholic edifice in the United States. Built in 1629, the church's *vegas* (roof beams) were transported from Mount Taylor. During the late 1800s, the church was served by priests from Seboyeta and San Rafael. In the 1920s, priests from San Fidel, which had by then became a parish, were sent to the Acoma church. Acoma was established as a parish in 1966, and it also serves the villages of Acomita and McCartys. (Courtesy of Aurelio Apocada.)

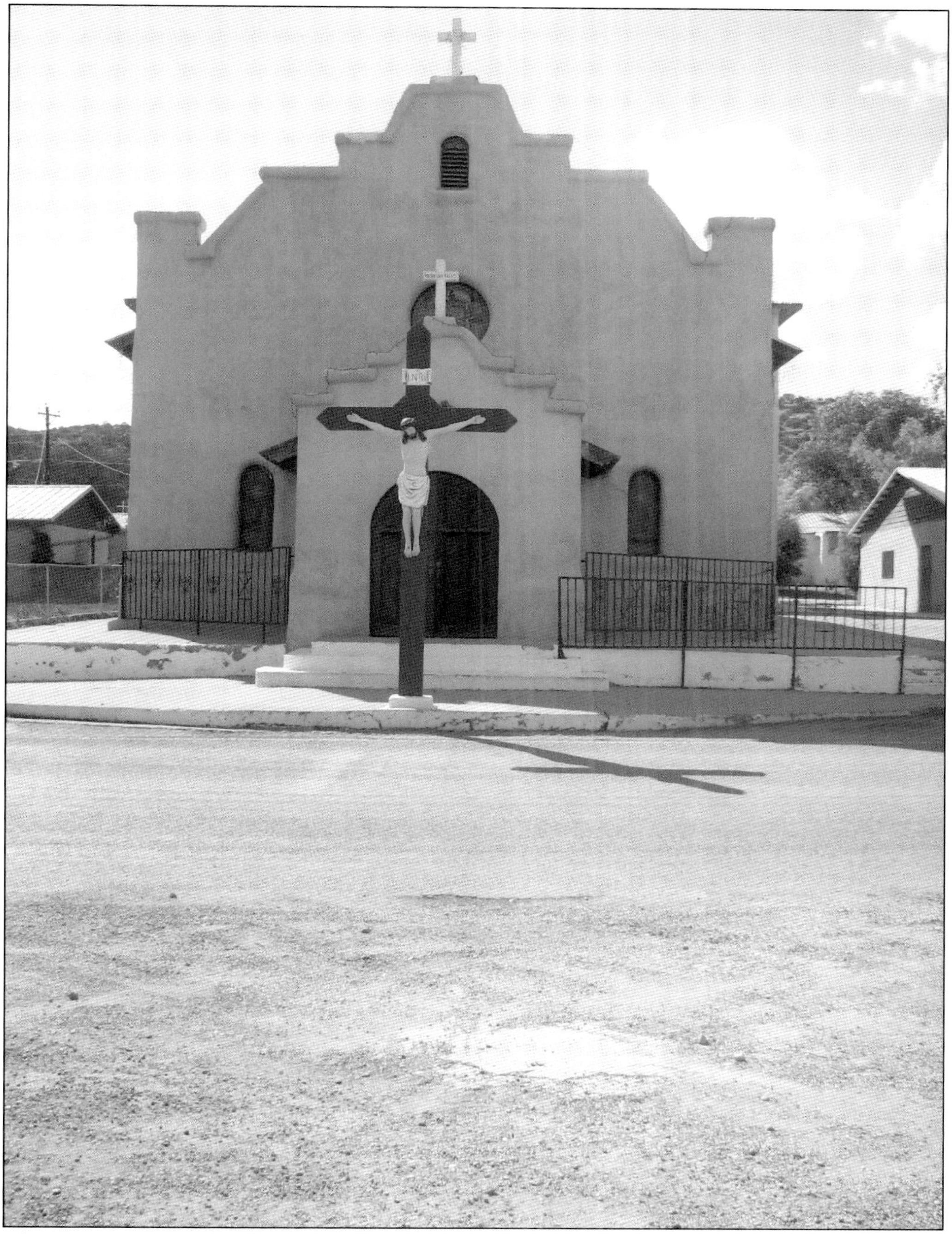

The Roman Catholic churches in Cibola County are now part of the Diocese of Gallup, founded in 1939. Prior to that, churches were under the order of the Diocese of Durango, Mexico. Mexico won its independence in 1821, and the Franciscan missionaries were expelled. New Mexico became a part of the United States in 1848. The Franciscan Order established nine missions in Native American pueblos and Spanish settlements. This mission is in San Rafael. In 1875, the diocese was elevated to the status of archdiocese. (Courtesy of Aurelio Apodaca.)

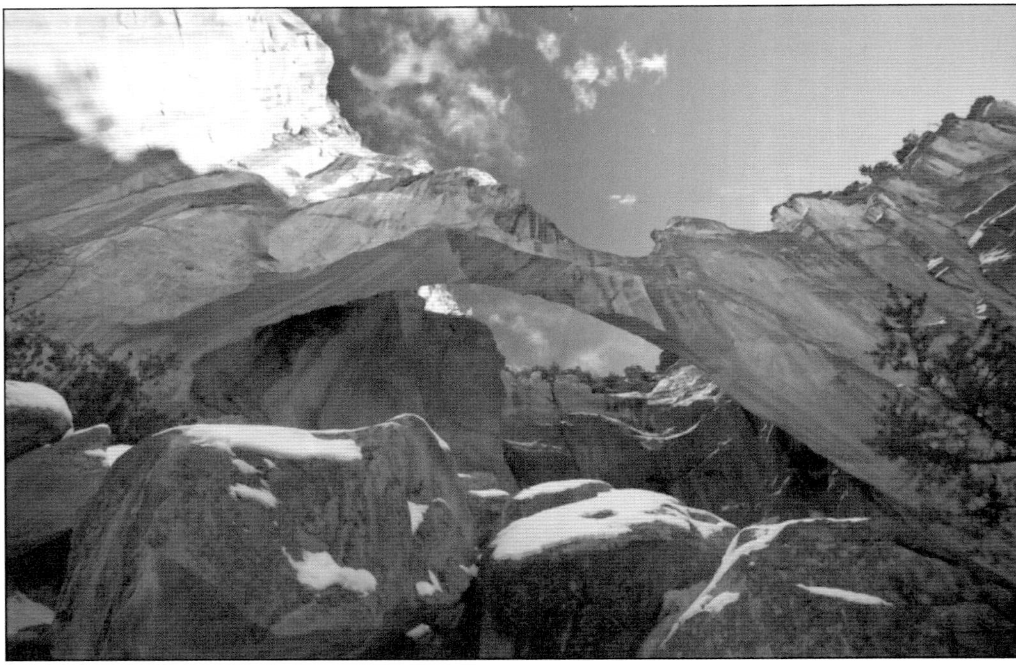

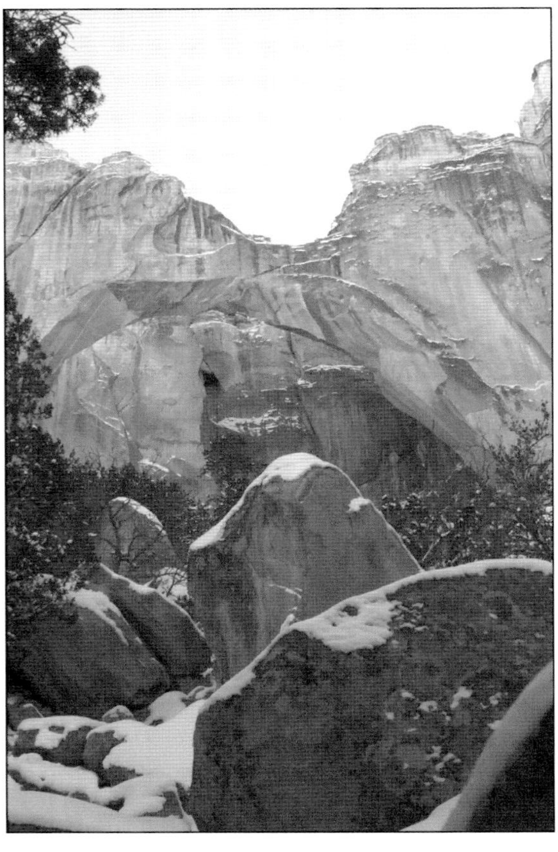

La Ventana (The Window) Arch is a natural rock arch within the El Malpais National Conservation Area. The arch is 165 feet wide. It is a highlight of the classic Southwestern scenery. These images capture the arch's unique beauty. (Both, courtesy of the US Forest Service.)

A unique phenomenon exists just 25 miles south of Grants. The "Land of Fire and Ice" is a beautiful area of twisted old-growth juniper, fir, and ponderosa pine trees covering an ancient lava trail. The Ice Cave, pictured here, and Bandera Volcano were formed when Bandera erupted around 10,000 years ago. (Courtesy of the US Forest Service.)

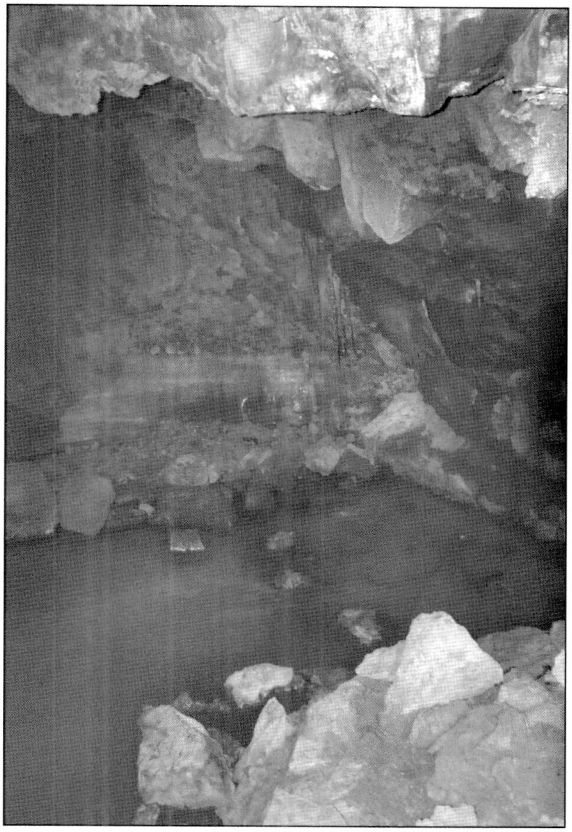

Only 25 miles from Grants and Milan in the Zuni Mountains is a beautiful oasis, Bluewater Lake State Park. The lake's dam was built by Mormons in the 1920s to irrigate their farmland. The water level at Bluewater is determined by the runoff from the Zuni Mountains and Bluewater Creek. Visitors can fish, boat, water-ski, swim, camp, and bird watch at Bluewater Lake. For the geologist, there are many fossils to be found around the lake. Grants and Milan residents have enjoyed the lake for decades. (Courtesy of the Bureau of Land Management/National Park Service.)

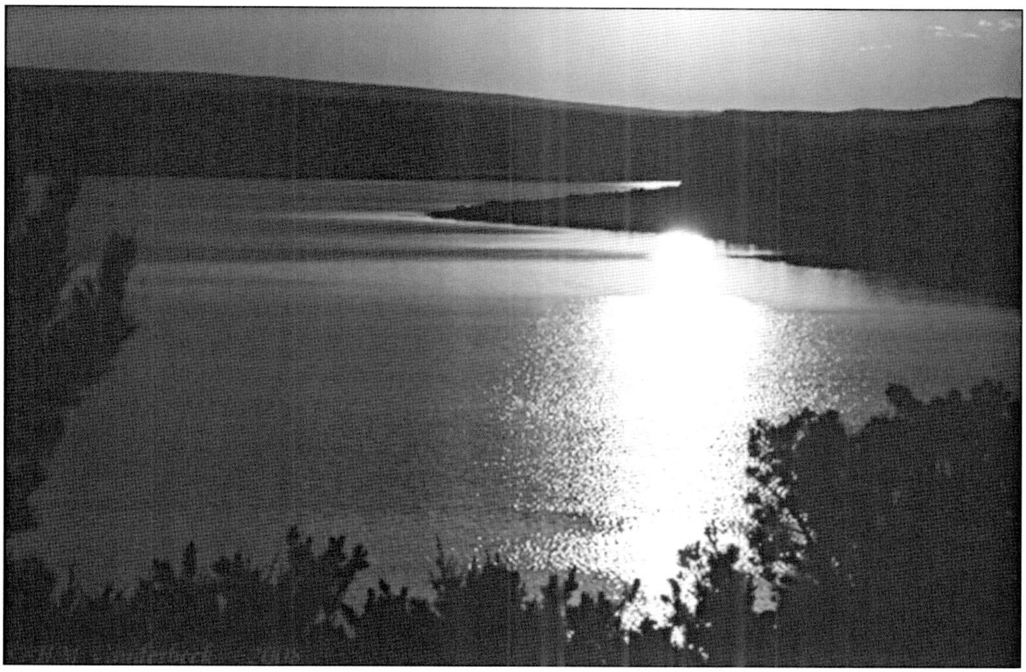

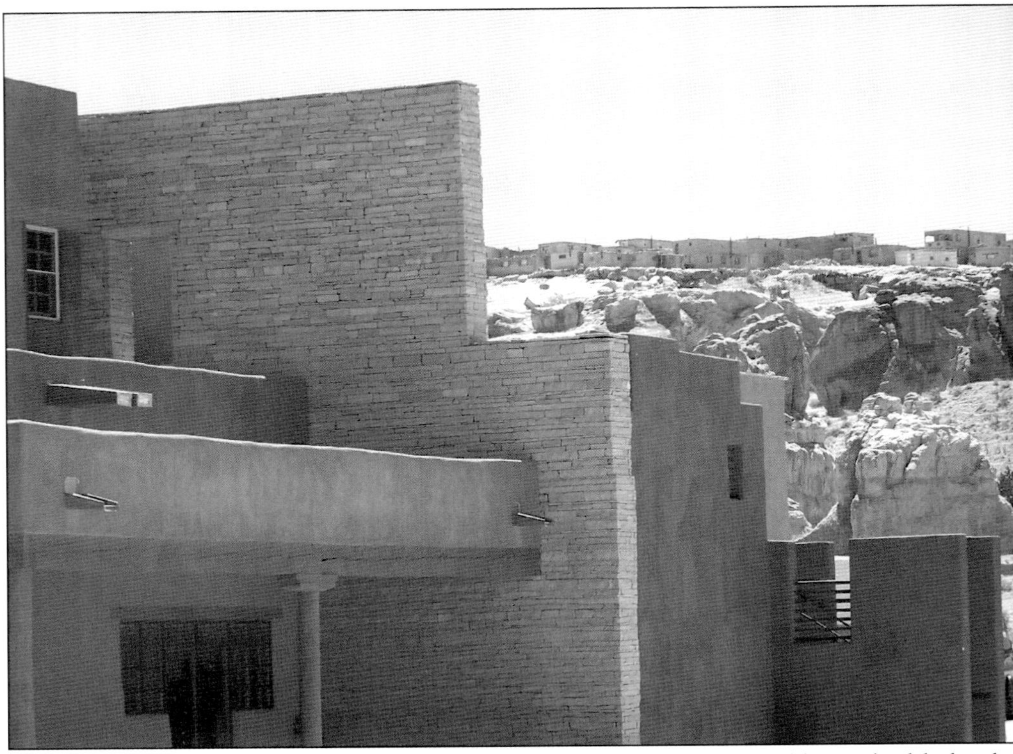

The history, family traditions, and cultural heritage of the Acoma Pueblo are highlighted at Acoma's Sky City Cultural Center and Haak'u Museum near the base of Sky City. In addition to exhibit space, the cultural center also has a plaza area, a 67-seat theater, a multipurpose room for community events, a library, conference room, and restaurant. A permanent exhibit showcases the people's history. (Courtesy of the *Cibola Beacon*.)

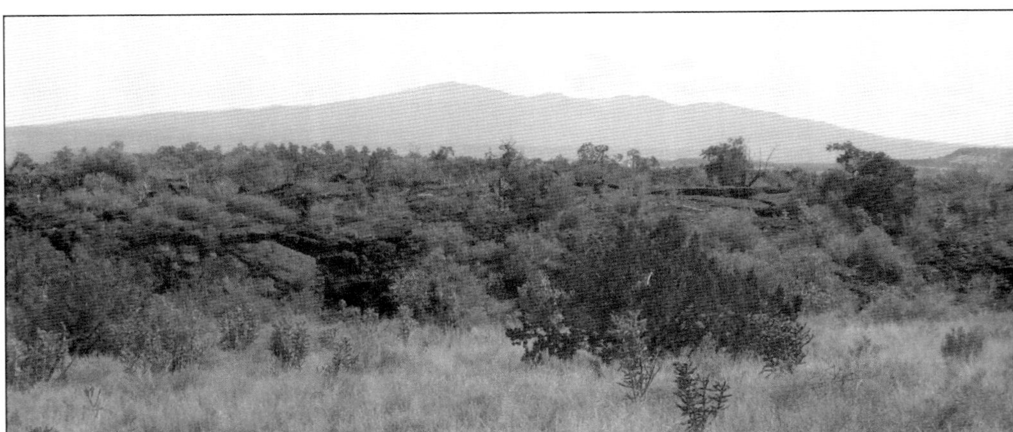

Mount Taylor (Navajo: *Tsoodził*) is a stratovolcano just northeast from Grants. It was named in 1849 for then president Zachary Taylor. Prior to that, it was called *Cebolleta* (tender onion) by the Spanish; the name persists as one name for the northern portion of the San Mateo Mountains, a large mesa. Mount Taylor is largely forested. It is the second-highest point in New Mexico. Its slopes were an important source of lumber for neighboring pueblos. (Courtesy of the *Cibola Beacon*.)

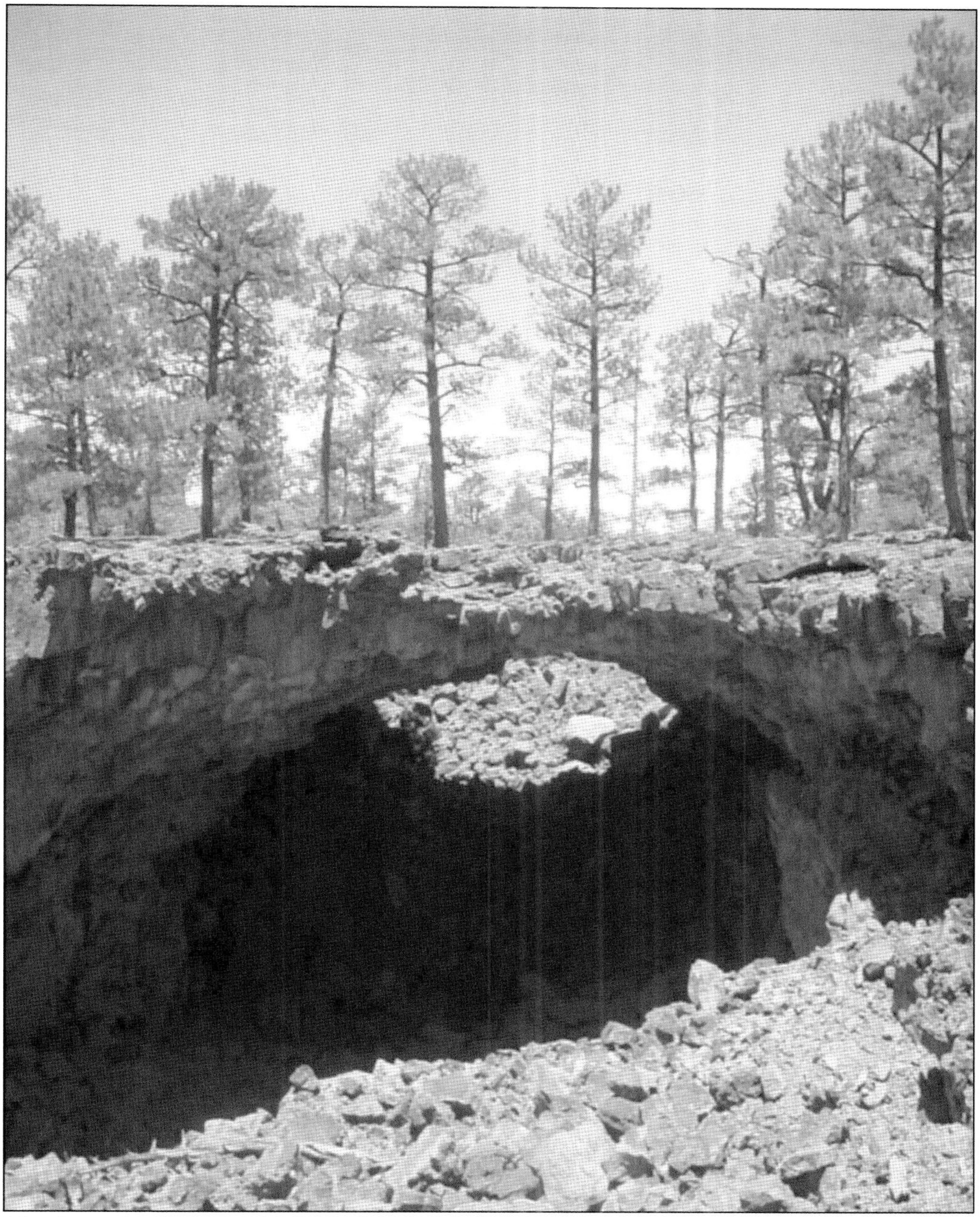

This formation is the result of lava flow in the El Malpais National Monument and Conservation Area. In 1987, Pres. Ronald Reagan signed legislation that granted national monument status to a remote and little corner of northwestern New Mexico. The wild and wooly lava flows south of Grants had been considered for national monument status back in the 1930s and have been a source of excitement to scientists of volcanology and geology for decades. Now that rangers and researchers have trod the many acres of the El Malpais National Monument and Conservation Area, much more is known about the various lava flows, their mineral composition, and how all of that relates to volcanism on a planetary scale. (Courtesy of the *Cibola Beacon*.)

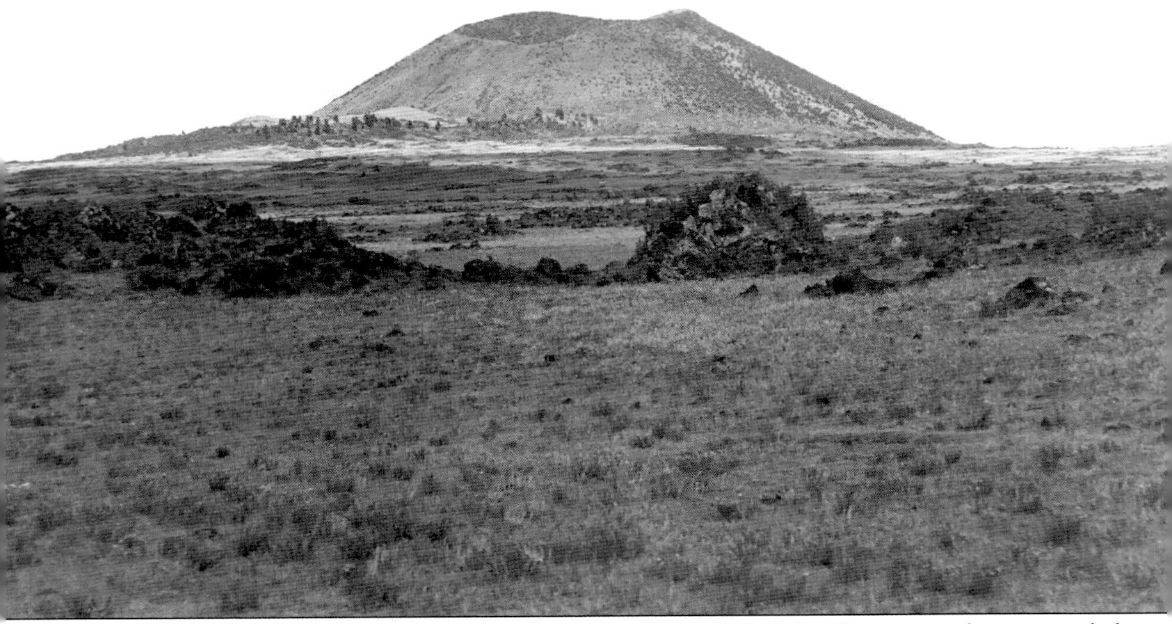

Mount Taylor was active from 3.3 to 1.5 million years ago during the Pliocene, and is surrounded by a field of smaller inactive volcanoes, shown above. Repeated eruptions built lava domes and produced lava flows, ash plumes, and mudflows. Estimates vary about how high the mountain was at its highest. Conservative estimates place its maximum near a similar pre-explosion height for the San Francisco Peaks of 16,000 to 18,000 feet (4,900 to 5,500 m.), and an extreme estimate places it near 25,000 feet (7,600 m.), nearly double its current height. (Courtesy of the *Cibola Beacon*.)

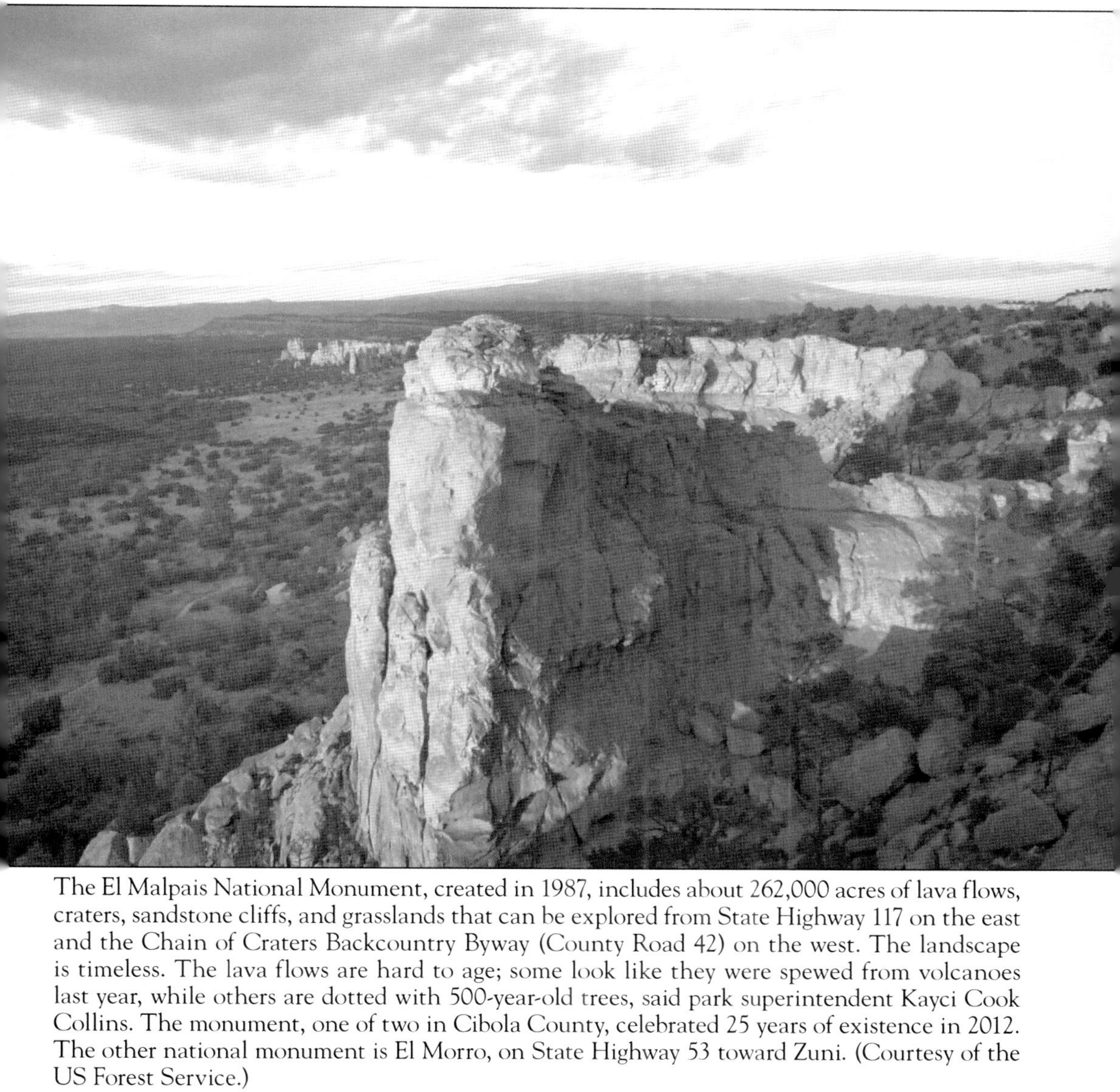

The El Malpais National Monument, created in 1987, includes about 262,000 acres of lava flows, craters, sandstone cliffs, and grasslands that can be explored from State Highway 117 on the east and the Chain of Craters Backcountry Byway (County Road 42) on the west. The landscape is timeless. The lava flows are hard to age; some look like they were spewed from volcanoes last year, while others are dotted with 500-year-old trees, said park superintendent Kayci Cook Collins. The monument, one of two in Cibola County, celebrated 25 years of existence in 2012. The other national monument is El Morro, on State Highway 53 toward Zuni. (Courtesy of the US Forest Service.)

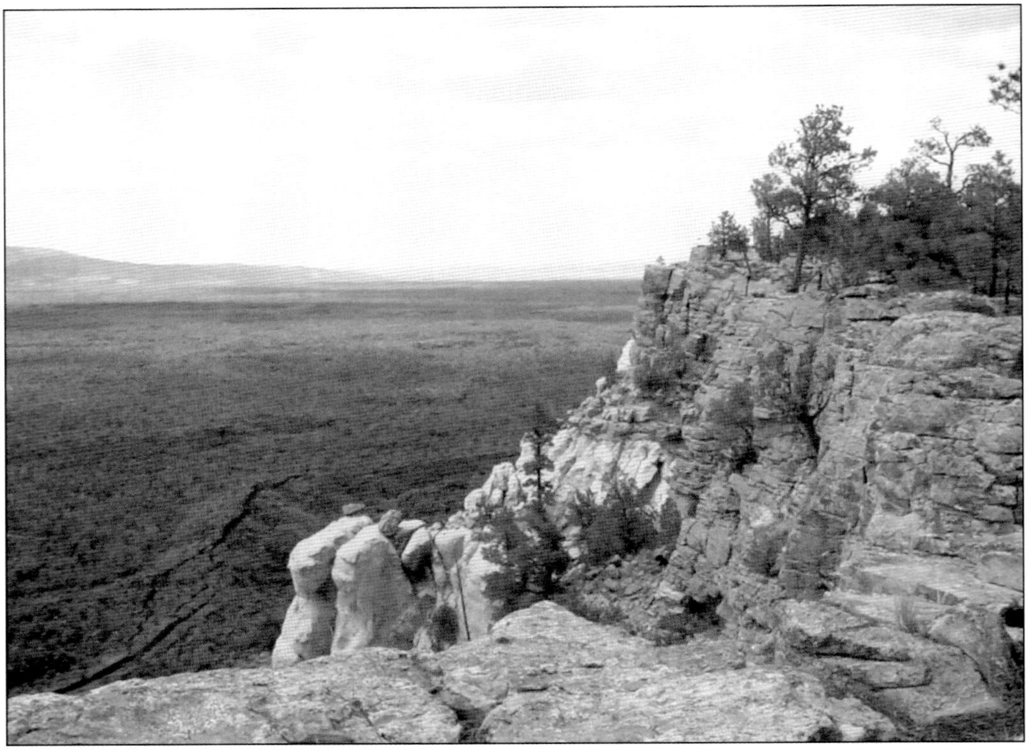

These cliffs, called Sandstone Bluffs, are just west of Highway 117 in the El Malpais National Monument. Famous because of the big panoramic views (above) that can be experienced from their heights, the bluffs are also a great place to wander around and explore on foot. The attractions of the bluffs are many. The big and colorful views allow orientation with the region's many landmarks and features. Up close, the little details provide lots of intrigue: aquatic creatures swimming in the sandstone *tinajas* (water tanks, below) after a rain, hidden petroglyph panels and arches, occasional potsherds, and the endless complexity of the sandstone geology. Sandstone Bluffs are a good synopsis of New Mexico's fascinating landscapes. (Both, courtesy of the *Cibola Beacon*.)

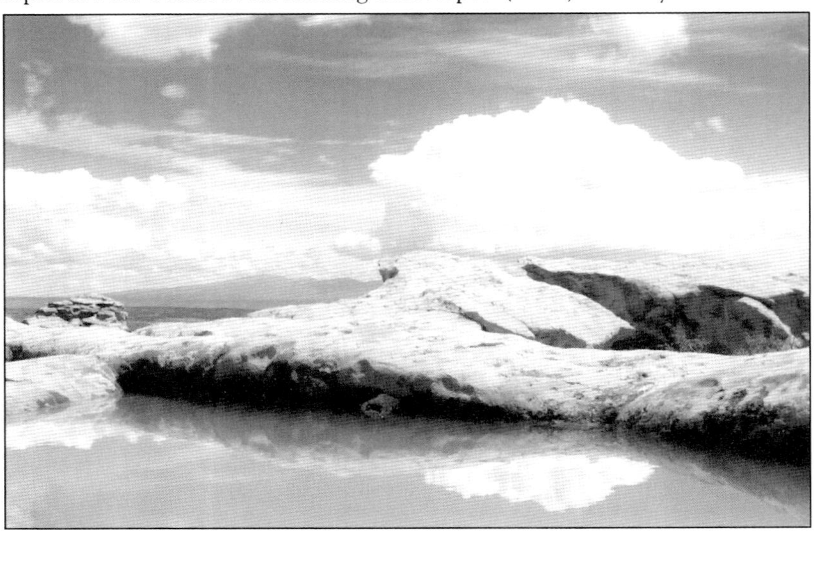

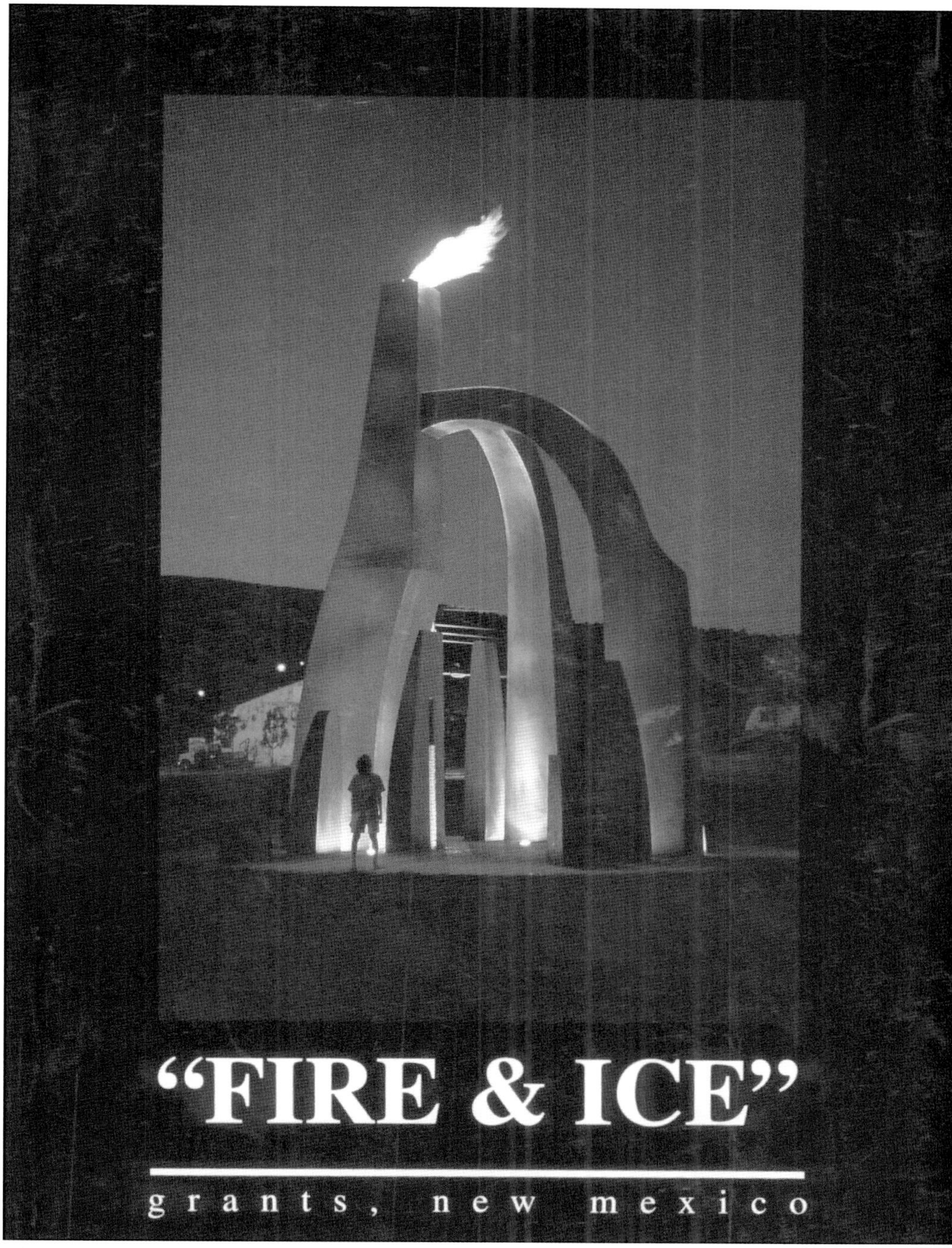

This poster was created to commemorate a new sculpture depicting the origins of the area with the phrase "Fire and Ice." The sculpture was the result of a contest in which 25 artists provided renderings of proposed art that was to be placed in the Grants Riverwalk Park. The proposal that was chosen depicted the fact that the area was surrounded by volcanoes and huge lava beds. A number of ice caves developed within the lava beds, and the artists felt that the area could be described as "Fire and Ice." (Courtesy of the Cibola Arts Council.)

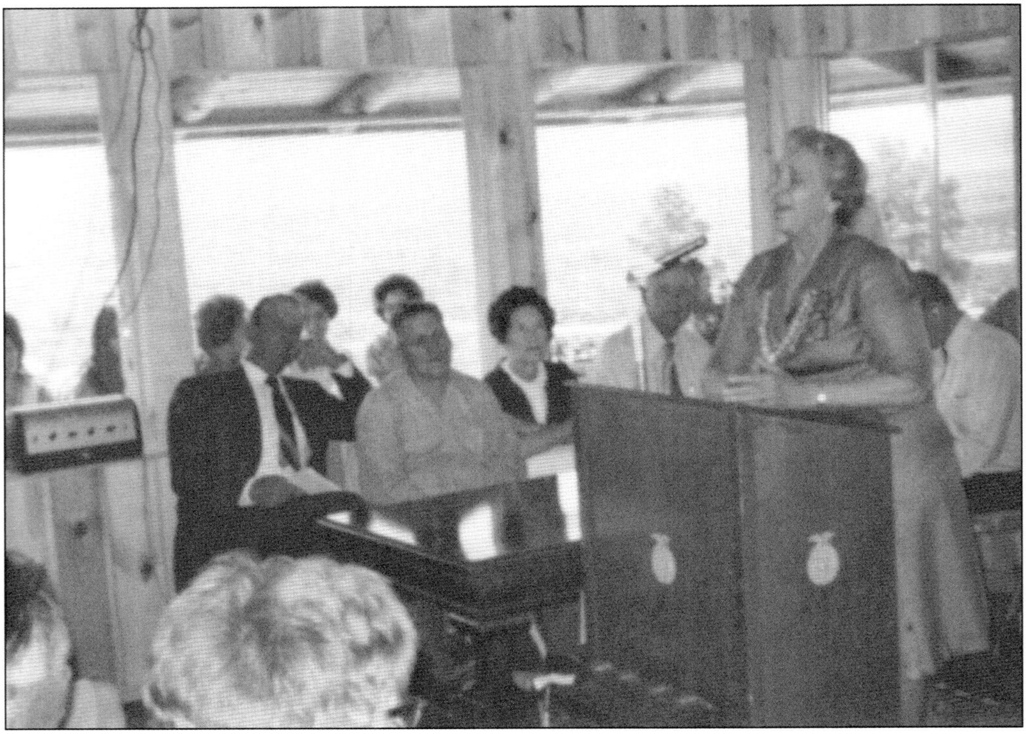

Above, Ina Tietjen Elkins speaks at the museum that the Mark Elkins family established in memory of the pioneers who moved to this area, especially the many homesteaders who helped develop the area's ranching and farming businesses. The area and facility, seen below, were sold to the Acoma Pueblo tribe, and the museum is now closed. (Both, courtesy of the Elkins family.)

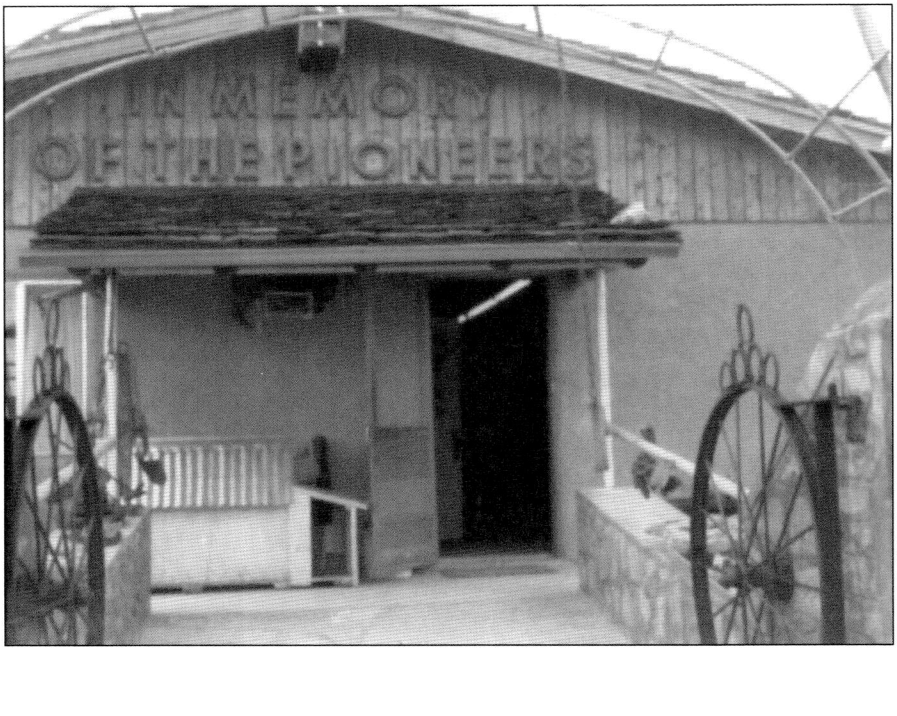

Two

Grants

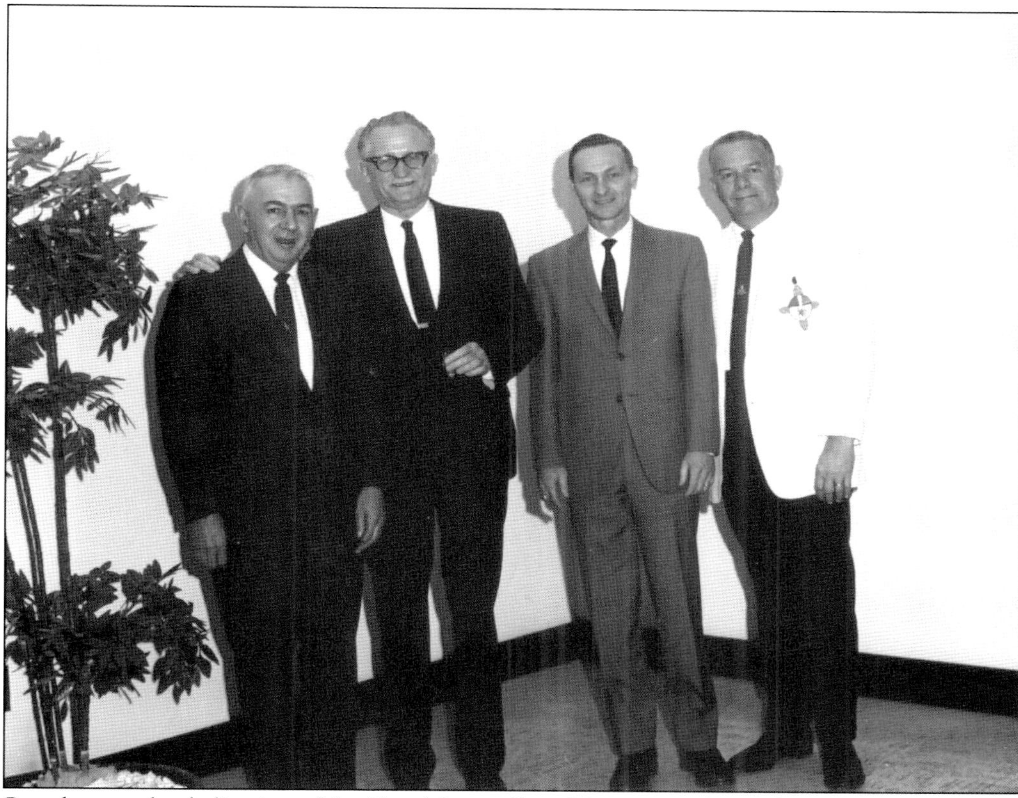

Seen here at the dedication of the New Mexico State University–Grants branch are, from left to right, Salvador Milan, mayor of Milan and president of the Grants School Board; New Mexico State University president Roger Corbett; New Mexico State University–Grants branch president Carl O. Westbrook; and Stuart Lydick, mayor of Grants and president of First National Bank of Grants. Classes were first held at the high school at night and were later moved to the Job Corps facility that was donated to the university by the federal government. Although it started as a two-year college, it is now able offer bachelor degrees in many disciplines. (Courtesy of the Milan family.)

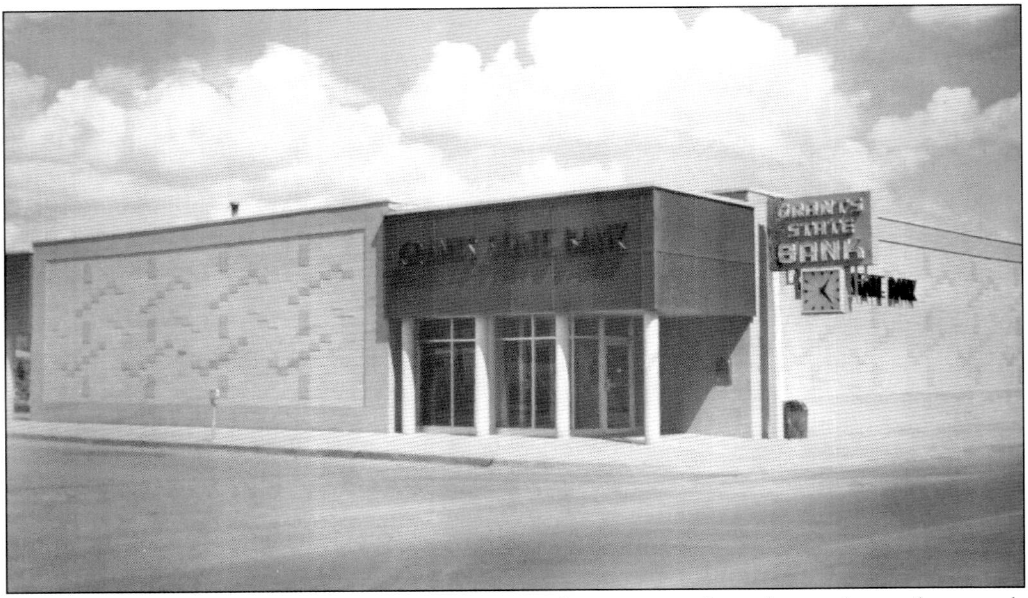

Grants State Bank was built in 1958 in response to the increase of population due to the growth in the uranium industry. The boom started in 1950 with the discovery of uranium in the area. The original designs of the bank were in color with Zuni symbols to celebrate the culture of the area. (Courtesy of the Grants State Bank.)

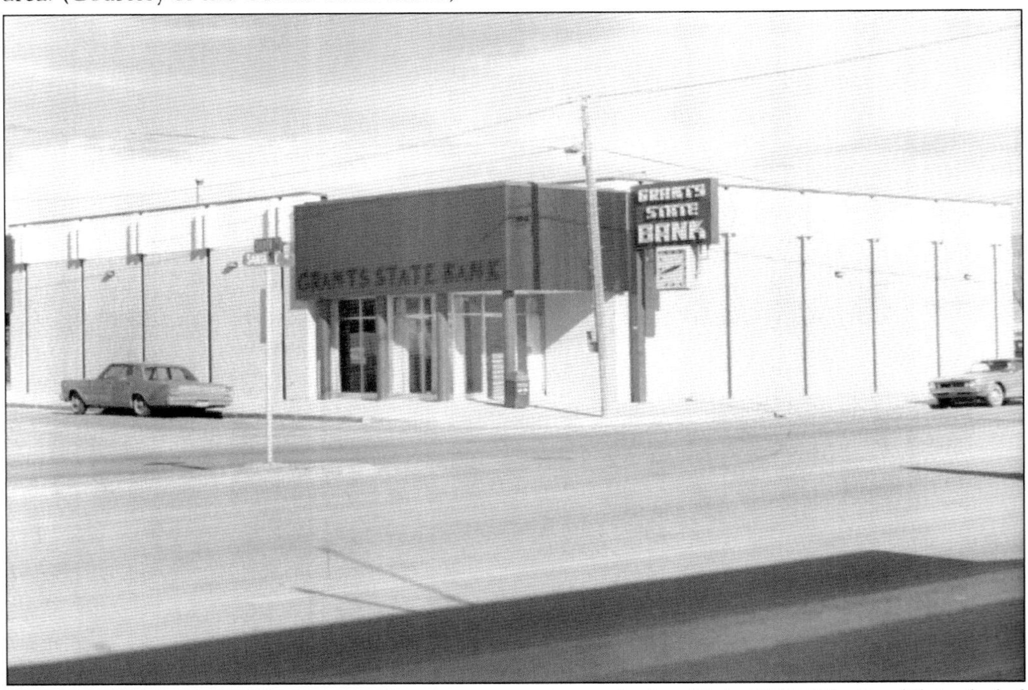

Grants State Bank's building received new construction and a facelift in 1969. The facelift included a new large community room to help the new growing population from all over the world to have access to a place to hold meetings and was also aimed towards competing with new banks. (Courtesy of the Grants State Bank.)

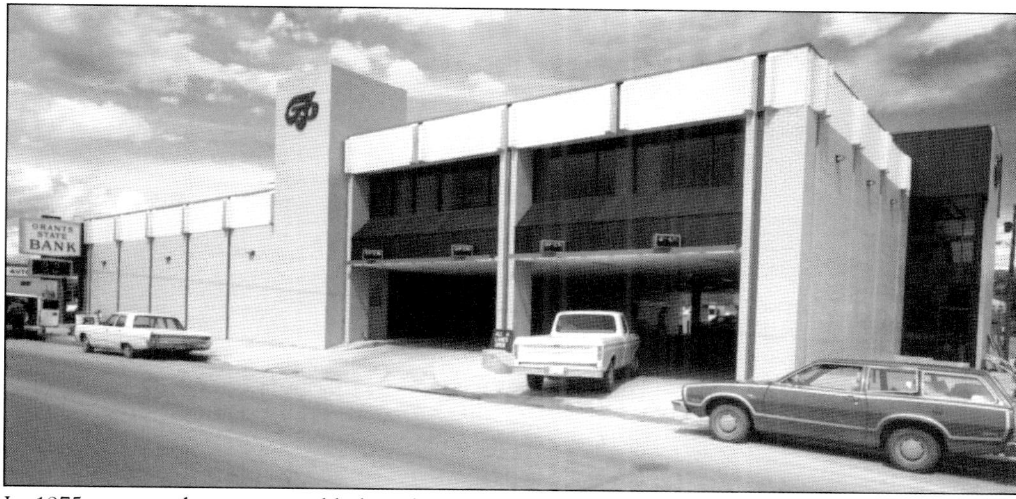

In 1975, a second story was added to the Grants State Bank due to the uranium boom and the large customer base that the bank enjoyed. The uranium boom of the 1950s busted in the 1960s because the Atomic Energy Commission was the only entity that was allowed to buy uranium and a large stockpile resulted, causing a huge slowdown in mining, consolidation of the uranium mills, and a loss of mining and milling jobs. (Courtesy of the Grants State Bank.)

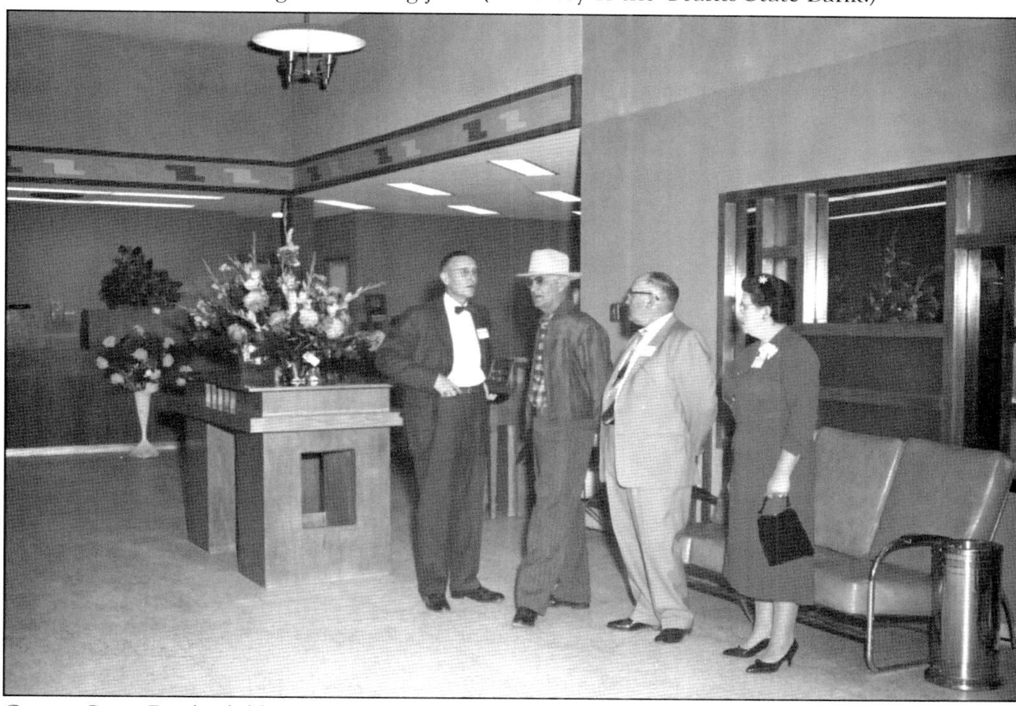

Grants State Bank's lobby was the site of the bank's grand opening in 1958. From left to right, executive vice president Norville Davis converses with Pablo Peña, Grants State Bank stockholder and local rancher; Monico Mirabal, chairman of the Grants State Bank Board; and his spouse, Belinda Mirabal. Bankers from all over the state, stockholders, and customers attended bank tours, and out-of-state bankers were given a tour of the uranium mines and mills. This was considered the biggest event of the year. (Courtesy of the Grants State Bank.)

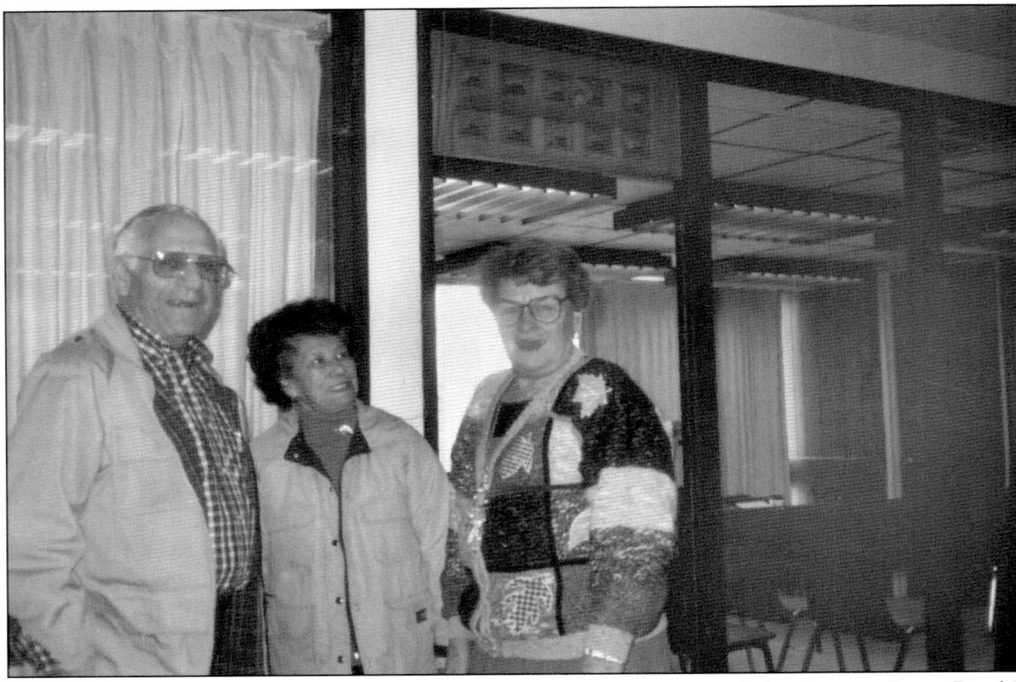

In 1982, the effects of the uranium bust began to take effect, and the Grants State Bank's ownership was taken over by a Dallas investment group that held the majority stock. The federal government did not approve the takeover and forced the stock to be placed in trust. The minority stockholders formed a holding company chartered under the name of Community Bancshares, Inc., and were able to take control in 1986. From left to right are state senator Joseph Fidel, stockholder; Flossie Rice, stockholder and director; and Birdye Abraham, director and secretary of the holding company, as they prepare for an annual stockholders meeting. (Courtesy of the Grants State Bank.)

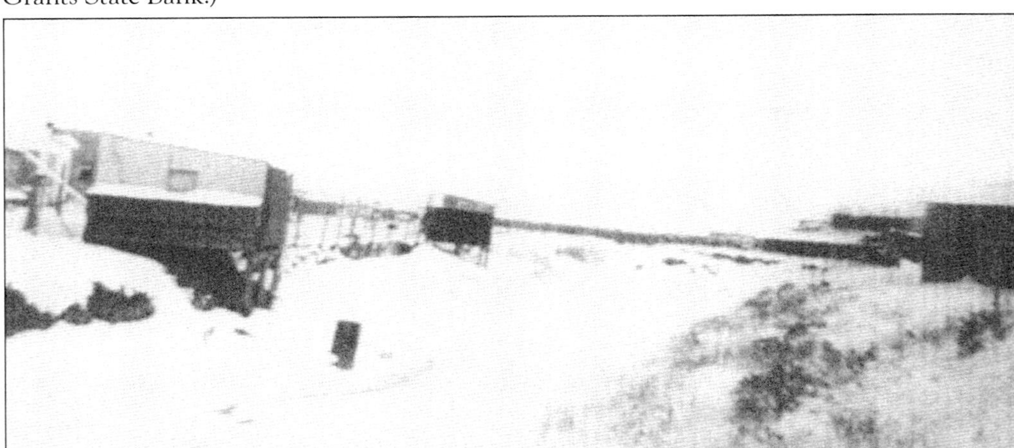

This was a scene of one of the areas in Grants during the 1940s. There were no housing developments, and houses were built wherever a person had land or could afford a lot. This area was close to the schools; therefore, there were a number of teachers who lived in rental homes. Grants was described by *Ripley's Believe It Or Not* as the "Biggest, Littlest Town in the World," one mile long and one block wide. (Courtesy of E.B. Dawson.)

A winter scene in Grants during the 1940s shows area that is now the Riverwalk Park. The house is typical of that time and would normally be rented to teachers, since the Grants Grade School and High School were in the vicinity. (Courtesy of E.B. Dawson.)

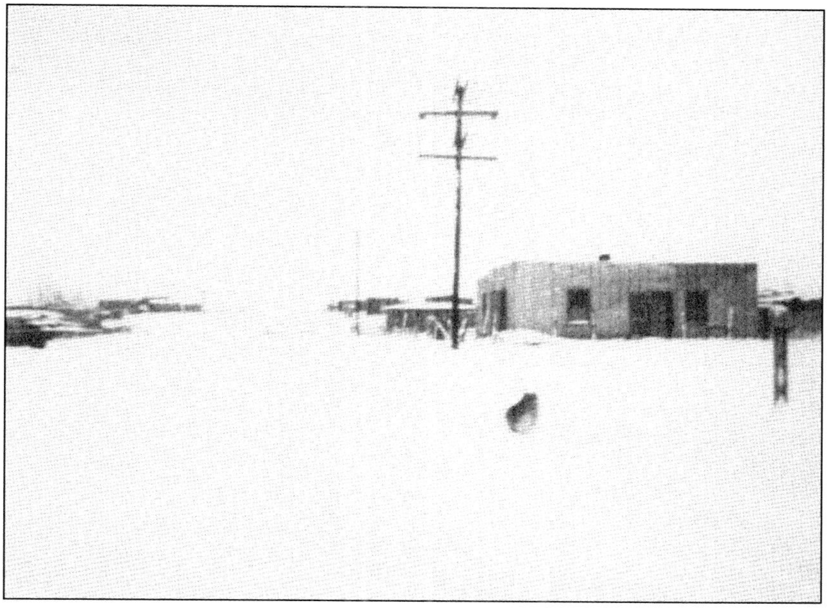

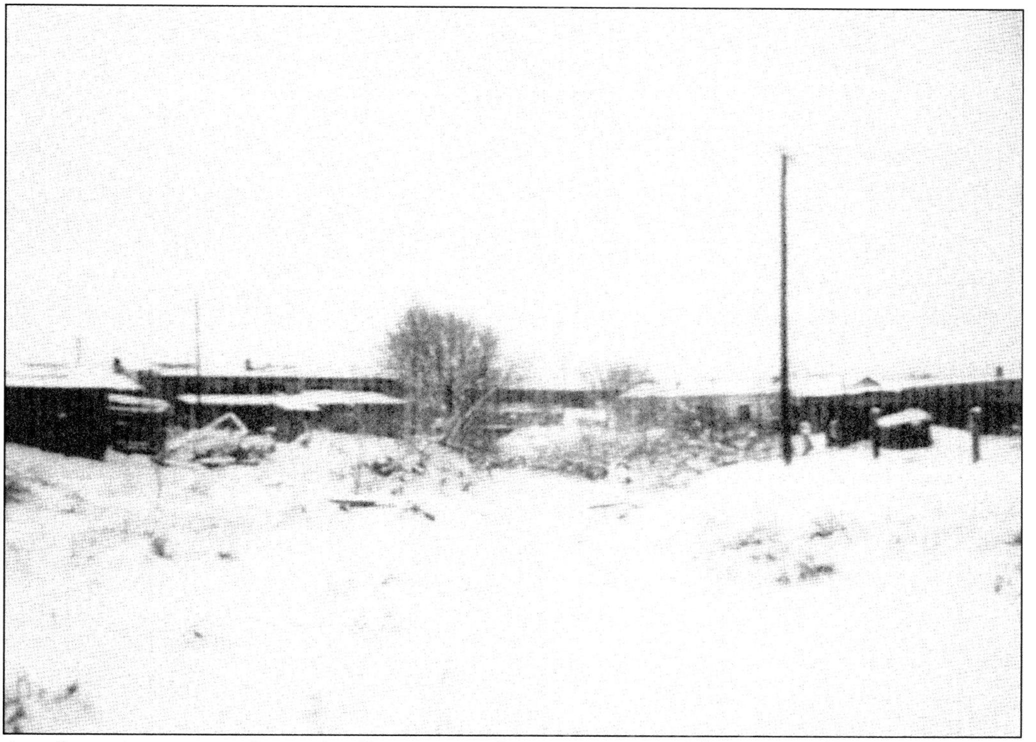

Another winter scene shows the Grants area that is now part of the Riverwalk Park. Since this area was bisected by the San Jose River and there was only one crossing from this side of the road to the school complex, bad weather would make it difficult to get to school by automobile or on foot. (Courtesy of E.B. Dawson.)

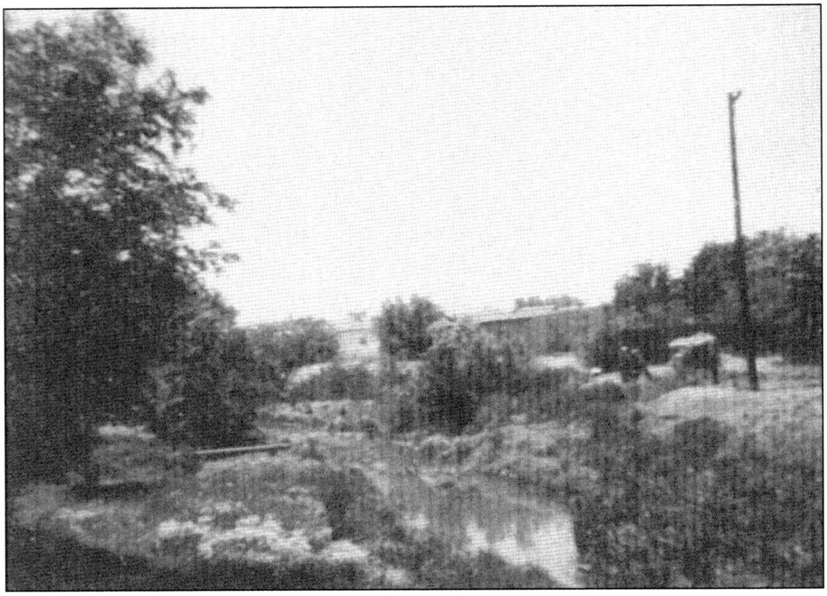

The San Jose River is pictured in summer. The water level was never too deep except during the monsoon. On one occasion, the Bluewater Dam burst, and the large flow of water caused some of the houses on the riverbank to collapse. (Courtesy of E.B. Dawson.)

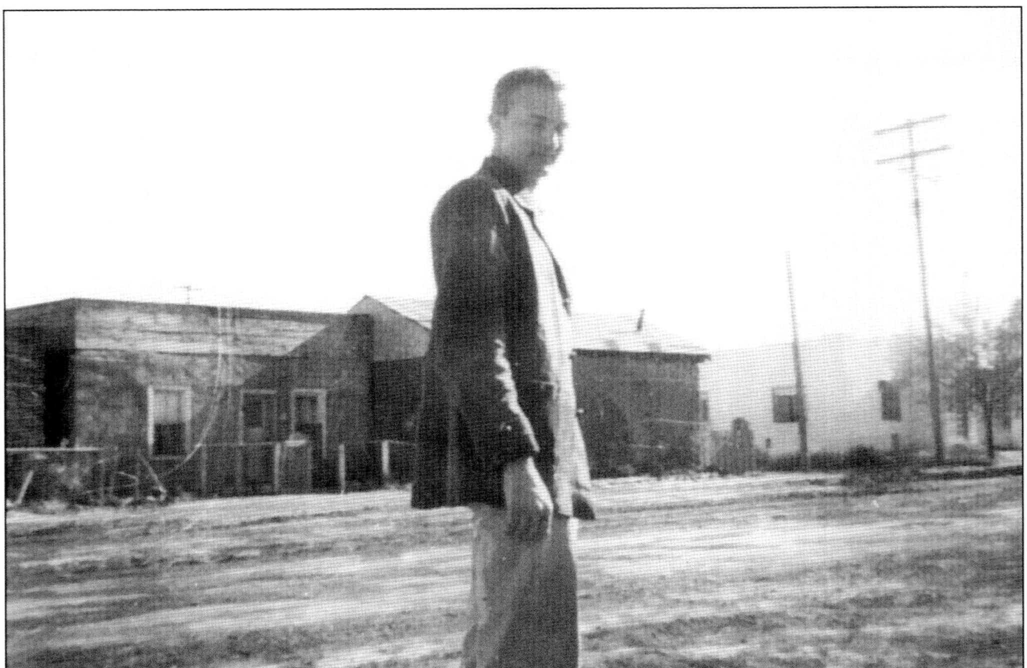

Gene Hodges, a teacher at the Grants High School, stands in front of his home along the San Jose River. Hodges had been drafted in the military and was saying goodbye to his students. (Courtesy of E.B. Dawson.)

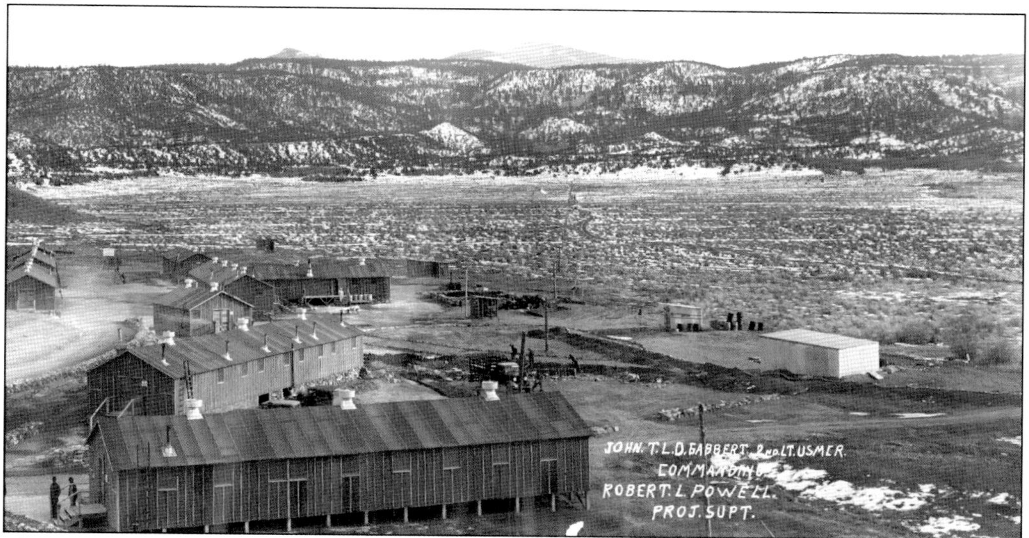

The Grants area was hit hard by the Depression, and the federal government setup a Civilian Conservation Corps (CCC) camp in the Grants area to provide jobs and to develop roads, trails, and bridges throughout the huge forests in the Grants vicinity. The employees stayed at these camps, and many of the members were very proud to have been part of this service. (Courtesy of George Rodriguez.)

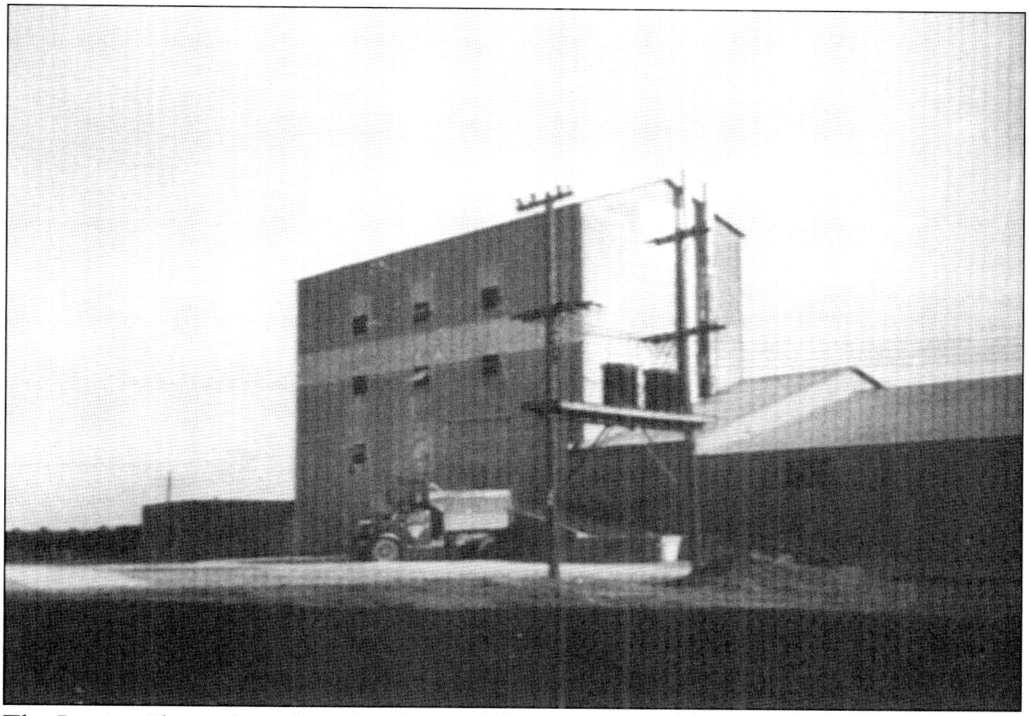
The Pumice Plant, also called the Gypsum Plant, was owned by the Pumice Corporation of America and was located between Highway 66 and the railroad tracks east of the railroad station. This plant was established in the late 1930s and was very valuable during World War II. The plant was demolished in the early 21st century. (Courtesy of E.B. Dawson.)

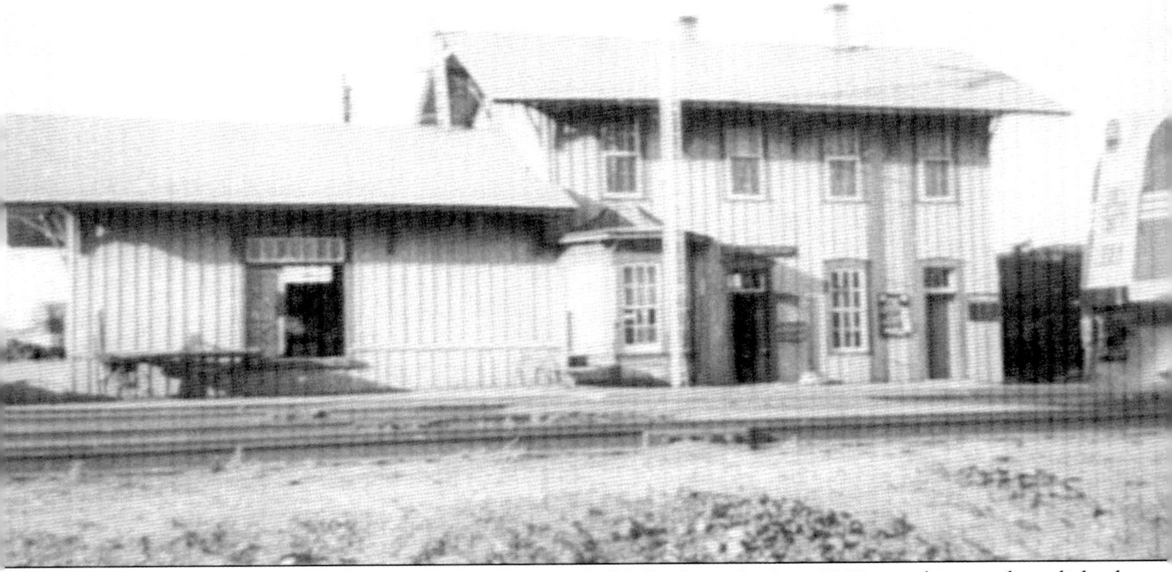

The original Santa Fe railroad station was probably built in the late 1800s, and it was demolished in the late 1950s. The replacement station was demolished in the early 2000s. This station was the center of all activity since its inception in 1865, which was the basis for establishing Grants. The railroad connected Grants to Albuquerque and Santa Fe, Kansas City, and Denver for travel and shipping livestock, wool, farm products, logging, and other materials. It resulted in a boom for the area. There was even a famous train robbery that took place nearby. (Courtesy of E.B. Dawson.)

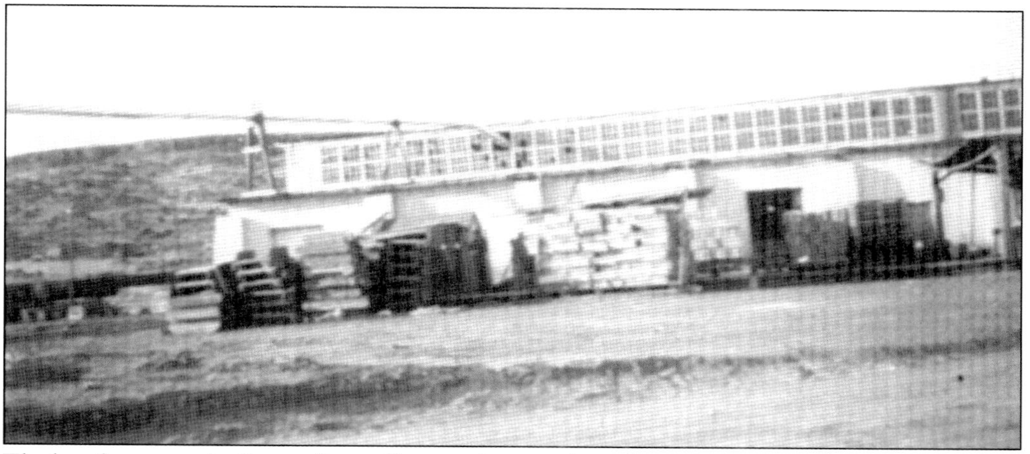

The box factory at the Breece Sawmill is seen here in the early 1940s. It is now the site of Diamond G Home Center. This facility was part of the railroad facility that was developed during the logging boom to haul logs from the Zuni Mountains, and later a sawmill was developed at this site. Housing was built for the employees across from this site, which was called Breece Town. Although all of the housing units are gone, some people still call the area Breece Town. (Courtesy of E.B. Dawson.)

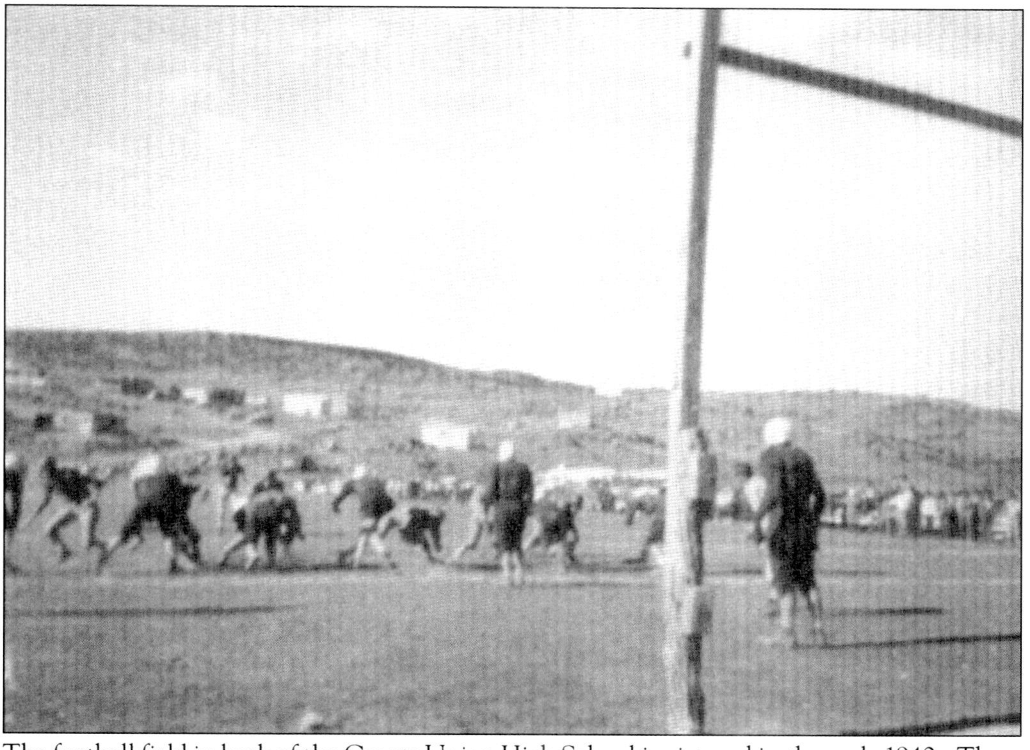

The football field in back of the Grants Union High School is pictured in the early 1940s. There is no grass, no bleachers, and no score sign, and spectators can be seen at the opposite side. Most of the games were played during the daytime, because lights were not available. On Thanksgiving or Homecoming, the games were played at the rodeo grounds, which had bleachers, although the dirt could be rough and most of the players did not have helmets. (Courtesy of E.B. Dawson.)

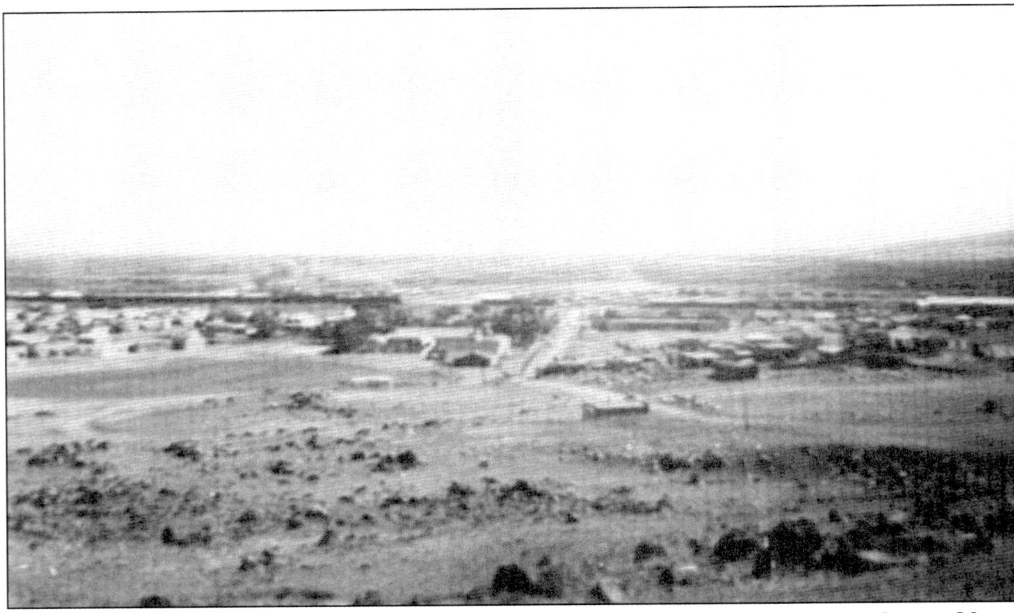

In this 1945–1946 scene of Grants from up the hill on Iron Street, one can see Grants Union High School, the railroad track, with a locomotive to the left, and a carrot shed to the right. The population was around 1,900, and this photograph reveals how sparse the buildings and housing was. There was very little construction during the Depression and World War II. (Courtesy of E.B. Dawson.)

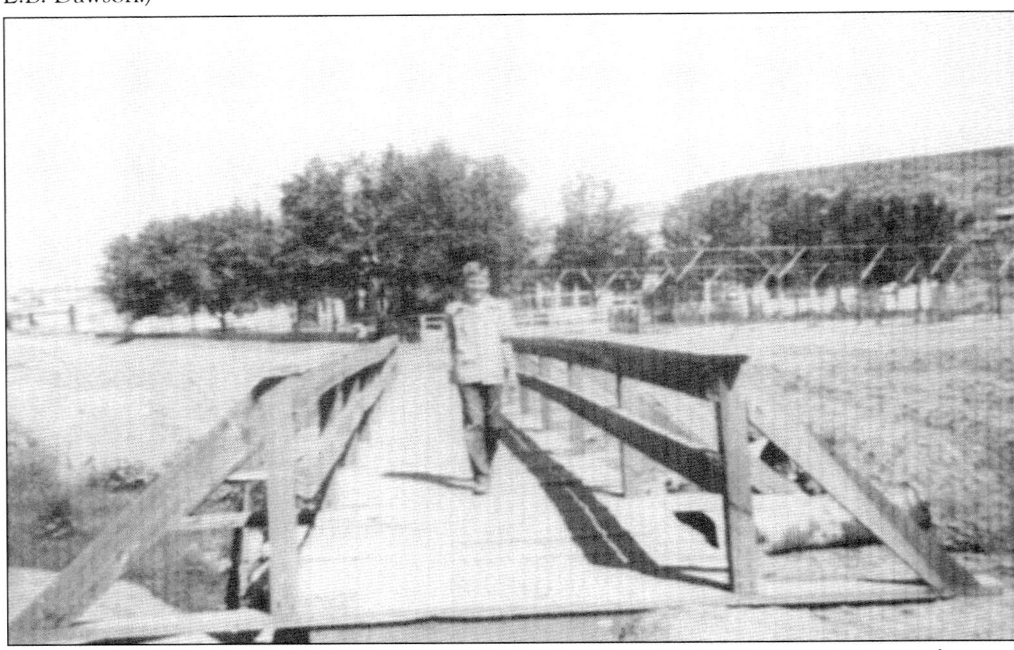

E.B. Dawson, the son of Emmet Dawson and schoolteacher Gladys Dawson, is pictured around 1945 or 1946 on the New Riverwalk Bridge, east of Grants Union High School. This bridge crossed the San Jose River, giving the population easy access between the housing area and the schools during the rainy season and winter snows. (Courtesy of E.B. Dawson.)

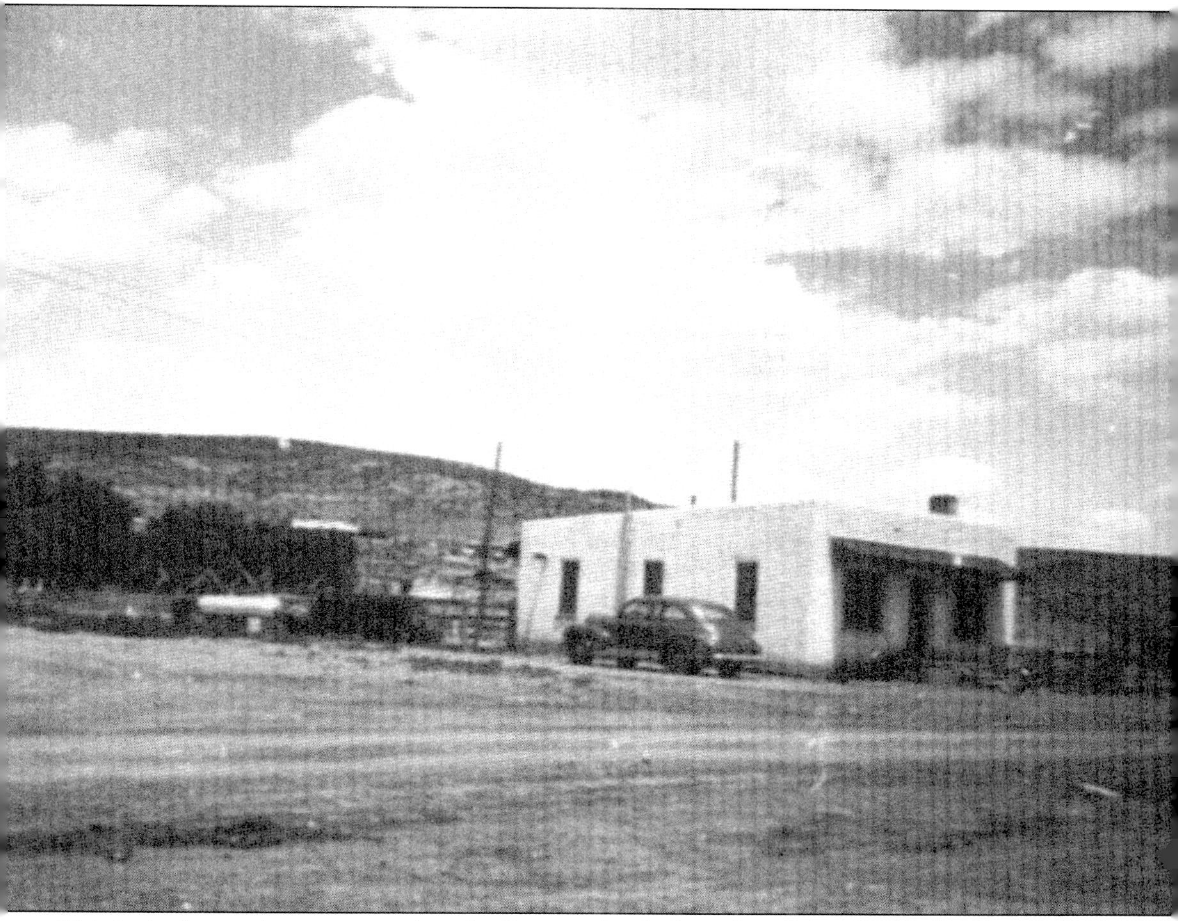

This is the house that was rented to the Dawson family for at least 10 years during the 1940s. Many of Gladys Dawson's students who rode the bus were invited to this house if a class program was taking place in the evening, and their parents would come to the program and take them home. Mrs. Dawson wanted to make sure that the students got to the program on time, so she fed them and got them there, especially if it was a program she was conducting and the students had a part in it. (Courtesy of E.B. Dawson.)

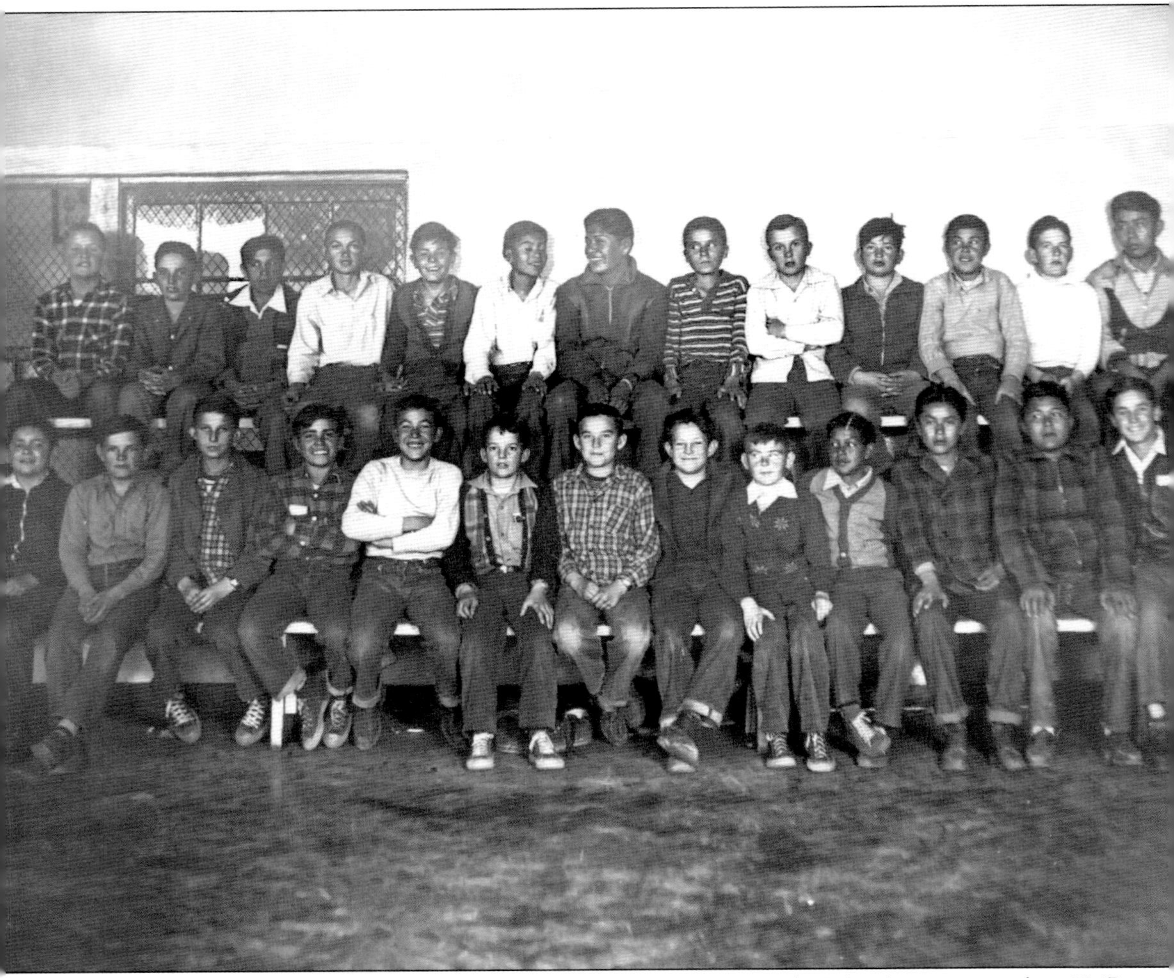

Boys who attended the seventh grade at the Grants Union High School are pictured in 1947. The junior high school was combined with the senior high school until about 1956, when a new high school was built. The majority of these students married and raised their children in the area. All of these students became very successful, and in their ranks were bankers, politicians, businessmen, government executives, ranchers, farmers, teachers, and military officers. (Courtesy of E.B. Dawson.)

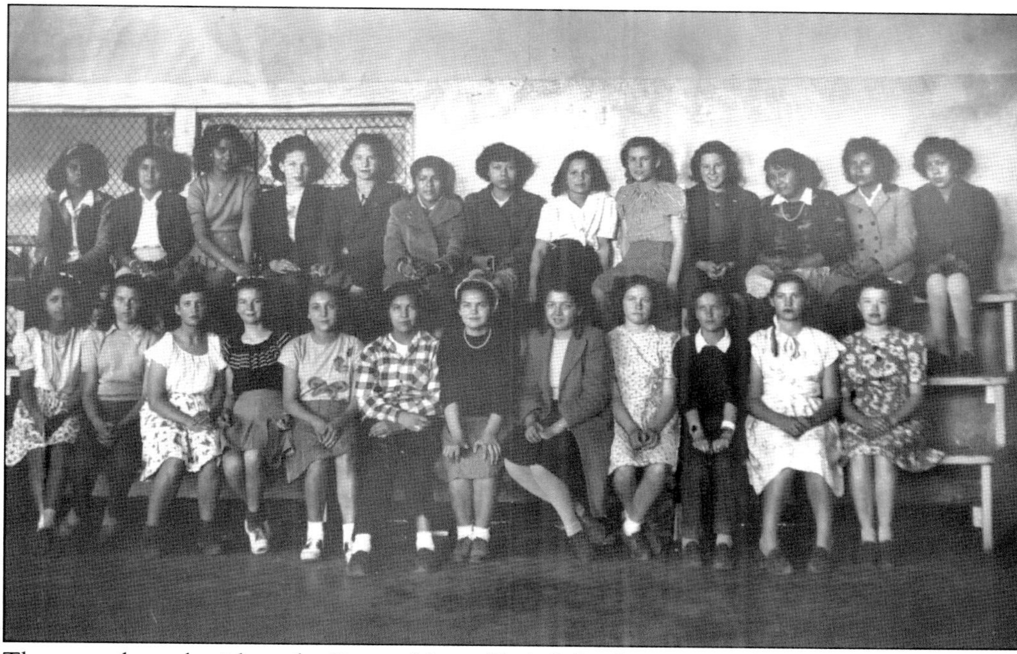

The seventh-grade girls at the Grants Union High School are pictured in 1947. These students, like their boy counterparts, were very successful as spouses, mothers, professionals, businesswomen, and volunteers. Like their boy counterparts, there has not been any derogatory information about them these last 60-plus years. In a small town, information moves rapidly, especially derogatory information. (Courtesy of E.B. Dawson.)

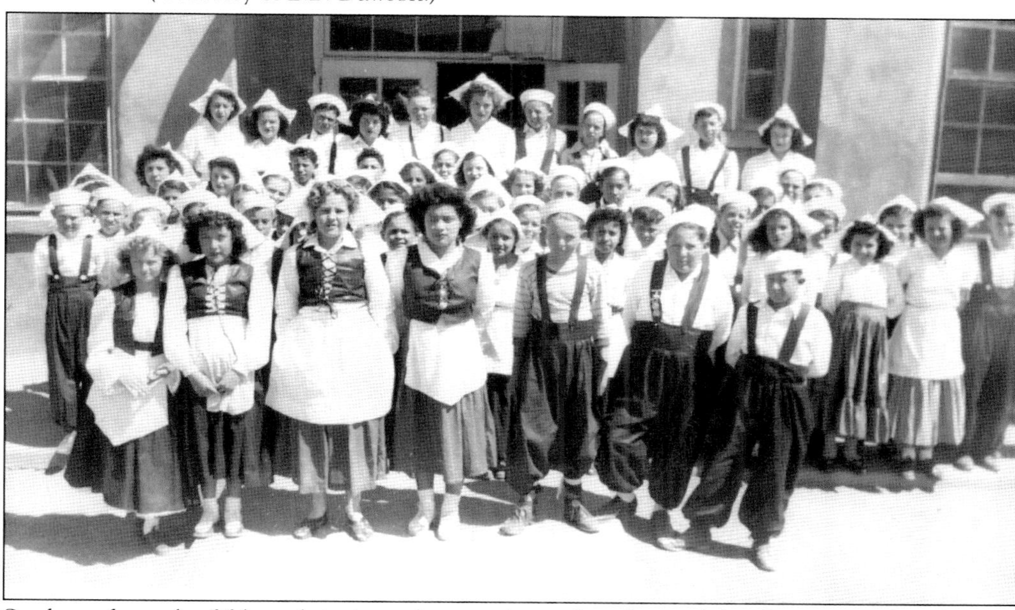

Students from the fifth and sixth grades are pictured in front of the Grants Grade School in 1945. The students performed the annual musical with a Dutch theme. The grade school was located where Grants City Hall is now. Most of the students have made their homes in this area and have been very successful. (Courtesy of E.B. Dawson.)

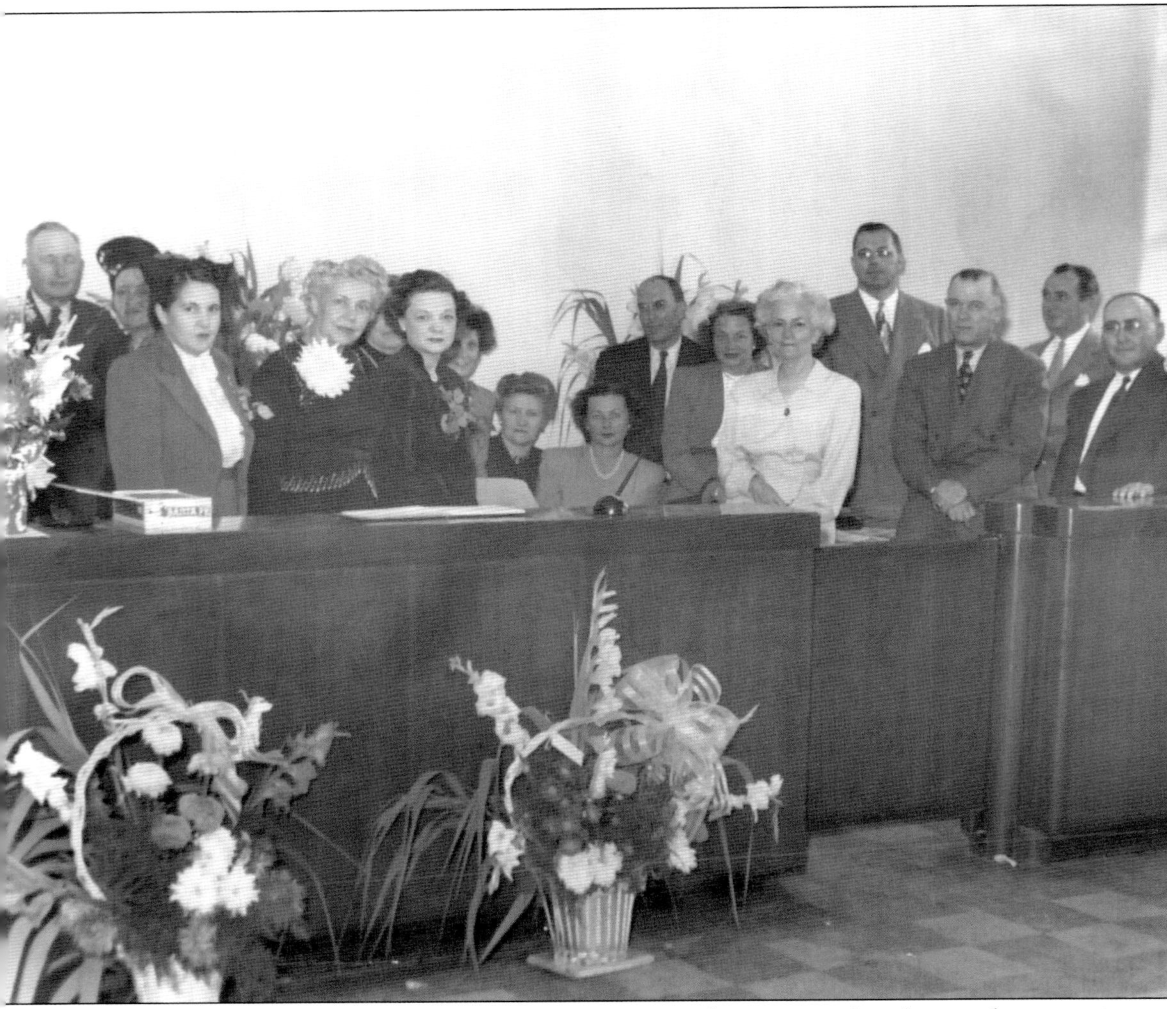

The stockholders and directors of the Grants State Bank are pictured at the grand opening in September 1947. This opening was celebrated by everybody in the area, as the bank was the first to serve the western part of the county. The celebration commenced with a parade, with the winning float by the high school business class featuring a giant sock and a safe with the theme "From Sock to Lock." All of the citizens of the area and out-of-town guests were invited to a picnic at the Ice Caves, which is one of the local wonders of the county. (Courtesy of the Grants State Bank.)

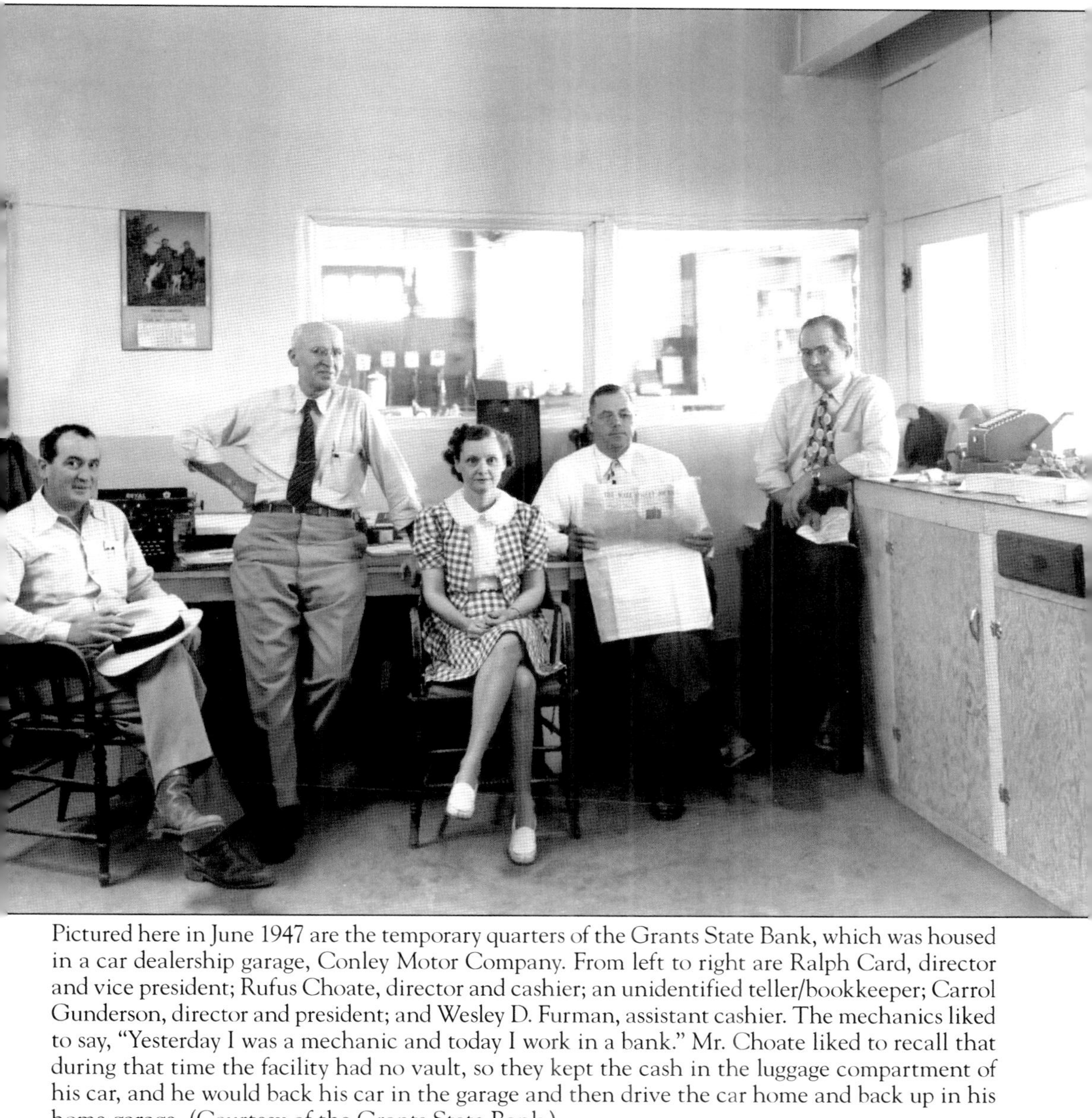

Pictured here in June 1947 are the temporary quarters of the Grants State Bank, which was housed in a car dealership garage, Conley Motor Company. From left to right are Ralph Card, director and vice president; Rufus Choate, director and cashier; an unidentified teller/bookkeeper; Carrol Gunderson, director and president; and Wesley D. Furman, assistant cashier. The mechanics liked to say, "Yesterday I was a mechanic and today I work in a bank." Mr. Choate liked to recall that during that time the facility had no vault, so they kept the cash in the luggage compartment of his car, and he would back his car in the garage and then drive the car home and back up in his home garage. (Courtesy of the Grants State Bank.)

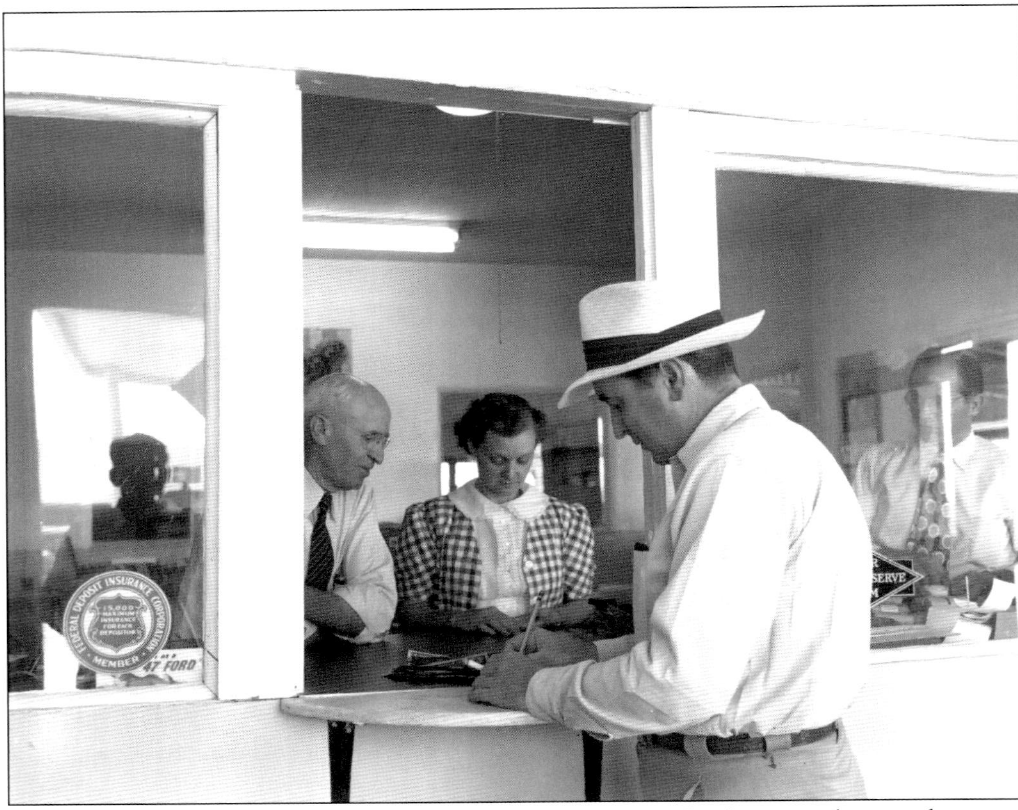

This action shot of the temporary quarters of the Grants State Bank was used as an advertising photograph. The manager and teller accommodate the president as he cashes a check to show to the public that services are now available. (Courtesy of the Grants State Bank.)

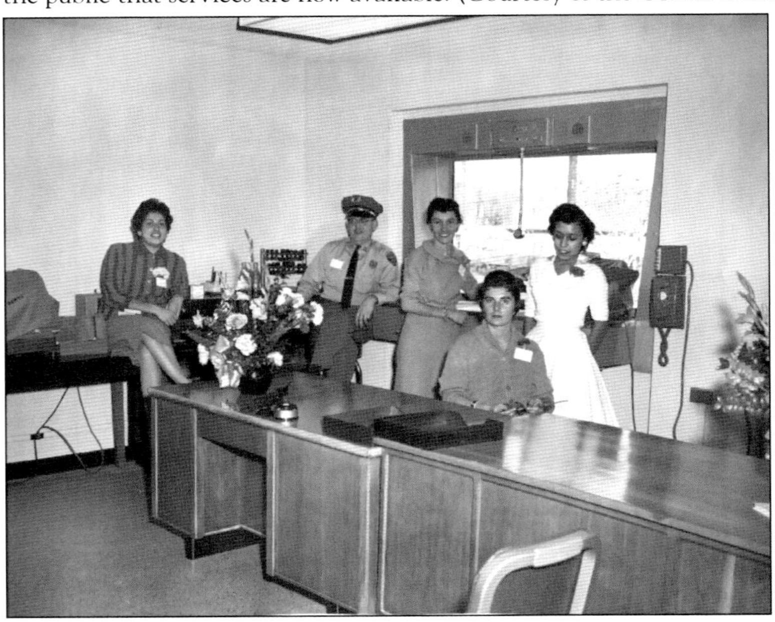

Tellers and bookkeepers celebrate the grand opening of the Grants State Bank built in 1958. The employees were on hand to give tours to the guests and explain how the new state-of-the-art drive-in teller functioned; it was the first in the area. (Courtesy of the Grants State Bank.)

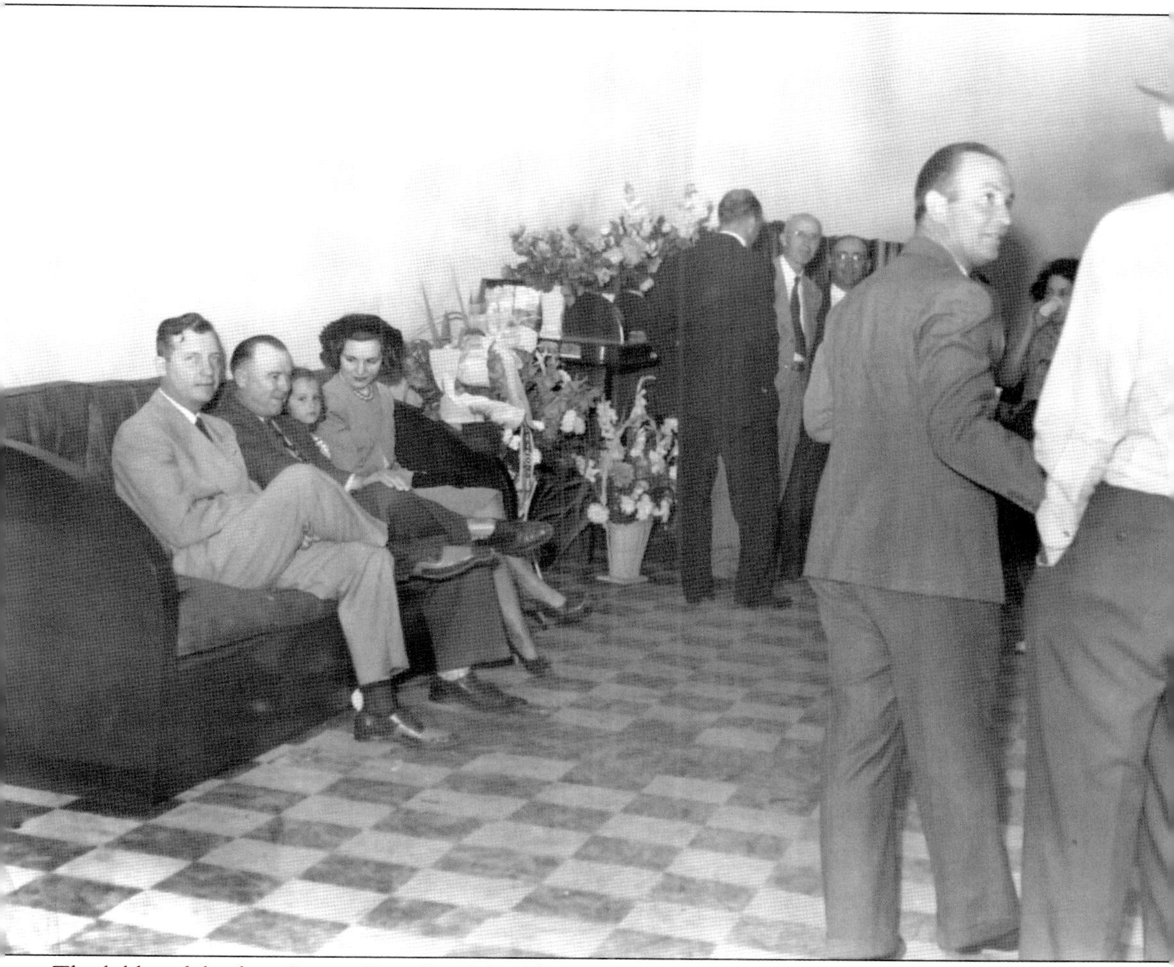

The lobby of the first Grants State Bank building is pictured after the parade held on September 1947 celebrating the opening of the bank. Customers lined up to open accounts on this historic occasion. (Courtesy of the Grants State Bank.)

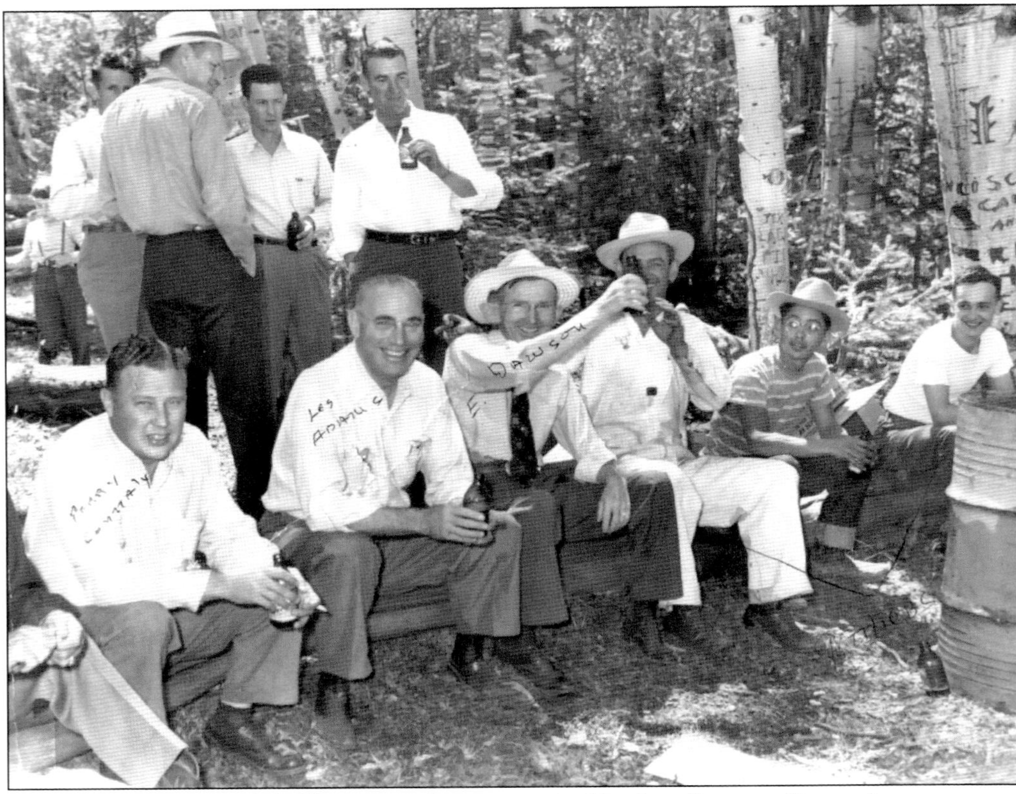

The Grants Lions Club held an annual picnic at the Harding Summer Camp that was one of the best events of the year. Pres. Emmet Dawson did not drink, but the members talked him into taking his picture with a bottle of beer. Although many of the members were farmers and ranchers, it was normal for them to picnic in what was then called Sunday clothes. (Courtesy of E.B. Dawson.)

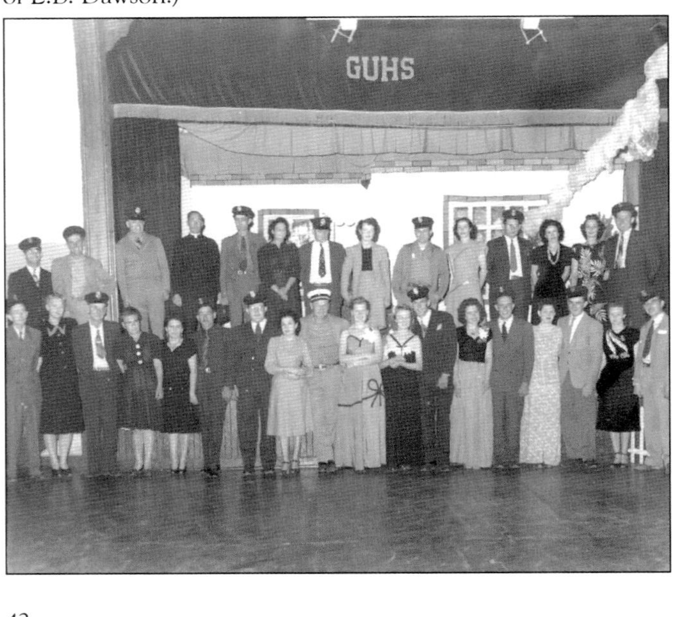

The Grants Volunteer Fireman's Annual Ball was held at the Grants Union High School gym. The ball was very formal, and an invitation was coveted. The members were prominent local businessmen and professionals, and to be selected to be a member was an honor. (Courtesy of E.B. Dawson.)

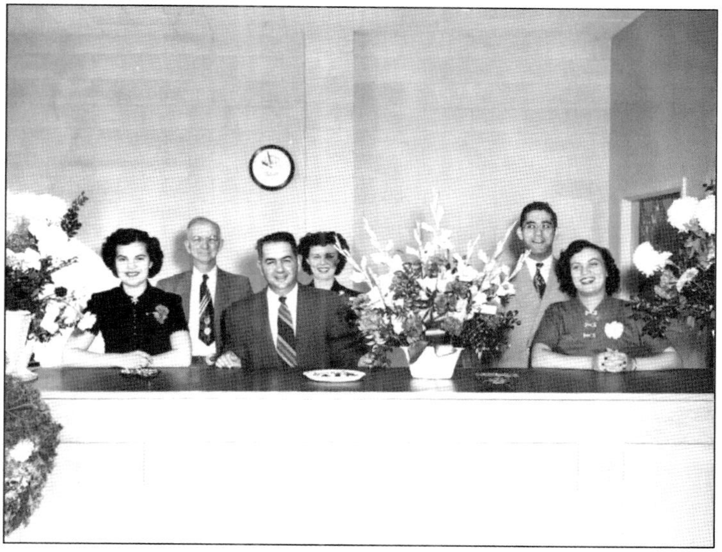

The longtime Fidel and Rouse Insurance Agency celebrates the addition of Mayor Salvador Milan as a partner. From left to right are (first row) Irene Baca Fidel, Salvador Milan, and Susie Sarracino Dominguez; (second row) Cy Rouse, Barbara Pegau, and Joseph Fidel. It was not unusual for businessmen at that time to be involved in multiple businesses as well as politics. (Courtesy of the Milan family.)

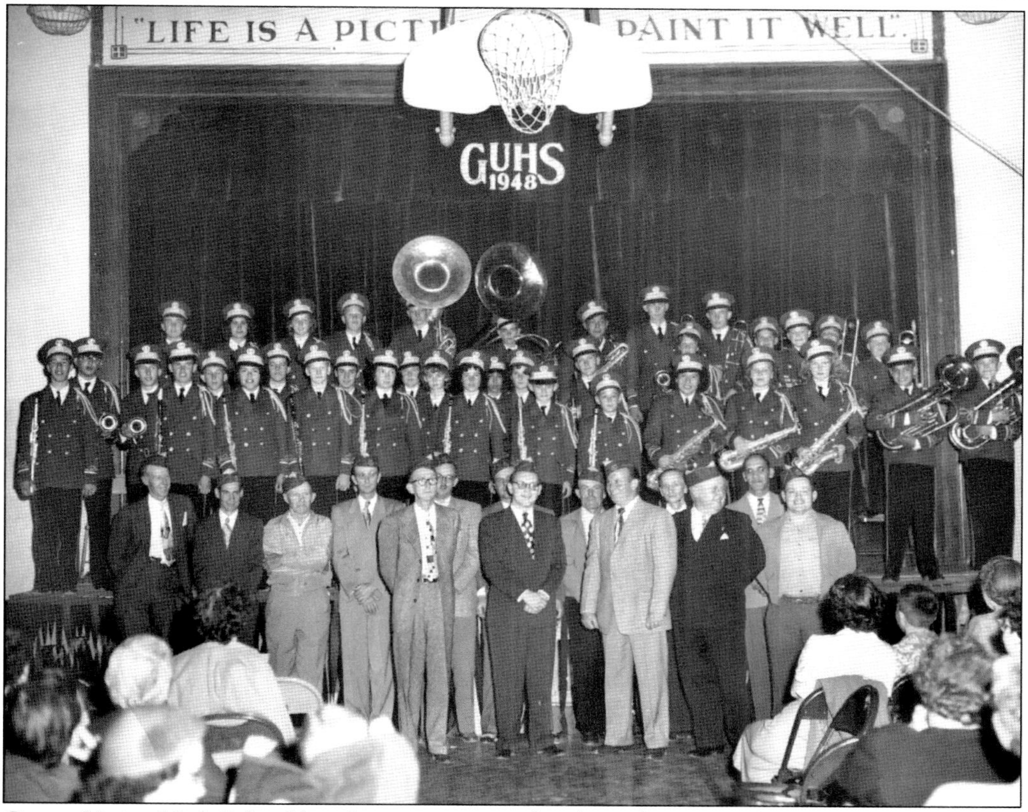

Grants Union High School band gives a concert thanking the Grants lions Club for purchasing the school's first band uniforms (1950–1951). The Grants Lions Club was one of the most active organizations in Grants and was responsible for supporting all causes that increased the quality of life in the area. They supported all youth activities as well as some Lion International causes, and it was an honor to be invited to be a member. (Courtesy of E.B. Dawson.)

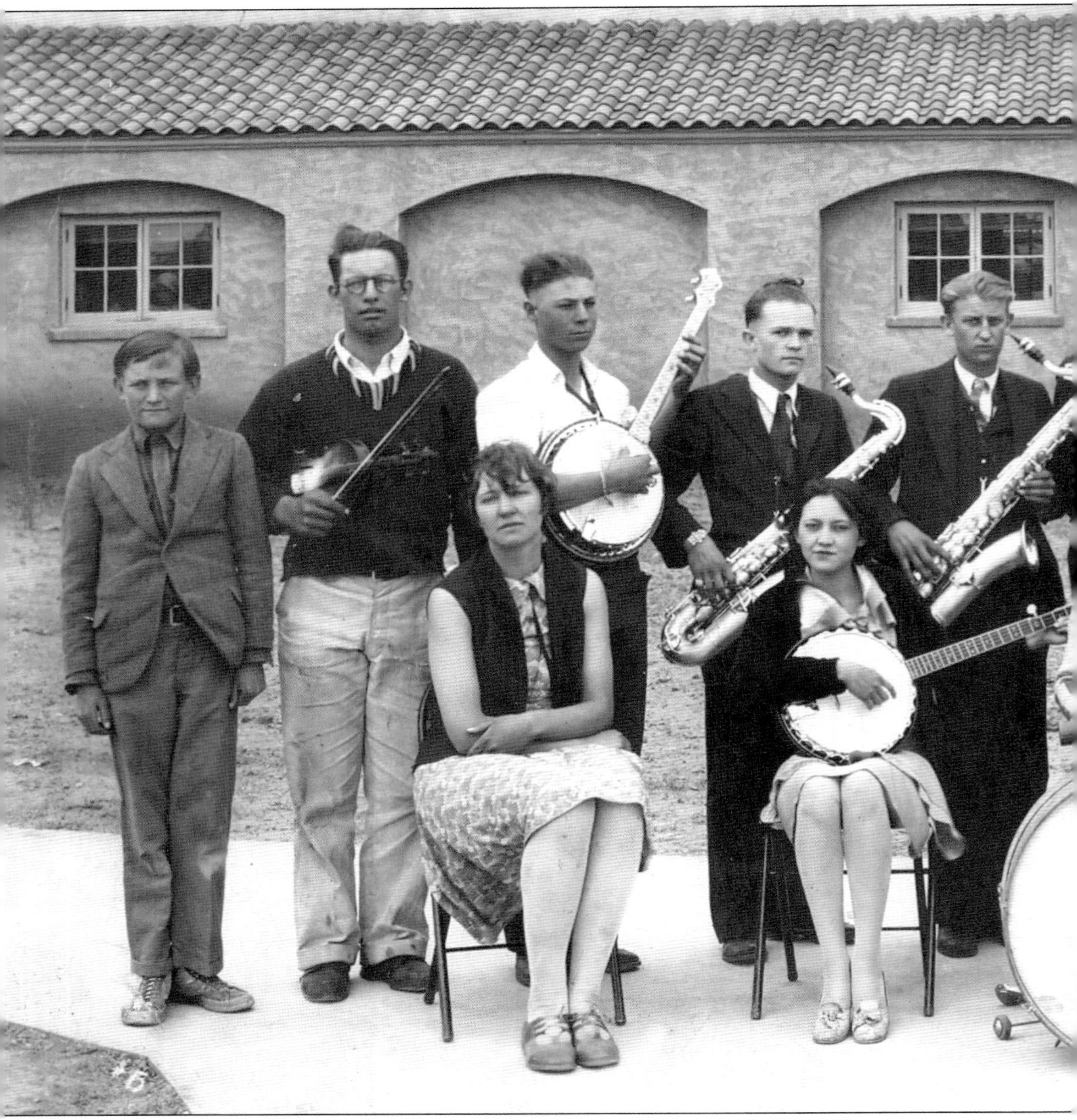

The Grants Union High School orchestra band is seen here in 1931–1932. This photograph was

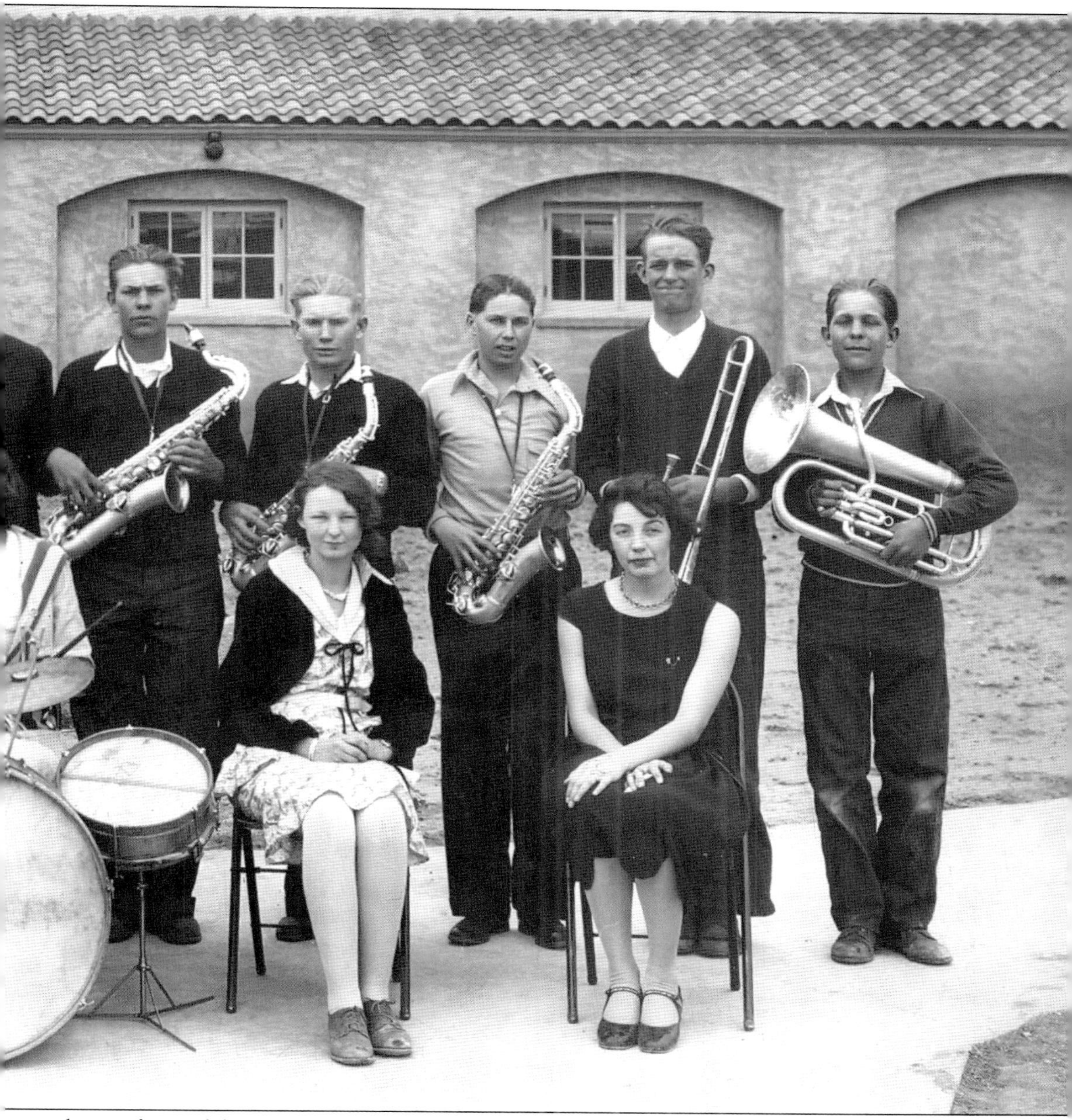

taken in front of the Grants Union High School. (Courtesy of the Milan family.)

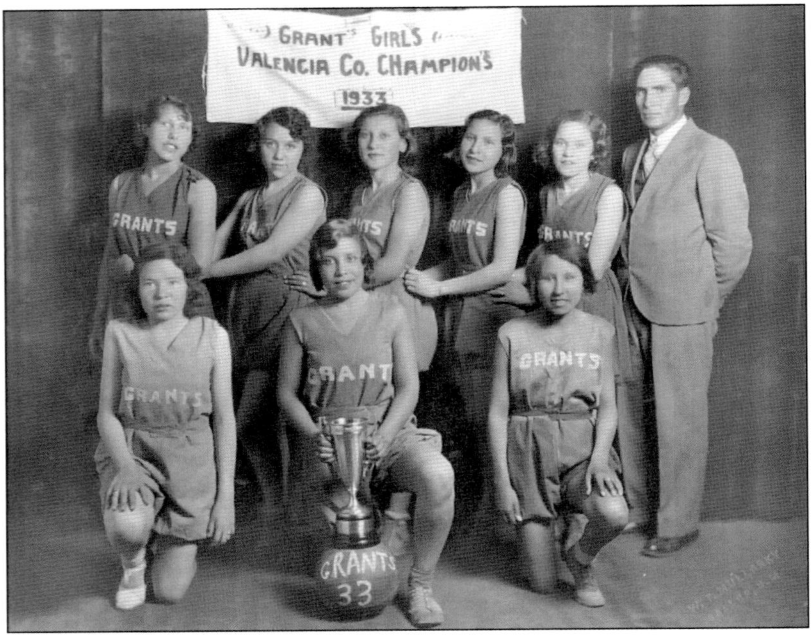

The 1933 Grants girls' basketball team was the county champs that season. (Courtesy of the Conklin family.)

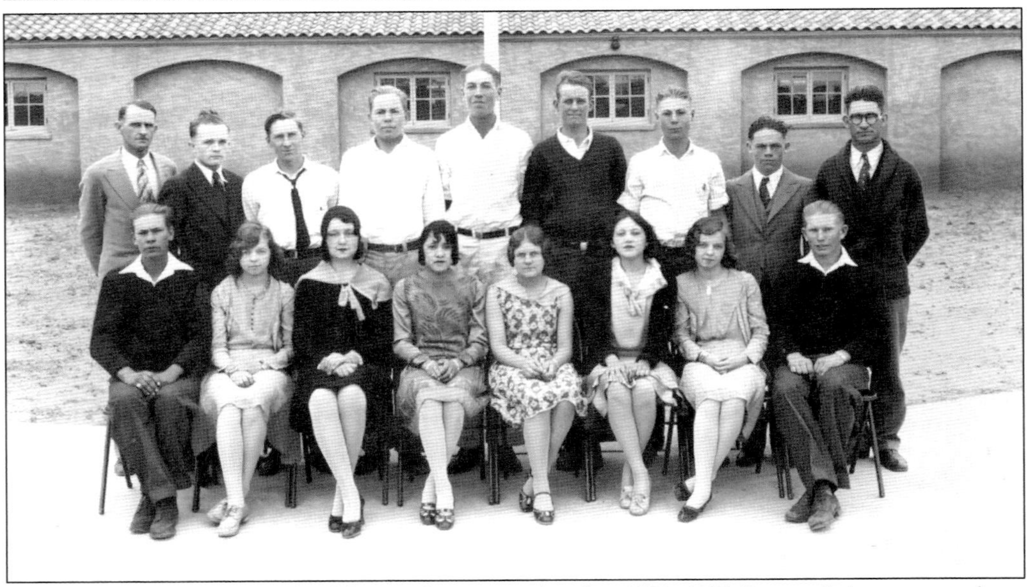

The Grants Union High School (GUHS) was completed in 1929–1930. Pictured above are students from the first graduating class of GUHS in 1931. Today, Grants High School, which used to be Grants Union High School, is part of the Grants/Cibola County School District. The district is larger than the state of Rhode Island. The old GUHS building is the Cibola County Office Complex as of 2012 and has been the center of events in the area for decades. Most of the small towns surrounding Grants had elementary schools up to the eighth grade, and most taught in Spanish except for the town of Bluewater, which was a Mormon community. Bluewater had the first high school in the area. There was a lot of negotiating as to where the union high school should be, and it was decided at that time that Grants would be a perfect neutral place for all of the communities, including the Native American reservations. (Courtesy of the Milan family.)

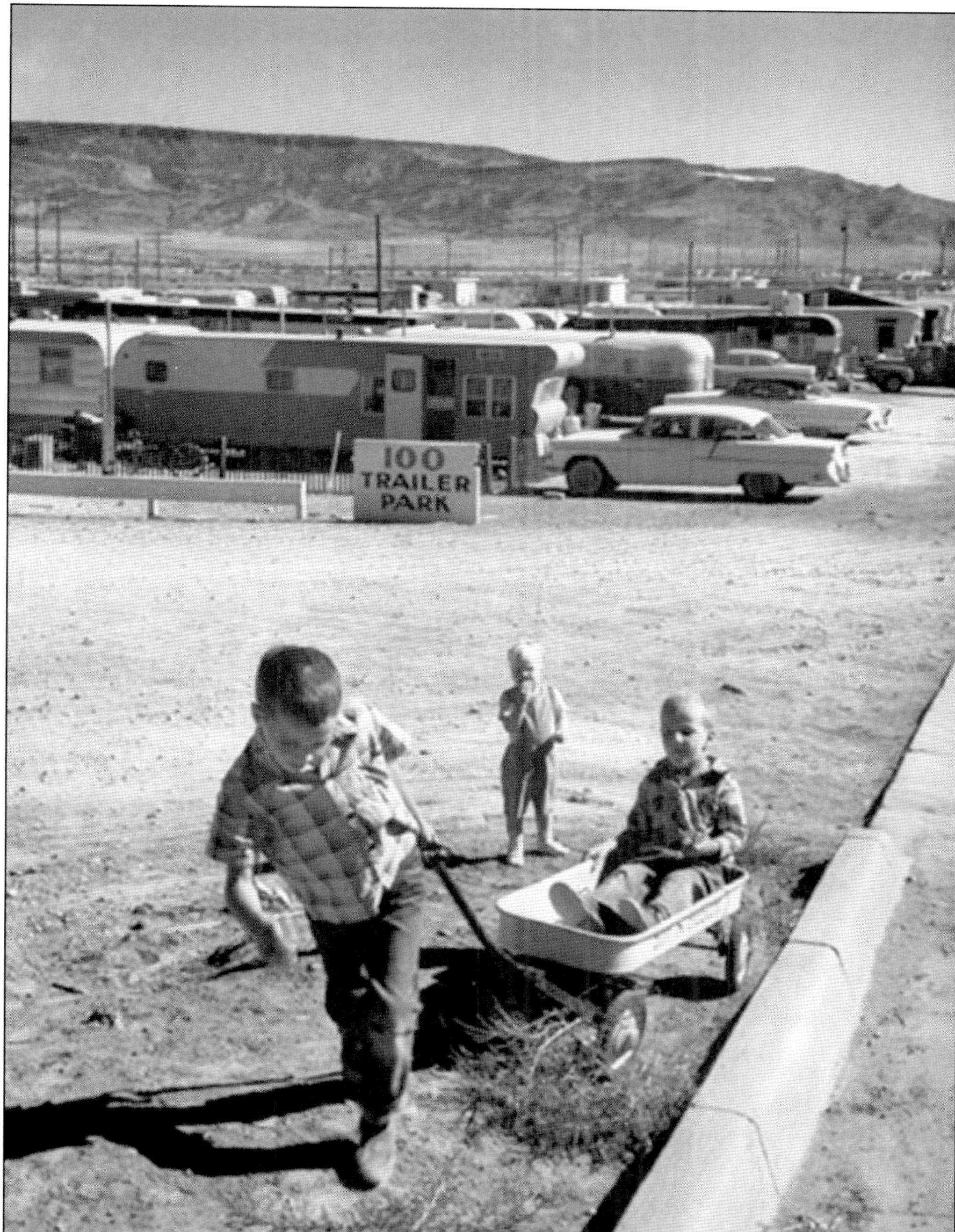

Pictured here is the uranium boom trailer park in Grants in the 1950s. The uranium boom created an immediate need for housing, and the solution was trailer parks like this one, which sprang up in Grants and Milan almost overnight. (Courtesy of the University of New Mexico, University Libraries.)

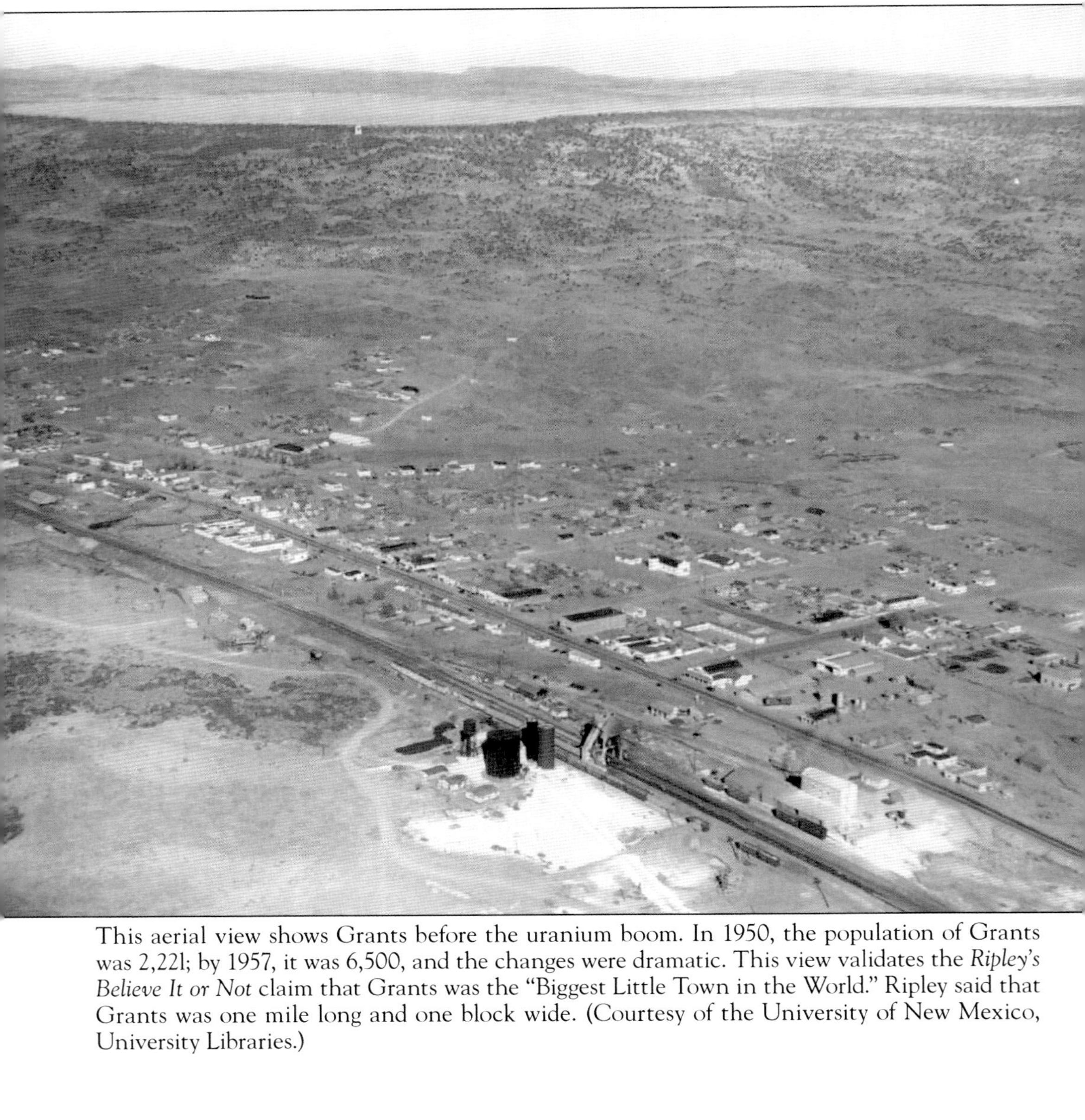

This aerial view shows Grants before the uranium boom. In 1950, the population of Grants was 2,221; by 1957, it was 6,500, and the changes were dramatic. This view validates the *Ripley's Believe It or Not* claim that Grants was the "Biggest Little Town in the World." Ripley said that Grants was one mile long and one block wide. (Courtesy of the University of New Mexico, University Libraries.)

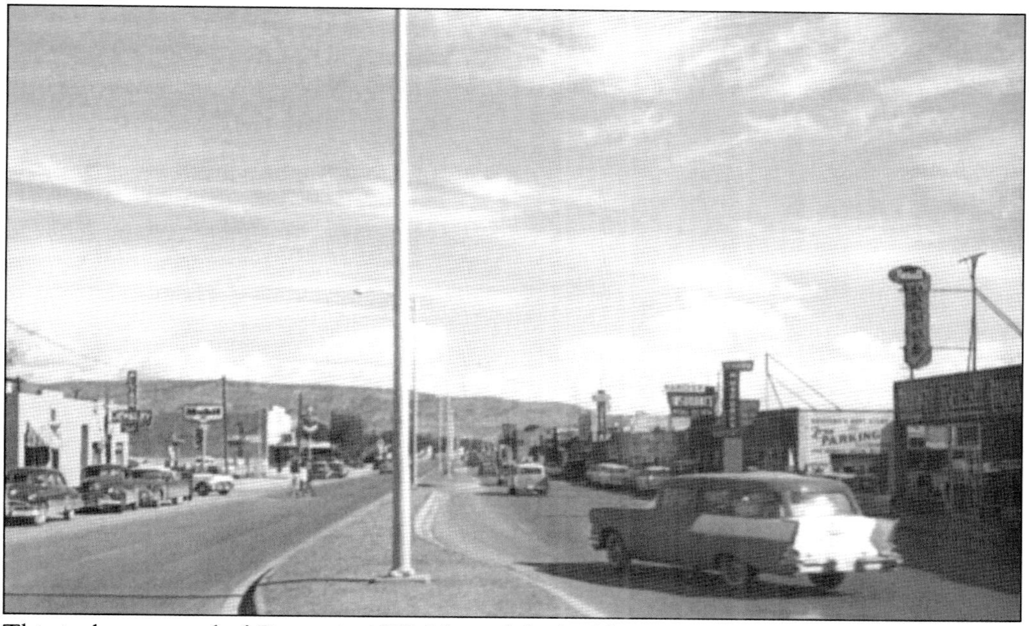

This is the west end of Grants in 1957. Most of the building are still present, although they are either vacant or are used for other businesses. On the right is the Thrifty Drug store, which is now vacant and was sometimes used as a second-hand store. Next to it was a clothing store that has been remodeled as the Double 66 Art Gallery. On the left are Allison's Jewelry, the Mobil station, Adams Department Store, and the Chevron station. During that time, there were service stations on almost every corner, a café and bar on every block, and a ma-and-pa store on every block. (Courtesy of Aurelio Apocada.)

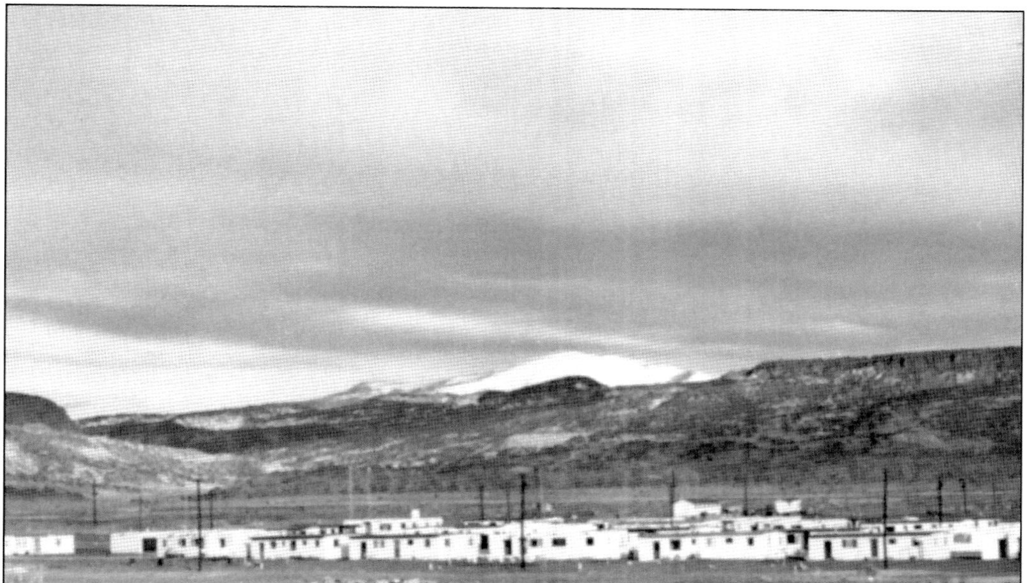

The first housing development in Grants that responded to the new uranium boom was developed by the Gunderson family. By 1960, there were housing projects in both Grants and Milan, including many trailer parks. (Courtesy of the University of New Mexico, University Libraries.)

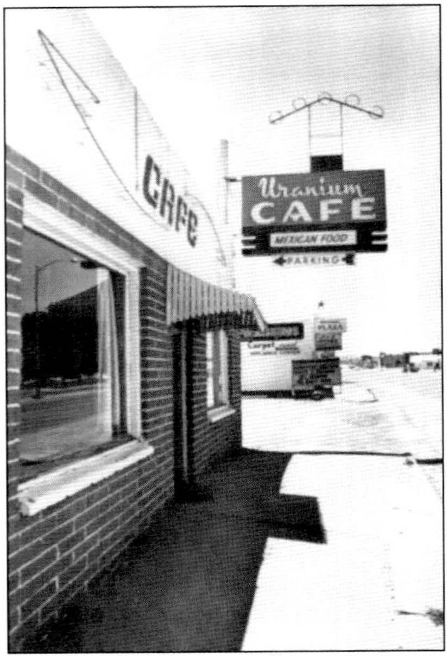

This was a café that responded to Grants designating itself the Uranium Capital of the World. The café was built by the Thigpen family and was rented and then bought by the Wu family, Chinese immigrants. The café has been very popular, and because of the nuclear attack on Japan, Japanese tourists come to see the café and have commented that it is well known in Japan. The café has changed hands and is now known as Badlands. (Courtesy Aurelio Apocada.)

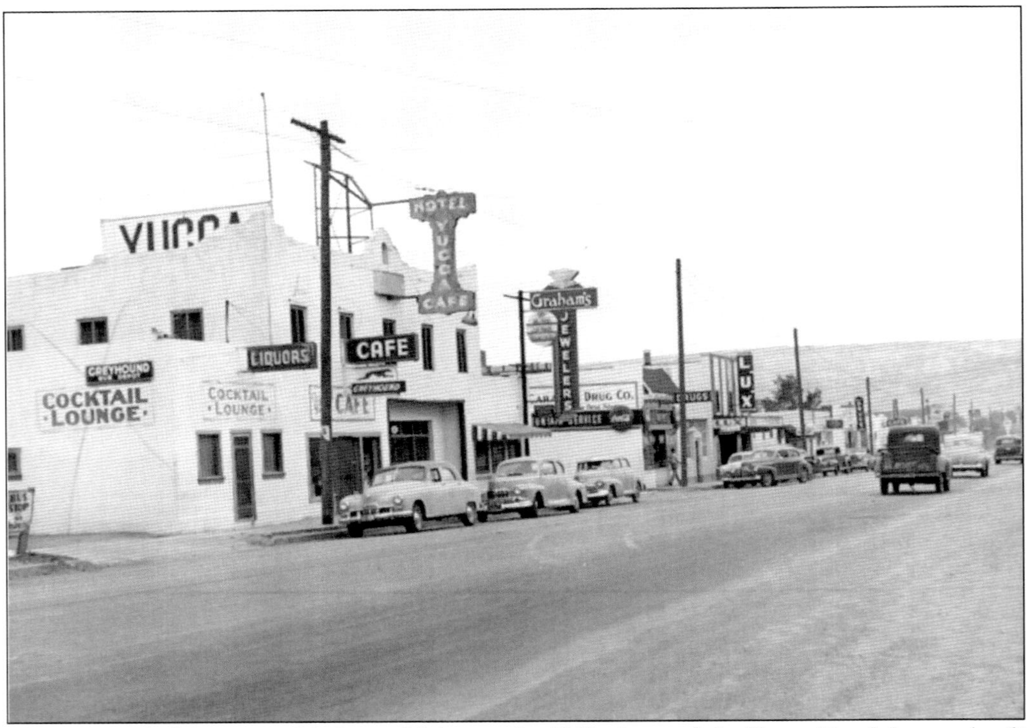

The west end of Grants on Highway 66 during the 1950s featured the Yucca Hotel, bar, and café and Graham's Jewelers. The Caradine Drugstore, the Grants State Bank, and the Lux Theater are also visible on the next block. The Yucca had had various owners. It was built by a Greek American by the name of George Ade, who also built the Lux Theater in the 1920s and early 1930s. The Yucca Hotel was the most popular meeting place in Grants during that era. (Courtesy of Aurelio Apocada.)

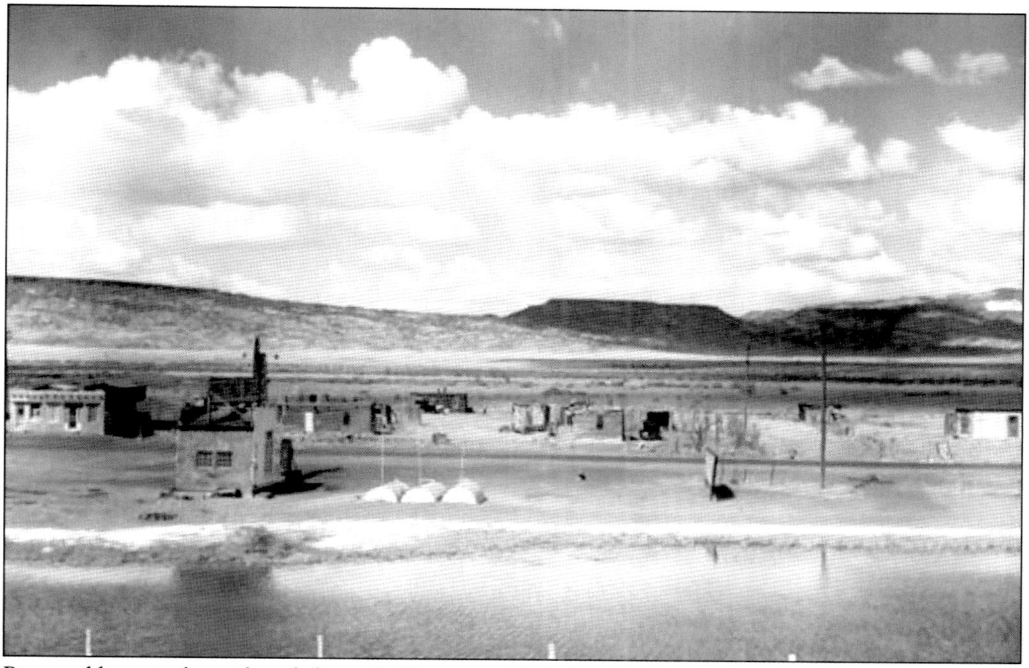

Pictured here is the railroad through Grants in 1943. This is the east part of Grants overlooking Highway 66 from the railroad tracks. There was a small service station with tanks, and the area between the highway and the railroad tracks was normally filled with water that ran off the east side of town from the south. (Courtesy of the University of New Mexico, University Libraries.)

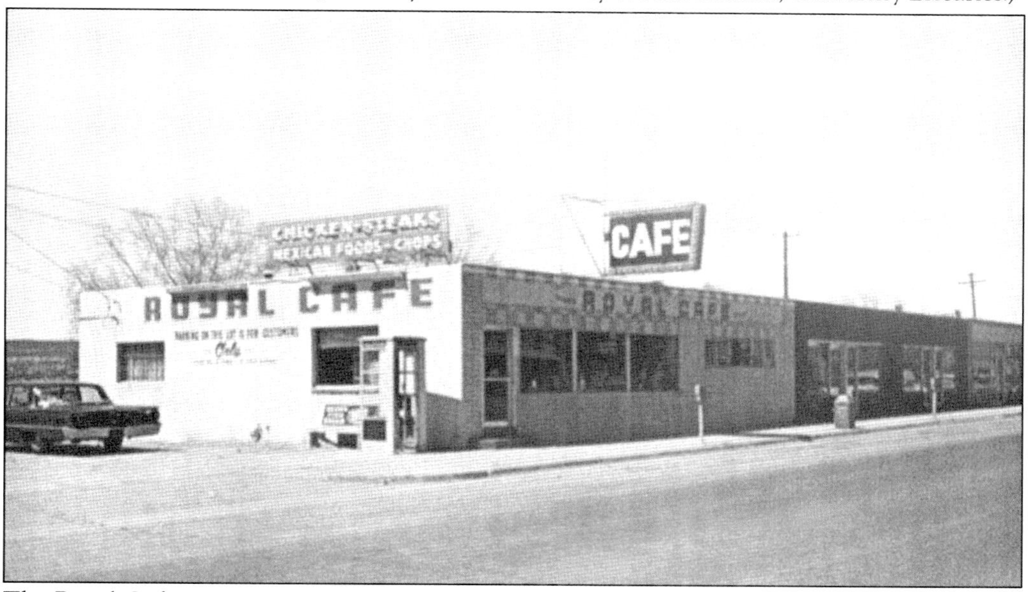

The Royal Café was one of the most popular cafés from the 1940s through the 1960s. It was a favorite hangout for many politicians, who met meet every morning to talk about their rivals (who met at the Grants Café to talk about them). The Royal Café had a number of owners, with the last ones being Greek Americans. During the uranium boom of the 1970s, it was replaced by a steakhouse. (Courtesy of Aurelio Apocada.)

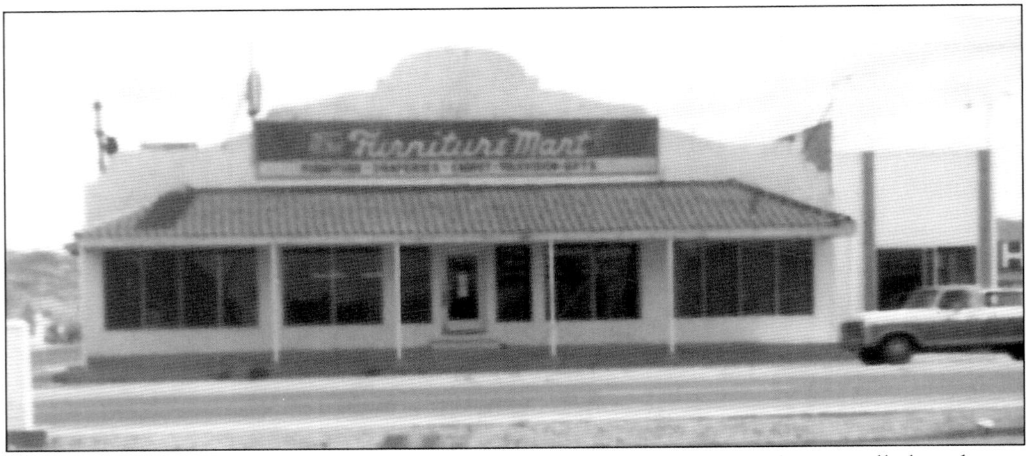

Mr. Carrol Gunderson came to work for the Bond store in the 1920s and eventually bought out Mr. Sargent and later Mr. Bond, but he initially kept the Bond-Sargent Mercantile name. The mercantile sold everything from shoes to screwdrivers and served as the local quasi-bank by cashing checks and keeping cash in its safe for customers. The store sold lumber and groceries, later served as a gasoline distributor, and maintained a bean cleaning facility for the farmers. It also bought wool and lambs from the sheep ranchers for shipment out of state. Eventually, Gunderson and his sons had multiple kinds of stores throughout the area and helped develop the local banks. The original facility became the Furniture Mart. The original building was demolished to give more room to the Hillcrest Shopping Center, which the Gundersons developed and which still serves the community under the third generation of Gundersons. (Courtesy of Aurelio Apocada.)

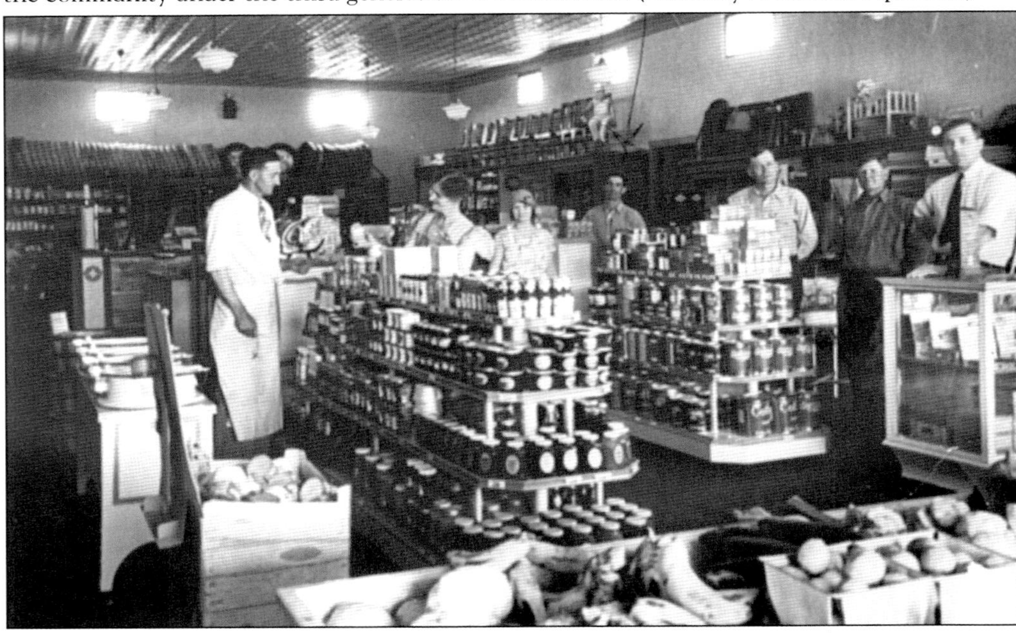

Inside the Bond-Gunderson Mercantile Store, the employees are standing in the grocery section. This photograph shows the variety of merchandise in back of the grocery department. Carrol Gunderson is on the far right, and Edwardo Baca is in the back of the store. Baca went on to open his own family store and ambulance service. Many of the employees of the Bond-Gunderson store went on to open their own businesses. (Courtesy of Aurelio Apocada.)

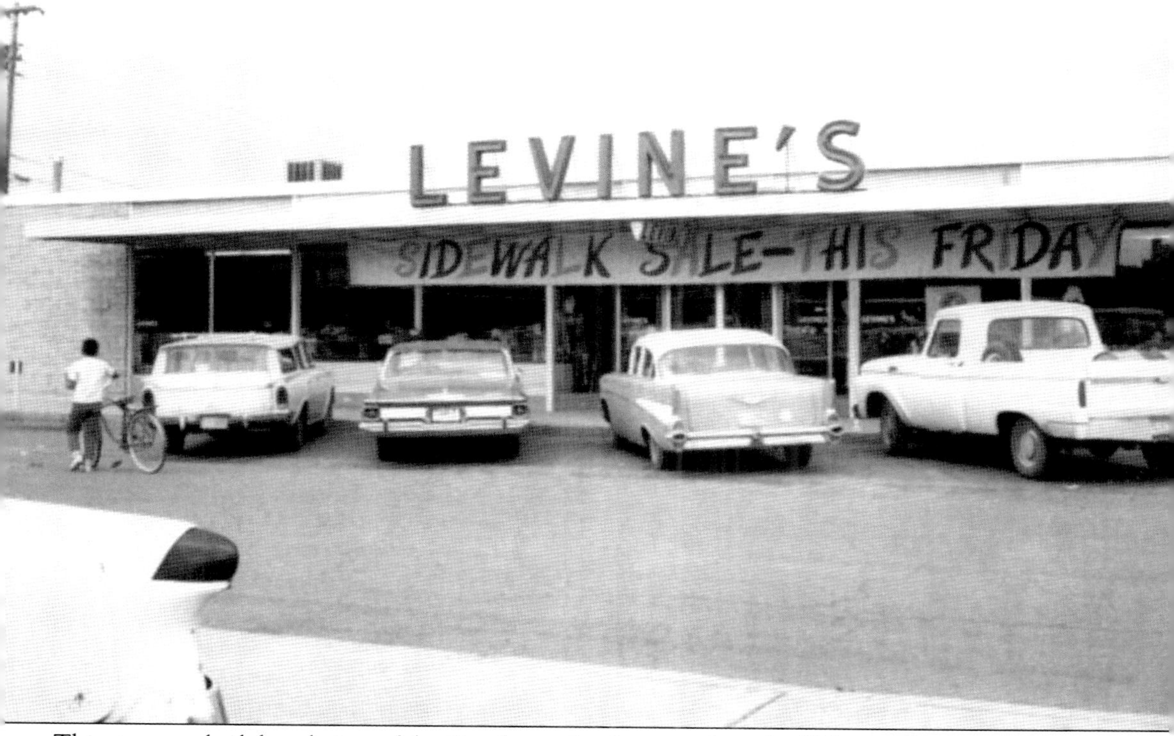

This store was built by relatives of the Gunderson family across from the Hillcrest Shopping Center in response to the growing population's need to buy a variety of clothing. It is now a furniture store. (Courtesy of Aurelio Apocada.)

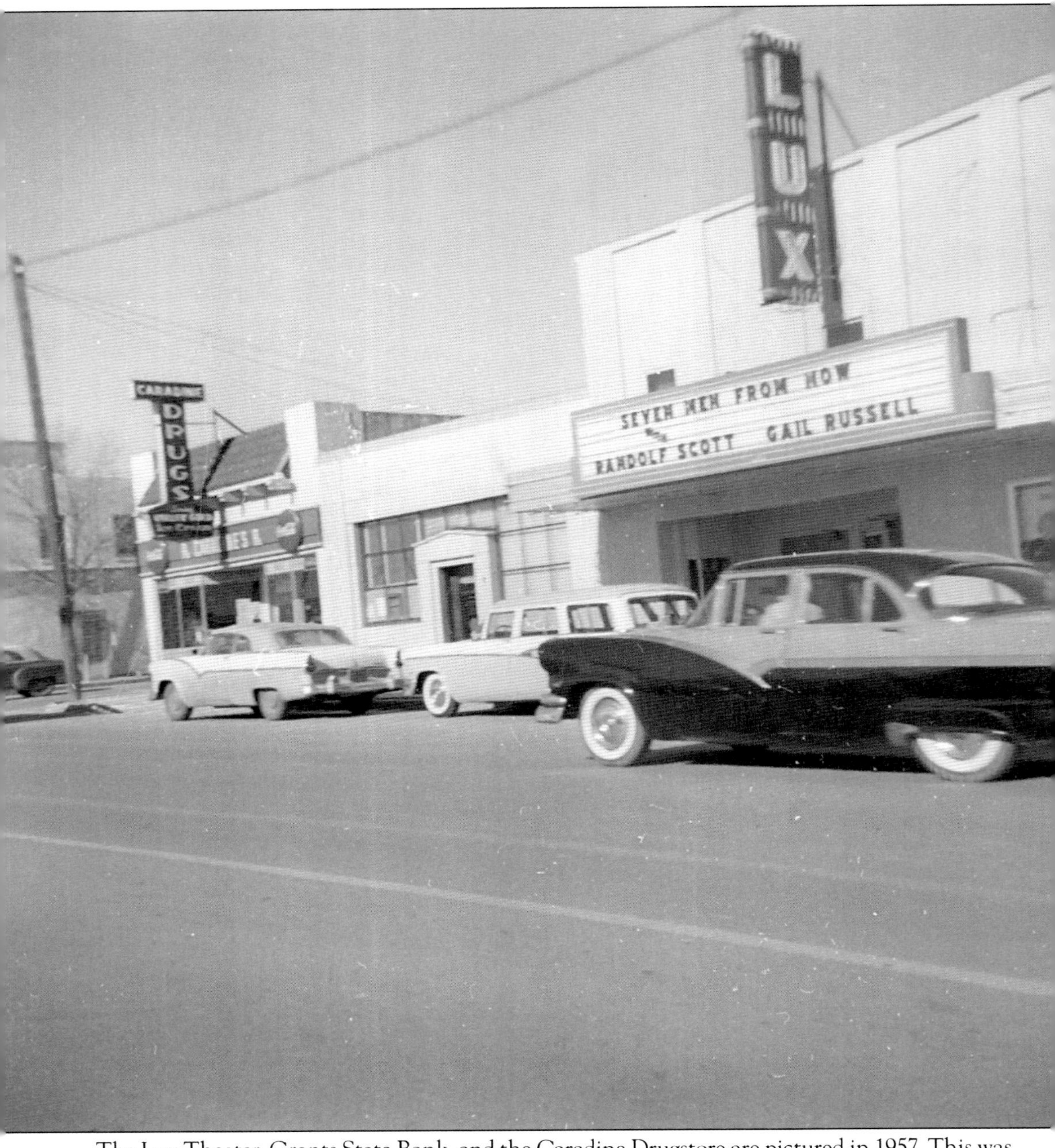

The Lux Theater, Grants State Bank, and the Caradine Drugstore are pictured in 1957. This was the most popular and active corner in town during the 1950s. Presently, these buildings are vacant and in a dire condition. Although they are candidates for preservation as historical buildings, funds to rehabilitate them have not been available. (Courtesy of Aurelio Apocada.)

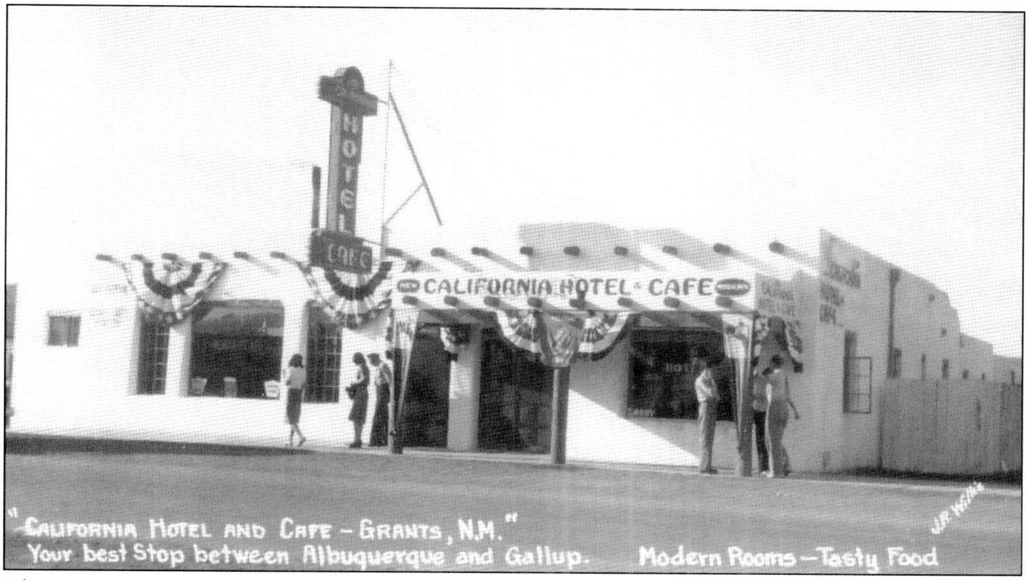

This was one of the finest hotels in Grants during the late 1930s. It was on the west side of town at First Street and Santa Fe Avenue (Highway 66). The California Hotel and Café was very popular and served as a bus stop for Greyhound and Trailways. Like with many hotels in small towns, new residents would live here until they found a home rental or built a home. Many of the local hotels and cafés were owned by Greek immigrants at that time. (Courtesy of Aurelio Apocada.)

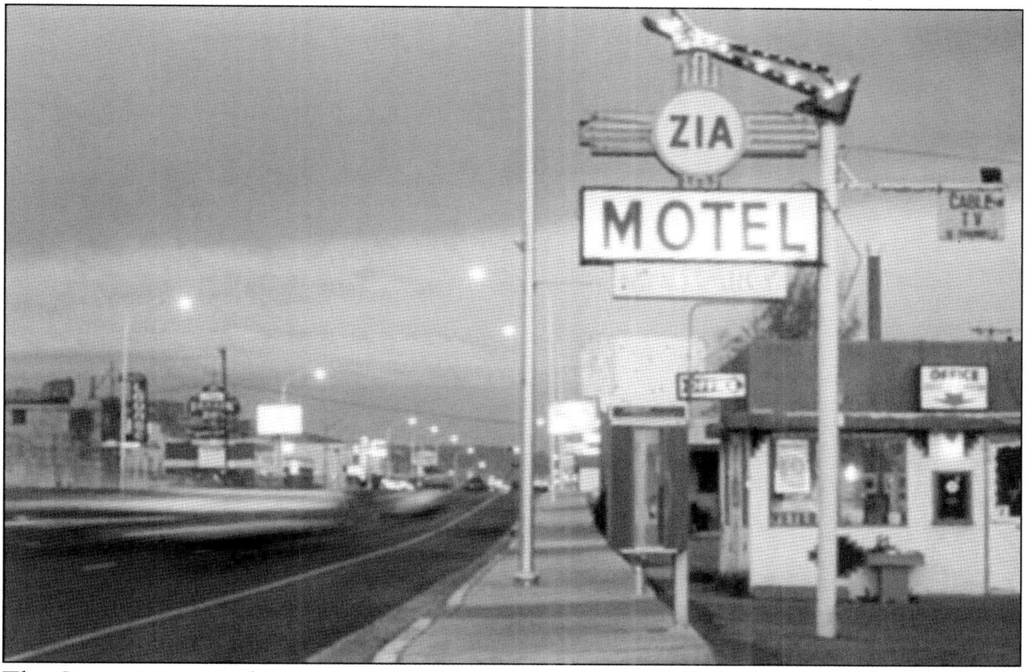

The Grants Motor Lodge was built by Bennie Sarracino in 1945. This was the first motel not called a campground in the east part of Grants. In later years, the name changed to the It'll Do Inn and then to the Wayside Motel. All that remains are the office and what were the living quarters on the second floor. (Courtesy of Aurelio Apocada.)

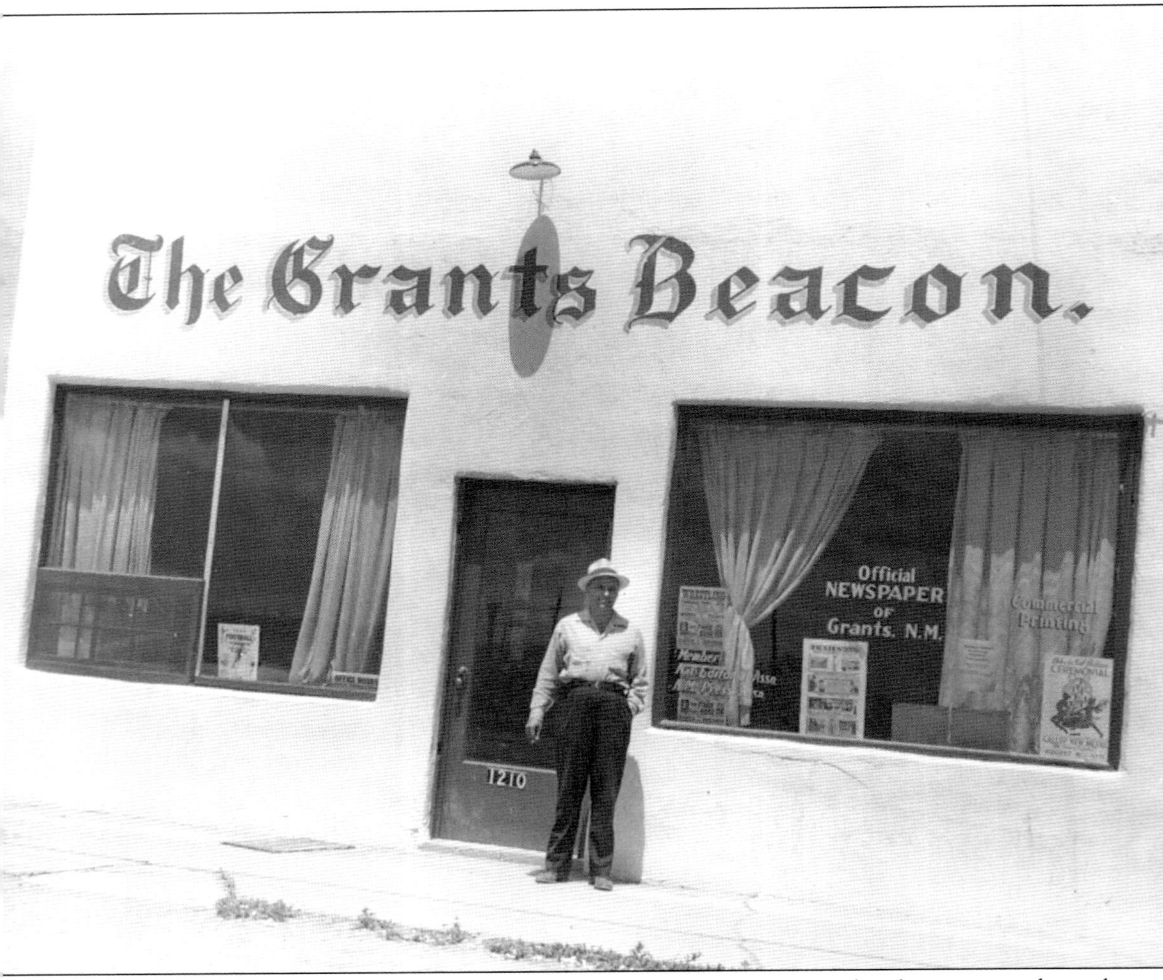

The *Grants Beacon*, now named the *Cibola Beacon*, has been reporting local news since the early 1930s. It is seen here around 1957. The first newspaper in Grants was the *Grant Review*, a weekly that was published by J.E. Williams of Gallup. The *Beacon* has had at least five editors and five or six locations and at one time was the *Grants Daily Beacon*. (Courtesy of Aurelio Apocada.)

The Sirloin Stockade was built in the 1970s in response to the new uranium boom that brought in a large population infusion. It was one of the first chain restaurants to enter the Grants area but closed when the uranium boom went bust. It is now a video store. (Courtesy of Aurelio Apocada.)

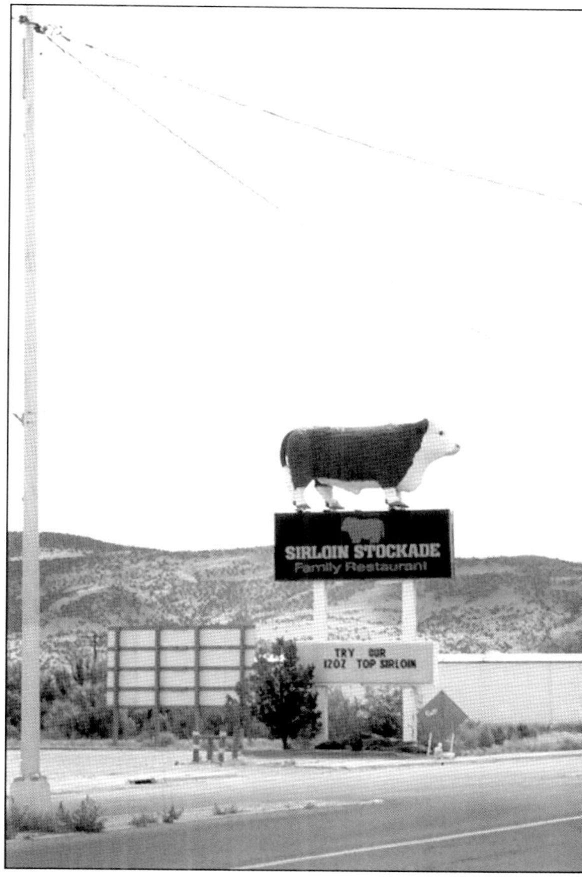

This was the first cafeteria-style restaurant and bar in Grants, built by the Pablo Peña family in the 1960s. It became a popular stop for tour buses and was also very popular as a meeting place because the building that could accommodate large groups. (Courtesy of Aurelio Apocada.)

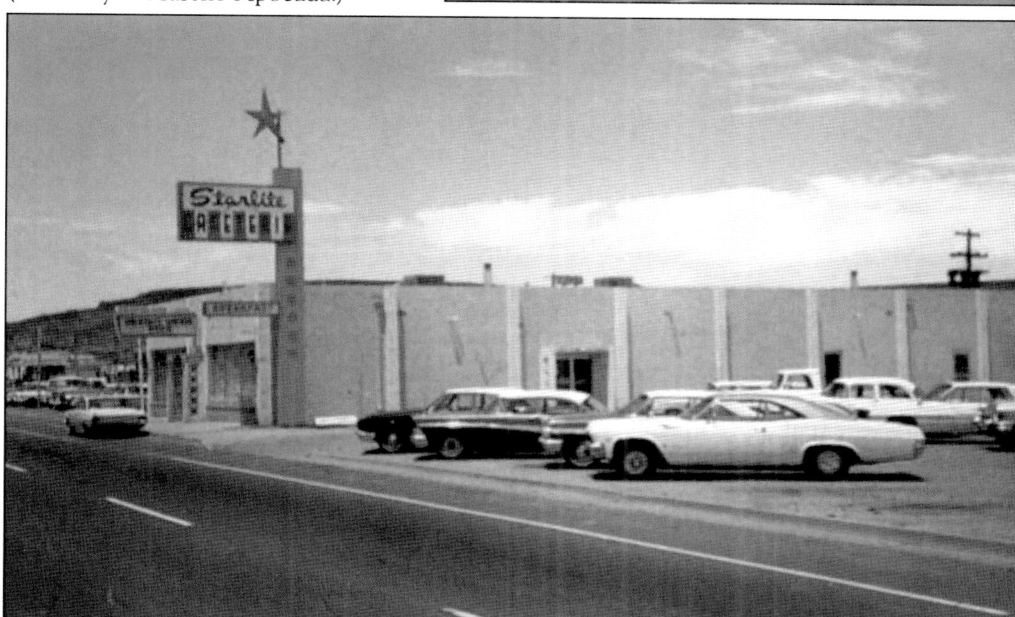

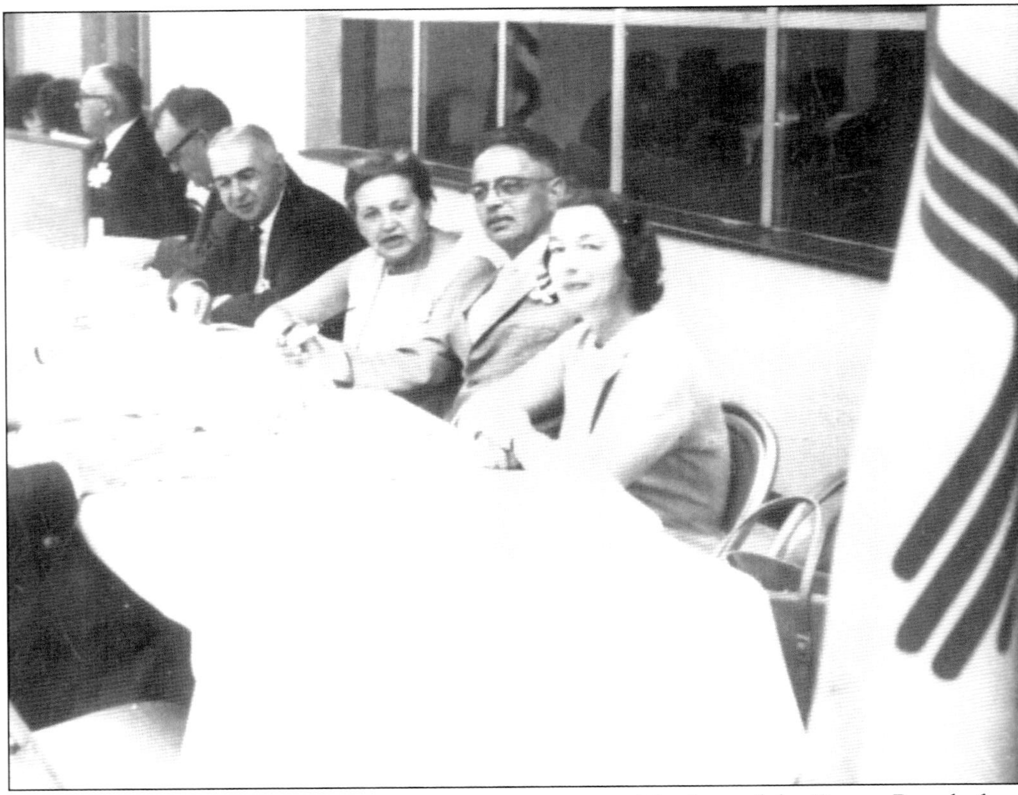

Members of the Grants Board of Education around 1967 included, from left to right, Manuel B. McBride, superintendent; unidentified; Salvador Milan, chairman; Bennie Milan; Robert Gottlieb; and Naomi Gottlieb. (Courtesy of the Manuel McBride family.)

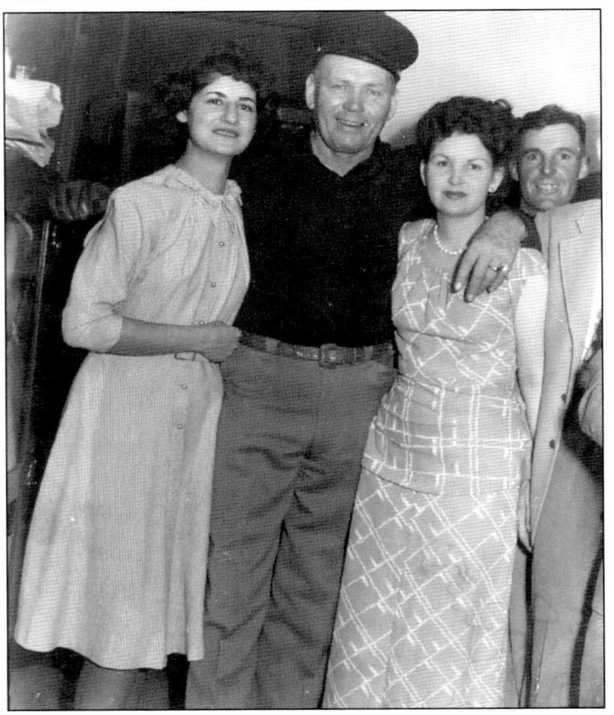

Mary Fidel (left) and friends attend one of the many dances held at the Grants High School gym. Mary was a sister to Sen. Joseph Fidel. Mary started as a teller at the Grants State Bank in 1947 and retired in 1997 after 50 years of service, ending her career as a senior vice president. (Courtesy of the Grants State Bank.)

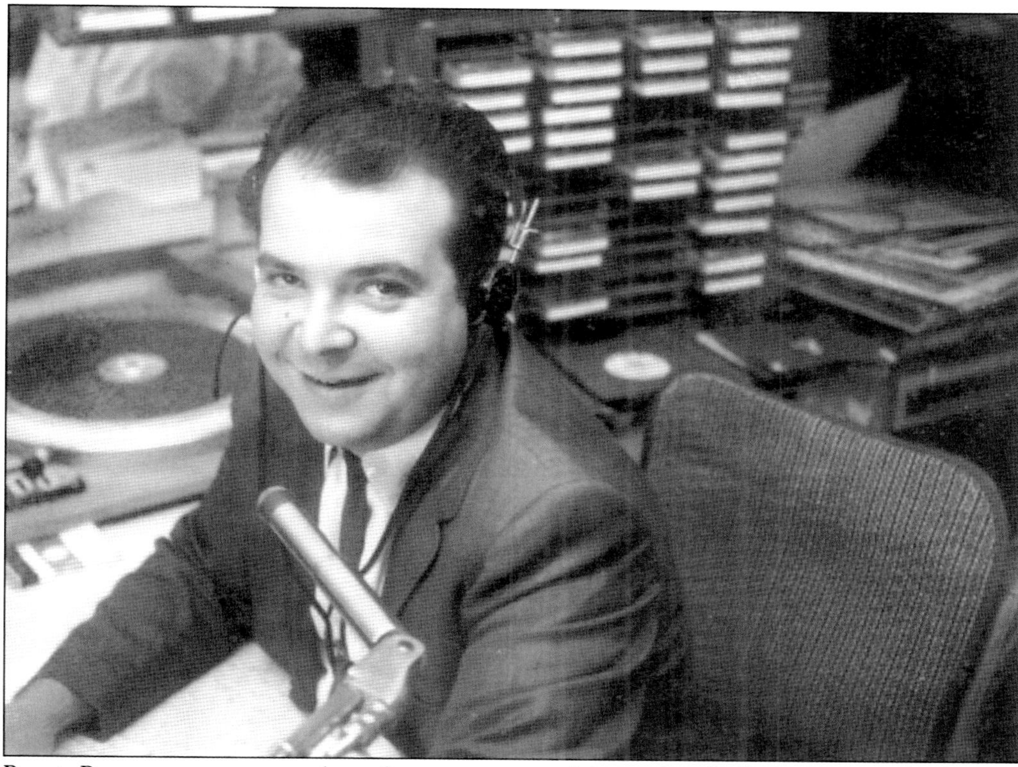

Bernie Bustos was a very popular radio announcer and disc jockey for Radio KMIN, which is still the local radio station of Grants, although new owners have expanded to other areas, including Albuquerque, the Los Lunas and Belen area east of Grants, and west on the Navajo reservation and Gallup, New Mexico. Bernie still utilizes his talent working with the Ramah Navajo tribe. (Courtesy KDSK/KMIN.)

This was KMIN facility south of Grants in the 1960s. The Big Rover and Bernie Bustos would be present at all events broadcasting to all the listeners. The new owners have moved to Grants and have developed a very nice museum featuring a lot of the old radio equipment that was in this facility. (Courtesy KDSK/KMIN.)

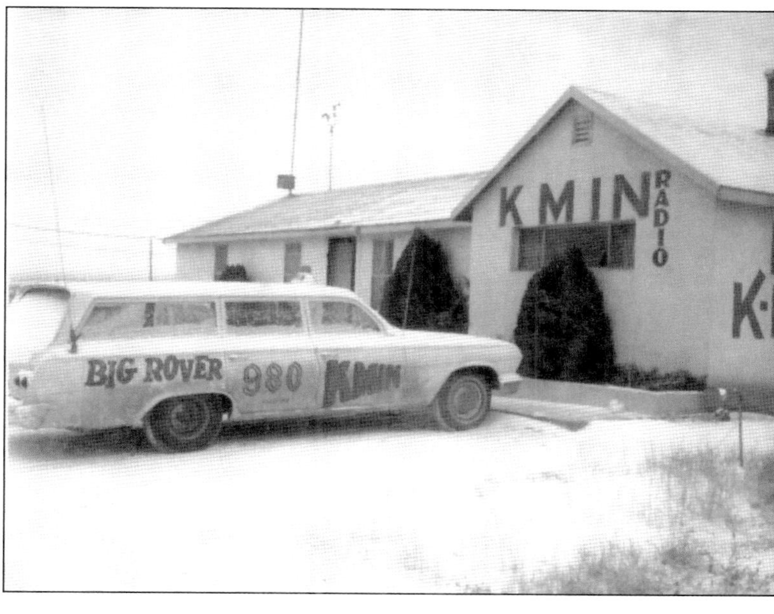

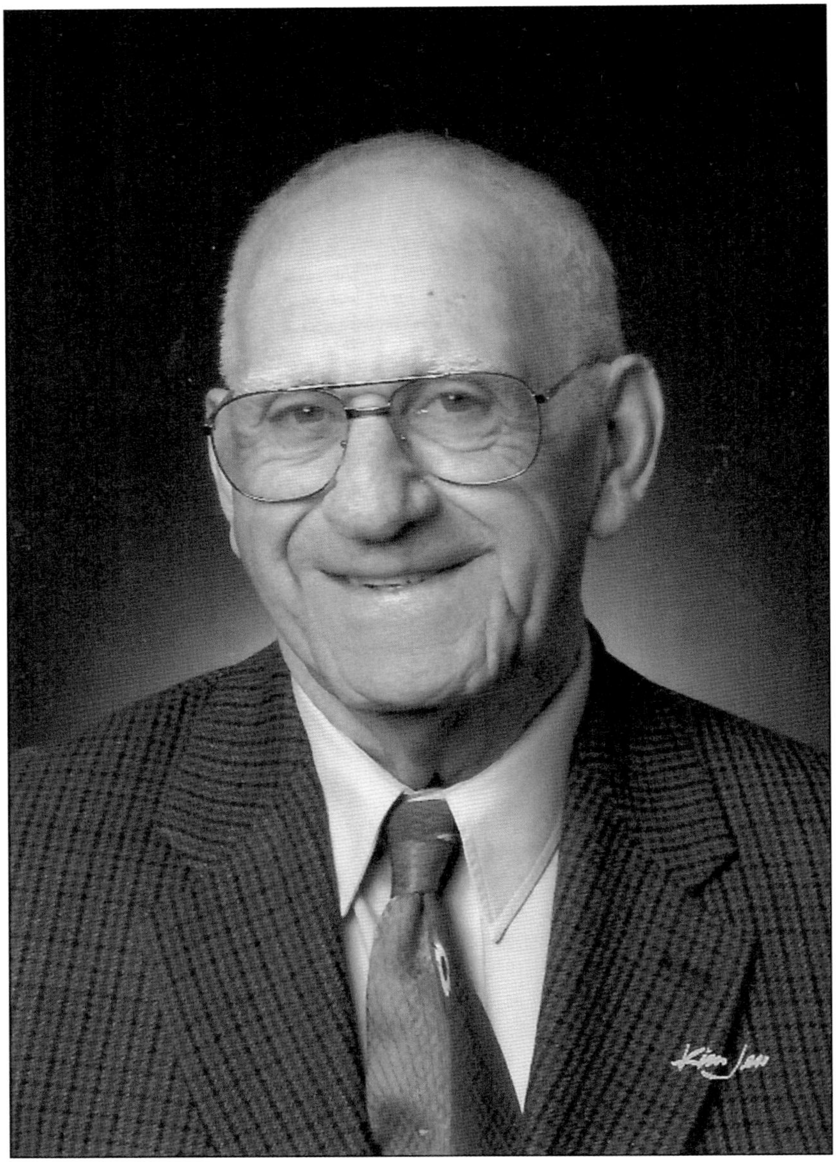

State senator Joseph (Joe) Fidel, a son of a Lebanese immigrant, moved to Grants from the small town of San Fidel 18 miles east of Grants after graduating from high school. Joe established himself in the insurance and real estate businesses and in politics. He started his political career as a county assessor and ran for any office that his party asked him to run in. He was a member of the city council and the school board. He ran for other offices that he lost, but after he won election as state senator, he won every election until he retired in 2012. Joe served during the uranium boom and then had to lead the road to recovery during the following bust as the area lost over 6,000 high-paying jobs and went into survival mode. Every project that originated in the Grants area had Joe's print on it. Joe and the local state representatives were able to work with state and local politicians and businessmen to keep the area from bankruptcy. Joe was the chairman of the State Senate Finance Committee, which was very important to the economic recovery of Grants. (Courtesy of the Fidel family.)

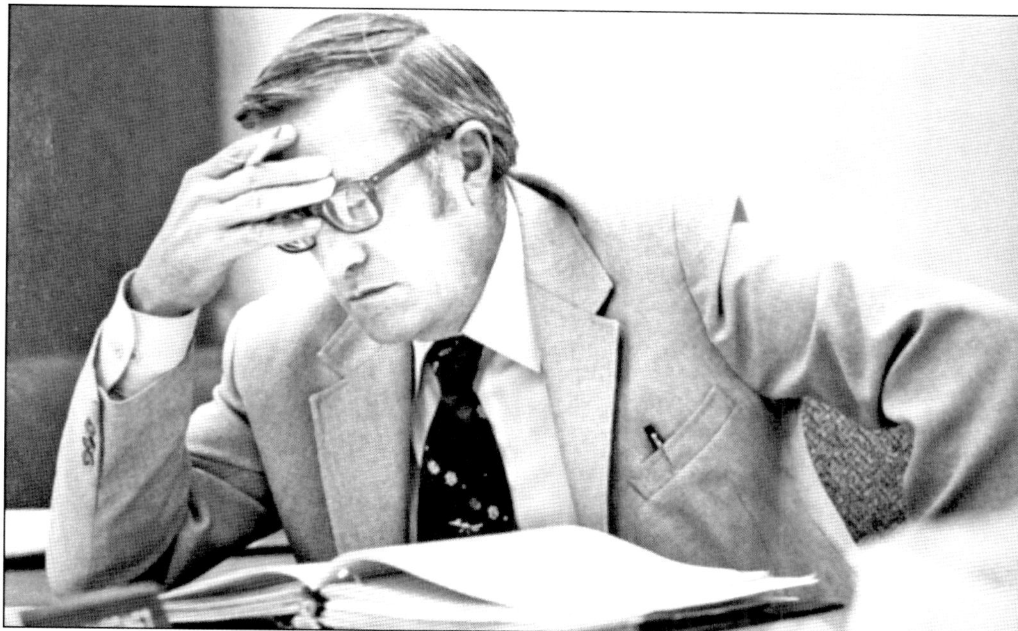

Walter Martinez was born in northern New Mexico and established his law practice in Grants after graduating from the University of New Mexico School of Law around 1956. Walter's only other office had been on the Grants Board of Education when he was elected to the New Mexico State House of Representatives. He eventually became the Speaker of the House, one of the most powerful positions in state politics. Walter was able to team up with Joe Fidel to help fund many projects in the area. He also did what everybody said was impossible when he sponsored legislation to split Cibola County from Valencia County, with Grants as the Cibola County seat. Although Walter died in his 50s, his legacy will live on. Walter's three children are lawyers, and his daughter is a district judge. (Courtesy of the *Cibola Beacon*.)

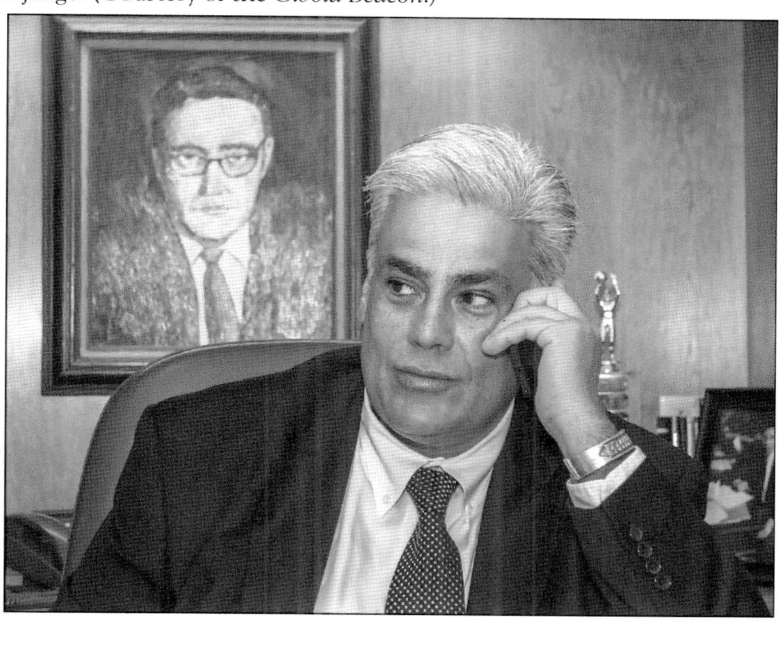

Ken Martinez is the oldest son of Walter Martinez. A graduate of Notre Dame Law School, he has been practicing law in Grants since passing the bar. Ken Martinez has been a state representative for years and was elected Speaker of the House for the 2013 session, following in his father's footsteps. (Courtesy of the *Cibola Beacon*.)

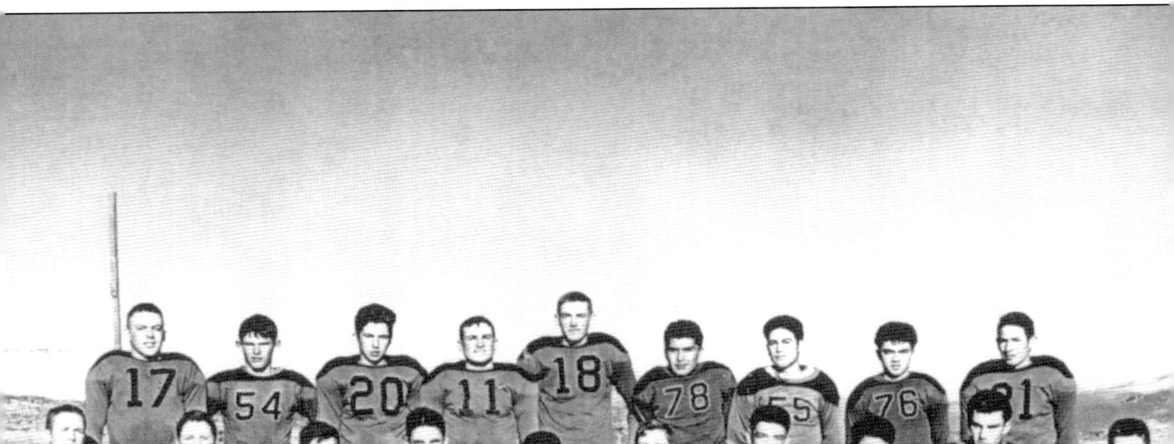

The 1949–1950 Grants Union High School football team is pictured in front of the grassless football field. Most of the players went into the service, returned to Grants, married, and lived respectful lives raising their children. They became teachers, bankers, miners, ranchers, businessmen, politicians, and government officials. From left to right are (first row) Eddie Duran, Bob Moore, Gilbert Saavedra, Billy Mohon, Paul Togami, Felix Baca, and Tommy Simpson; (second row) Keith Elkins, Buddy Elkins, Larry Leach, Ed Baca, three unidentified, Joe Sanchez, and Alex Baca; (third row) Otis Sullivan, Henry Andrews, Dick Morrow, Jack Elkins, Henry Elkins, Roy Koyona, Sikey McBride Jr., Tranqalino Padilla Jr., and Edward Sarracino. (Courtesy of the Elkins family.)

Three

Milan

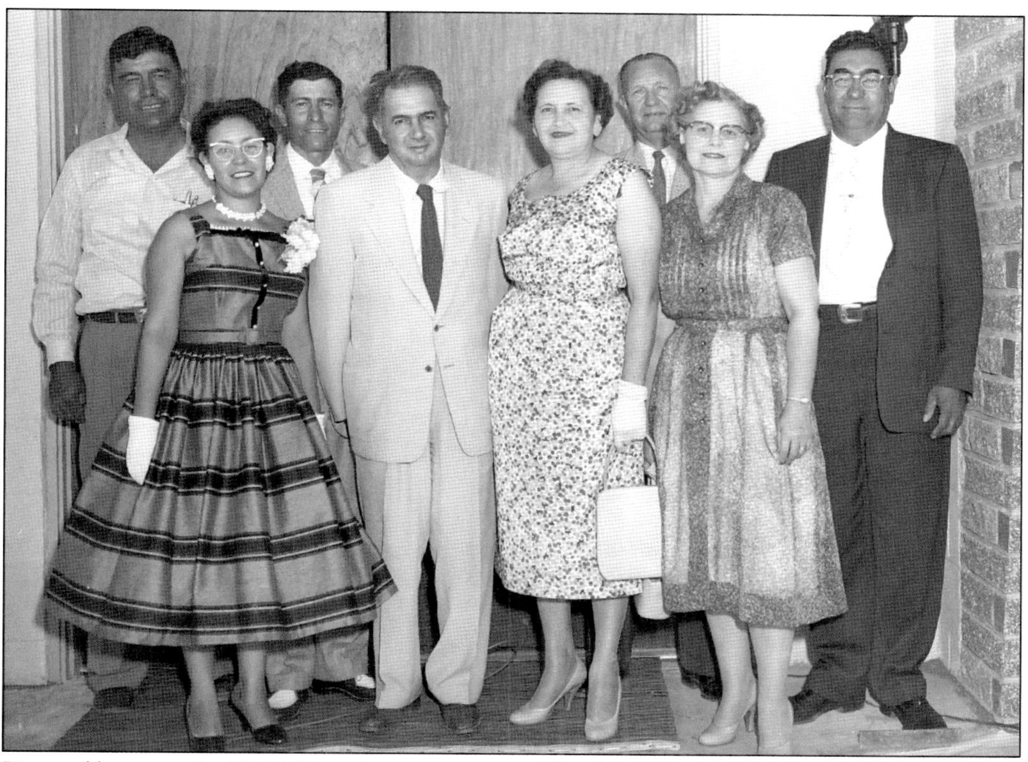

Pictured here are the 1957 Milan election winners. The election of the new officers occurred after the incorporation of the village of Milan. From left to right are building inspector E.C. Trujillo, village clerk Vera Lynn, trustee Joe Kie, Mayor Salvador Milan, Bennie Milan, trustee Claude Chambers, Blanche Chambers, and Judge Joe Dominguez. (Courtesy of the Milan family.)

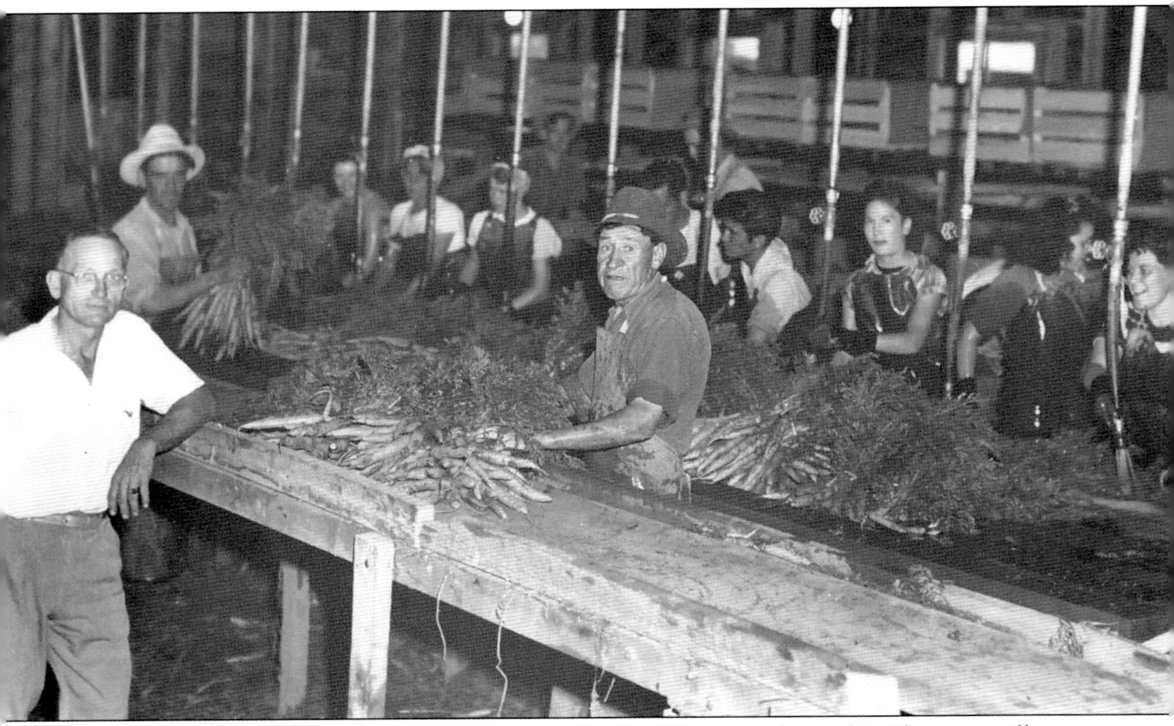

This carrot packing shed, owned and operated by Fred Freas, was located in Bluewater village, near the original Anaconda Company town site and mill. This photograph was more than likely taken in the early 1940s. This was the only carrot packing shed that was not in Grants. In the late 1950s, a packing shed was built in what was known as Breece Town and one in Milan to accommodate the new system of using cellophane bags and removing the tops of the carrots. Grants boasted at least four or five carrot packing sheds during the carrot boom. (Courtesy of Jack Freas.)

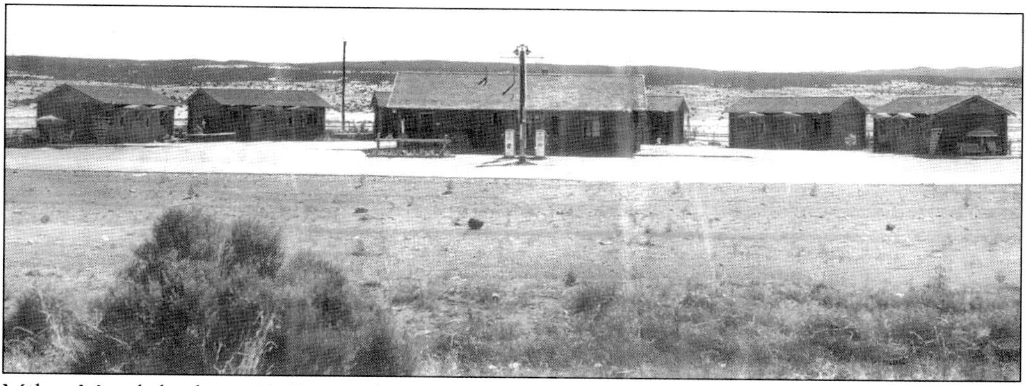

Milan Motel, built in 1947, was the second business built on Highway 66 in Milan to take advantage of the traveling boom following World War II. The motel consisted of 12 rooms within six cabins. When Interstate 40 bypassed Milan businesses, the motel changed its original purpose. Today, the old motel is Kachina Traders, specializing in manufacturing kachina dolls, a favorite of many tourists, especially Europeans. Notice there is not a tree in the area. (Courtesy of the Milan family.)

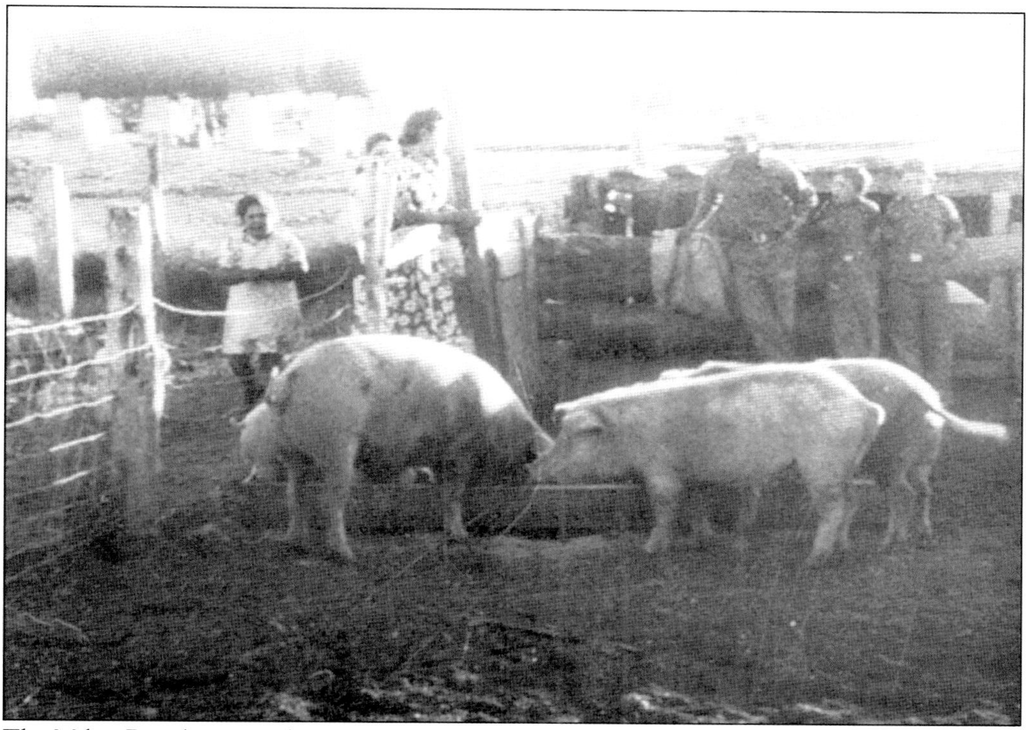

The Milan Ranch in seen here in 1943–1944. From left to right are a daughter of a ranch hand, Bennie Milan, a ranch hand, and Paul and Peter Milan. The water tank was a rail tanker car that was left from the logging-era railroad from Grants and the Zuni Mountains. The rails were hauled away for scrap and eventually sold to the Japanese before World War II. The hogs were well received by the local population during the war, since meat was rationed. (Courtesy of the Milan family.)

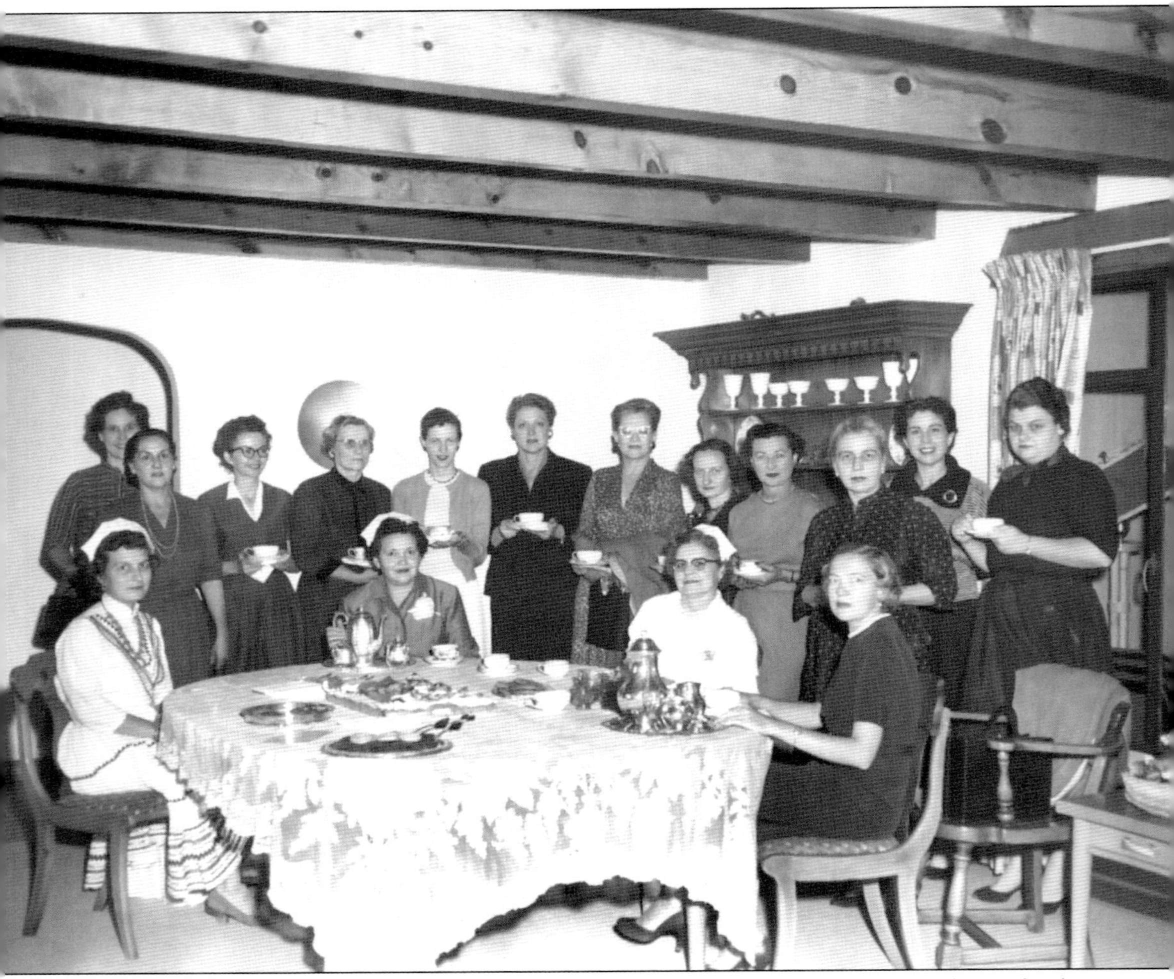

Members of the Pilots Club of Grants (a business/professional ladies' organization) host a fundraiser for the proposed hospital in 1958. The hospital was built by 1961. Some of the participants were also members of a new hospital women's auxiliary that made the new hospital possible. This particular tea was held in the home of Veneranda Milan, wife of the first mayor of the village of Milan. (Courtesy of the Milan family.)

In 1968, the Grants State Bank established a Milan branch by utilizing the front part of the Save-on Drug Store. The branch was to be established in the early 1960s, but the first bust of the uranium industry delayed the plans until the mining returned in the late 1960s. (Courtesy of the Grants State Bank.)

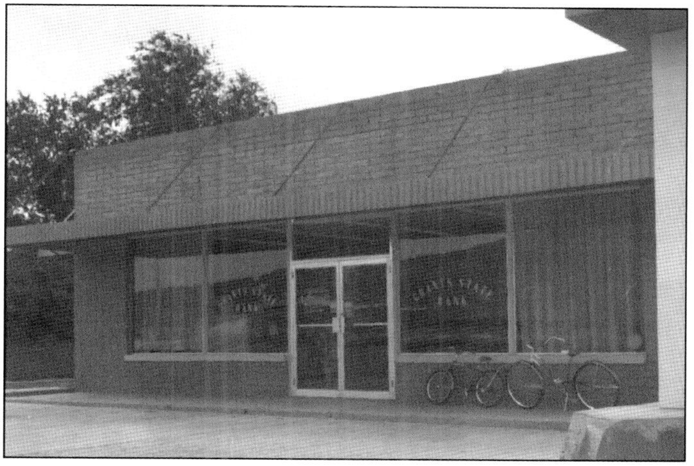

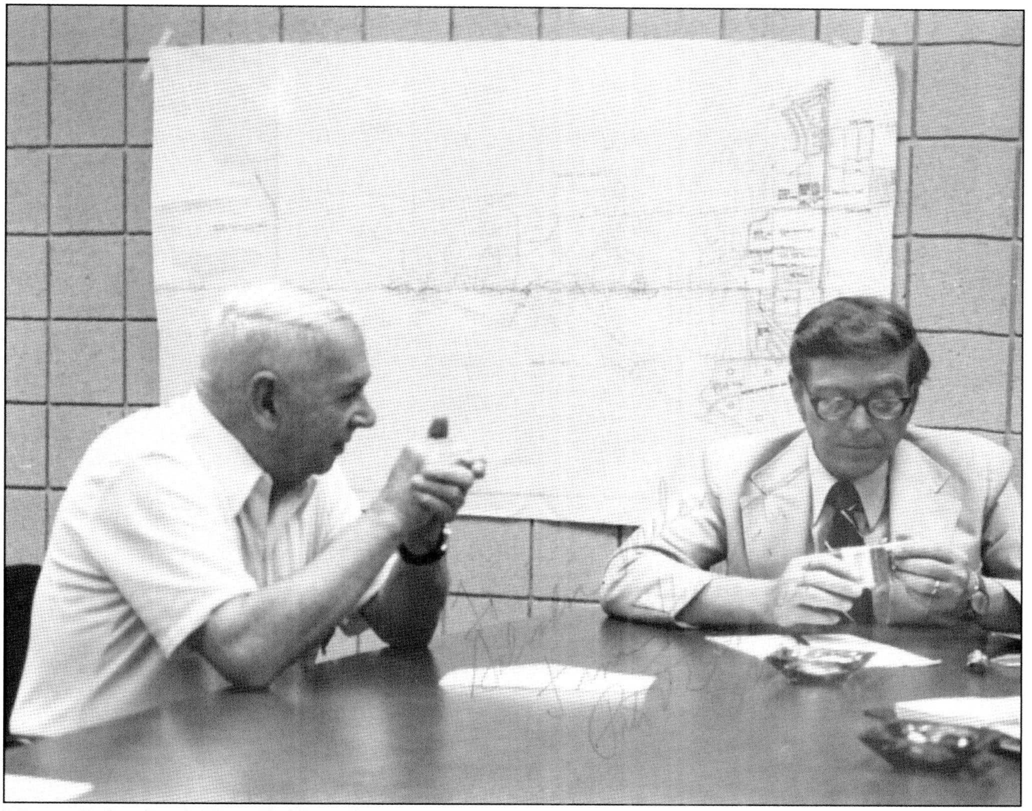

Mayor Salvador Milan (left) and Sen. Pete Domenici are pictured during one of the senator's many visits throughout New Mexico and the village of Milan. Pete Domenici ran for the US Senate after he lost his race for the governor of New Mexico in 1971. The senator reluctantly ran for office but was urged on by his supporters, and when he won, he said that he was going to be a one-term senator as a Republican in a Democratic-majority state. Senator Domenici was in his late 30s when he won his first election, and he won every election until he retired in his 70s. The senator never forgot his supporters and was very helpful in the development of the village of Milan. (Courtesy of the Milan family.)

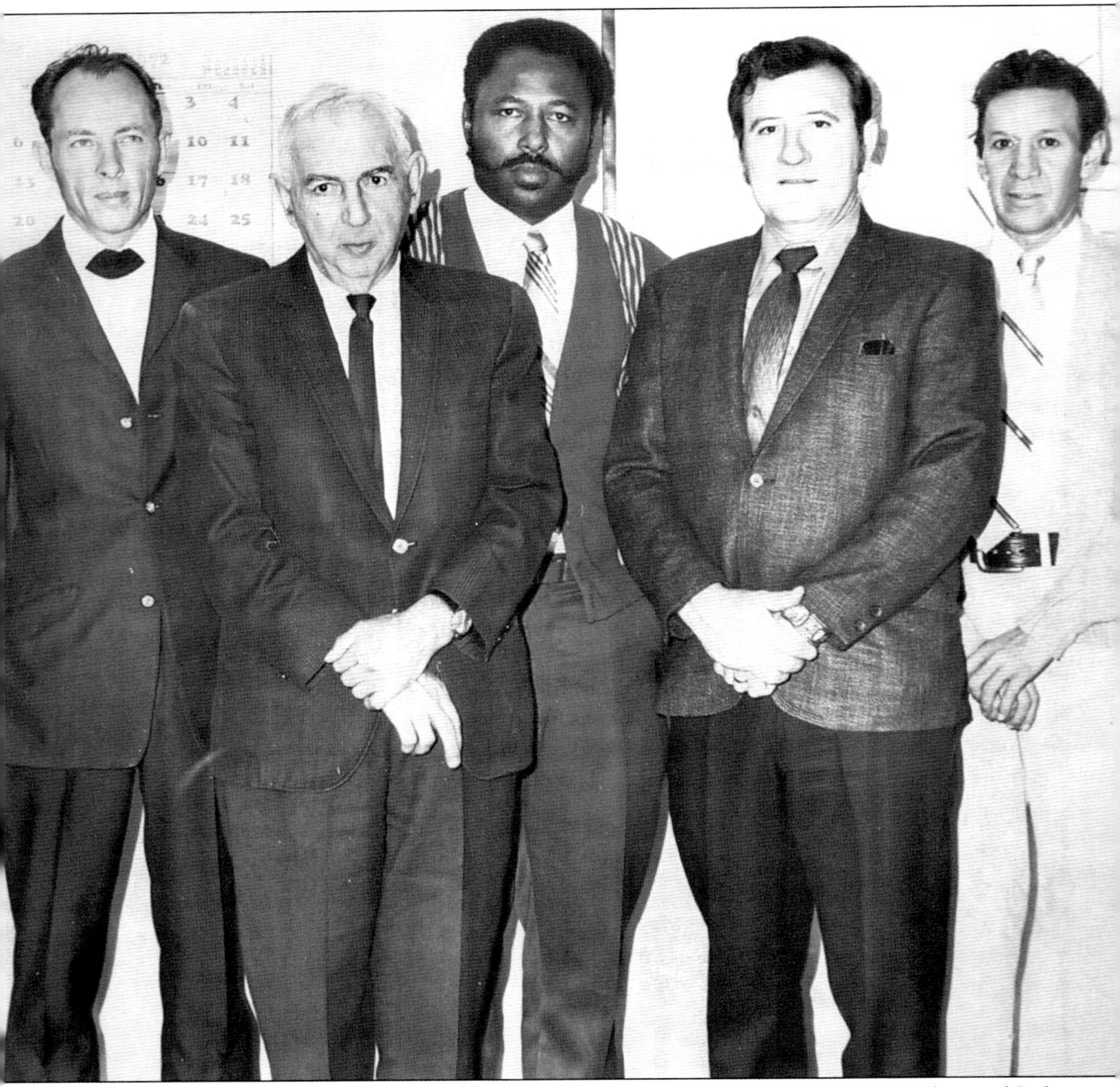

The 1972 election winners were, from left to right, (first row) Mayor Salvador Milan and Judge Kelly Kregger; (second row) trustees Wayne Spurgeon, Eddie Corley Sr., and Eddie Jaramillo. (Courtesy of the Milan family.)

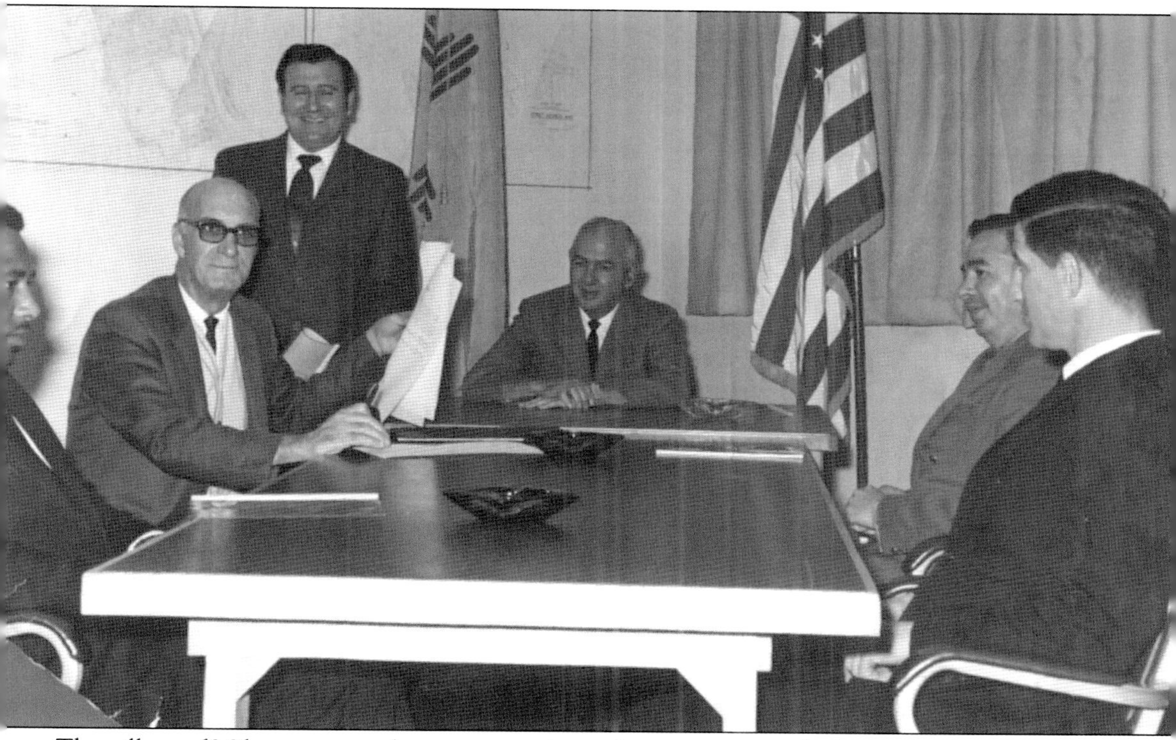

The village of Milan mayor and trustees are pictured at a meeting with the newly elected judge and appointed attorney. From left to right are trustee Eddie Corley, attorney W.P. (Bill) Kearns, Judge Kelly Cregger (standing), Mayor Milan (sitting in the middle), trustee Jessie Barela, and Wayne Spurgeon. Attorney Bill Kearns was a strong supporter of boys' baseball, and the village recognized his contributions to the youth by naming Kearns Baseball Park in his honor. (Courtesy of the Milan family.)

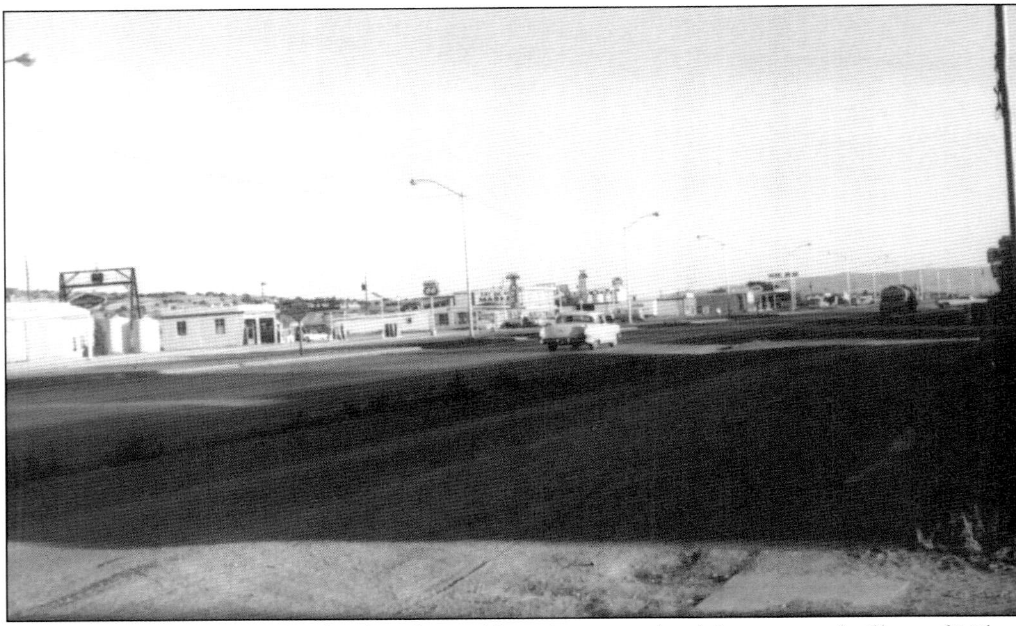

This is a scene of the north side of Highway 66 on the west side of the proposed village of Milan. The original development was to cater to the traveling public going from coast to coast. The first attraction in the area was the Cobra Gardens, featuring the largest collection of cobras in the United States. Service stations, restaurants, and motels began to develop for the traveling public. The uranium boom brought mine workers from all over the world, and the demand for housing and trailer spaces prompted the incorporation of the village of Milan in 1957, which aided in the demise of the vegetable farms. (Courtesy of the Milan family.)

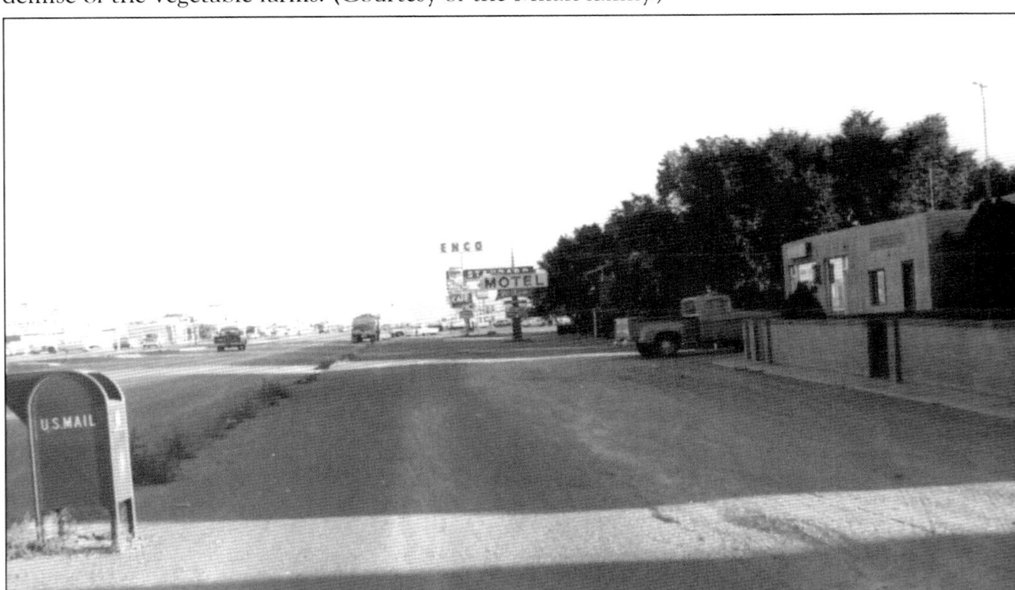

This photograph of the south side of the proposed village of Milan was taken from the west on Highway 66. Note the motel on the right and the trees. In 1946, there were no trees in the area that became the village of Milan. (Courtesy of the Milan family.)

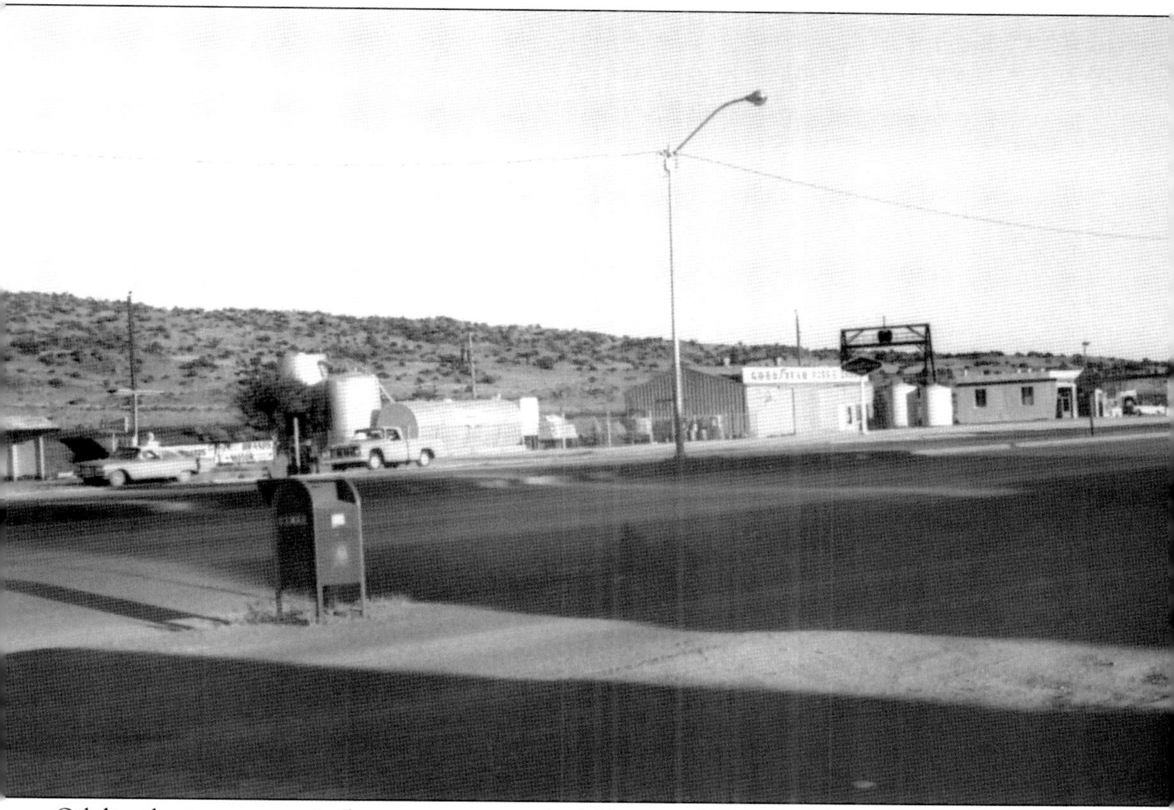

Oil distributing companies began to move to the Milan area because of the space needed for the growth of Highway 66 traffic and the needs of the population, which was expanding due to the uranium mining boom. This scene is on the west end of the village of Milan, and the oil company is on the left side of the highway. Eventually, the Chevron Distributing Company, the Phillips 66 Company, the Texaco Distributing Company, and Kerr McGee Distributing Company moved to the village of Milan. (Courtesy of the Milan family.)

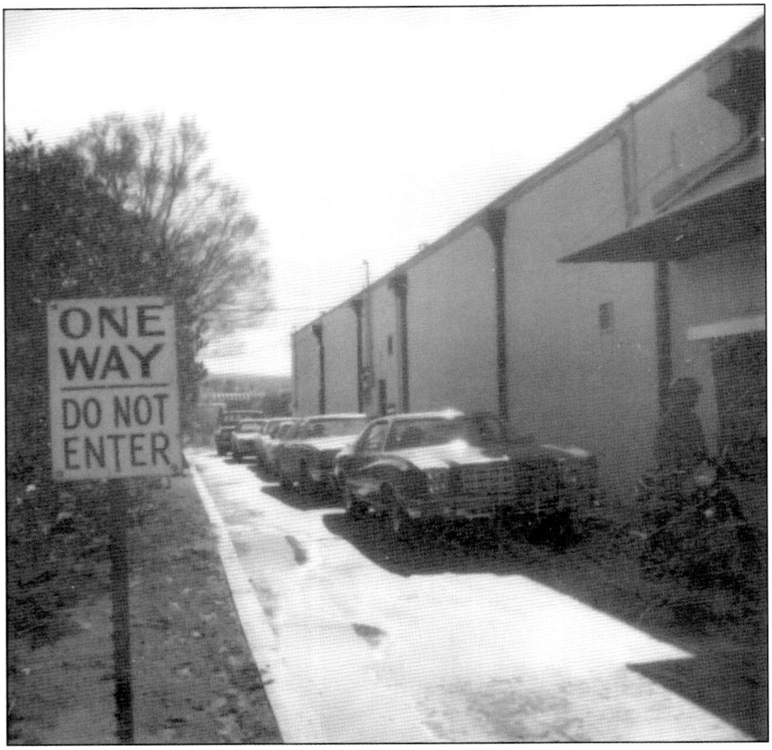

In 1968, the Grants State Bank opened a Milan branch to cater to the expanding population. The uranium mining industry was slowly building up after the bust of the early 1960s. The new drive-up banking became very popular on paydays. (Courtesy of the Milan family.)

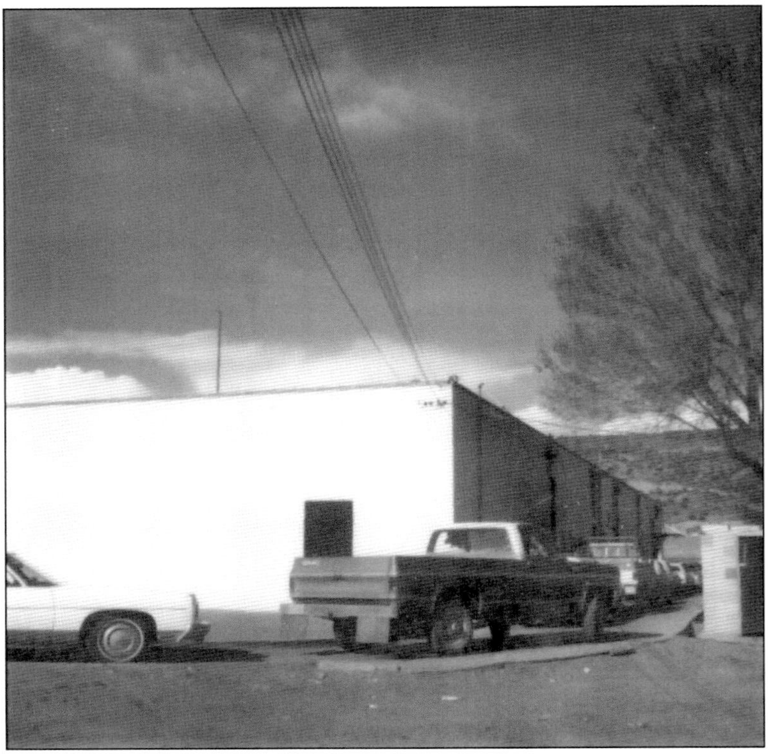

During payday at the mining companies, the lines to cash checks were enormous, and the banks would close at 7:00 p.m. on Fridays to accommodate the miners, who worked three shifts during the boom. This photograph was taken of the drive-up facility at the Milan branch during one of those paydays. (Courtesy of the Milan family.)

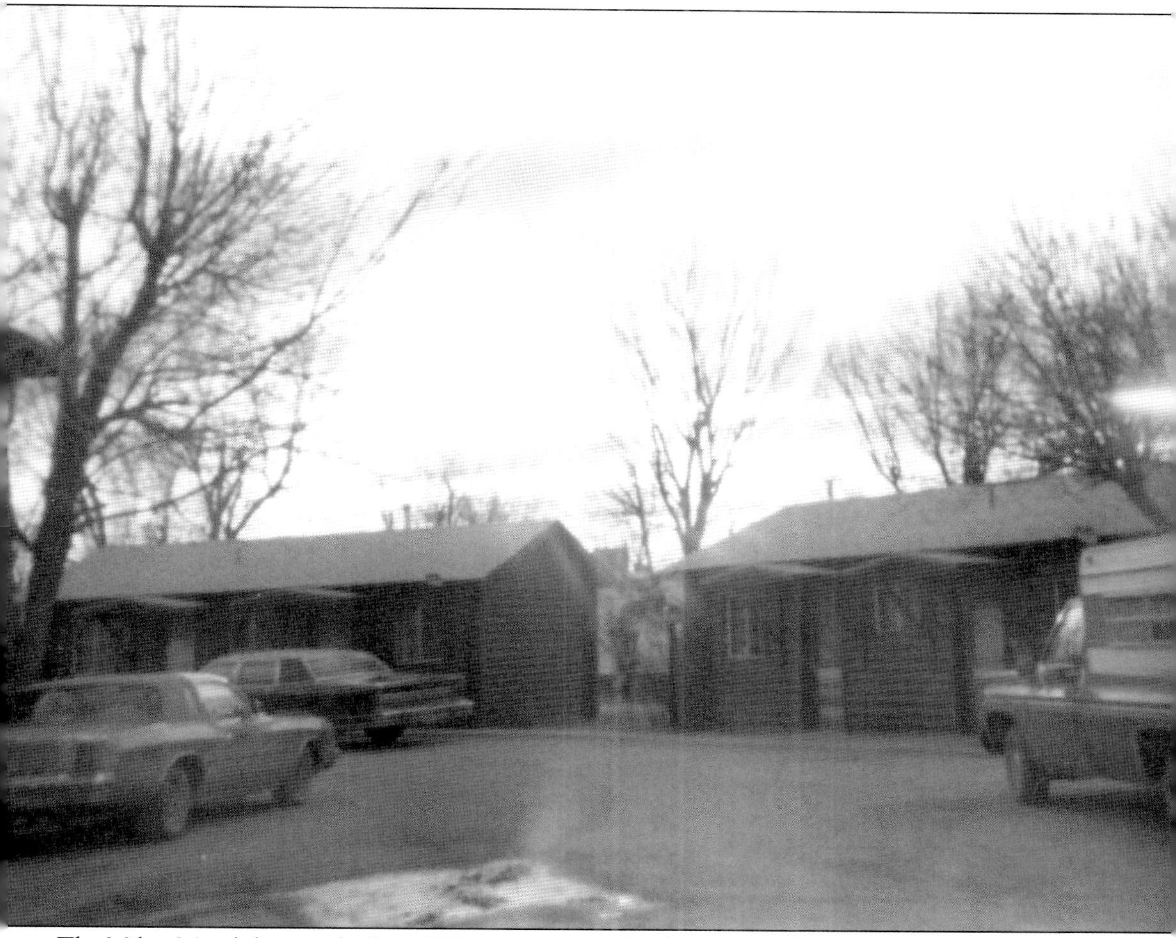

The Milan Motel that was built in 1947 in response to Highway 66 traffic was the second building constructed in what was to become the village of Milan. The first building was a tourist attraction called the Cobra Gardens. This photograph was taken in 1956, prior to the incorporation of the village. The trees were planted in 1950; before then, time there were no trees in the area that became the village. During the 1950s, there were five motels built in the Milan area to respond to the traveling public on Highway 66, while Grants had about 12 motels, and there were service stations almost on every corner. The interstate highway built in the 1970s caused a bust of the tourist trade in the Grants-Milan area. Presently, motels and a few service stations have been built around the interstate exits. (Courtesy of the Milan family.)

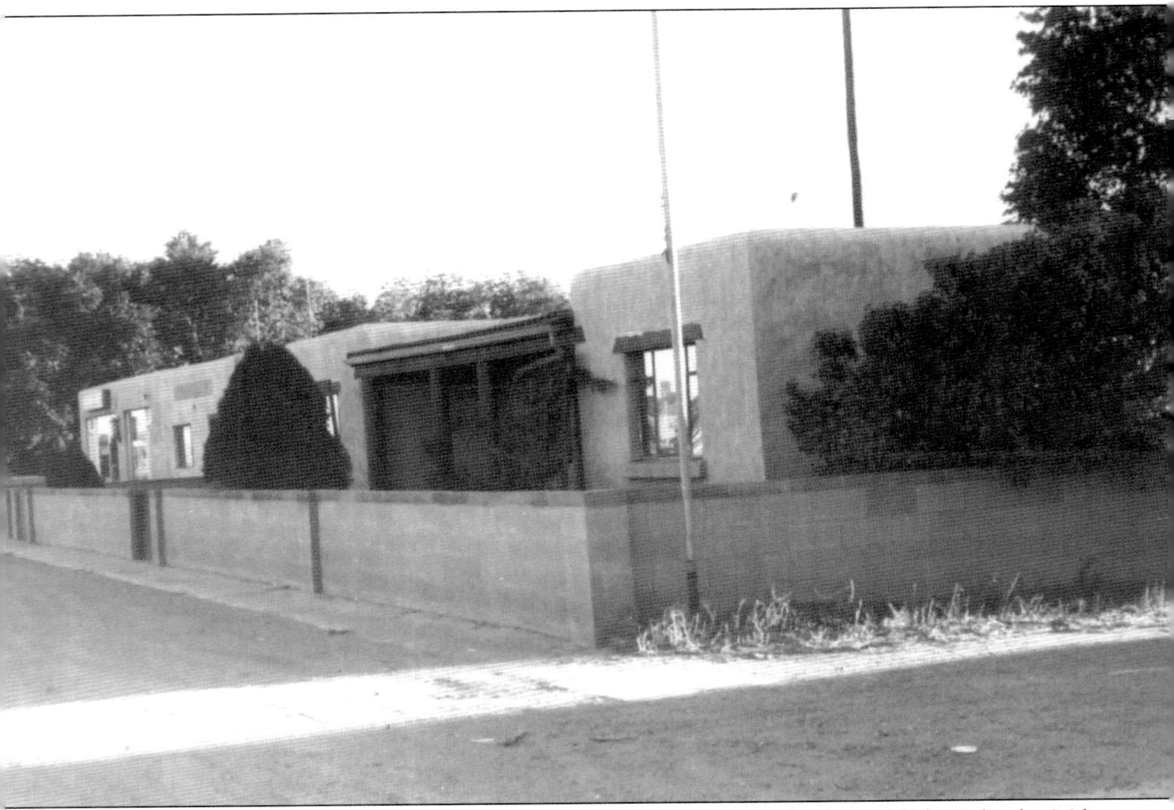

The second home in what was to become the village of Milan was built in 1951 by Salvador Milan. He moved his farming operation to this area after he had built the motel, a service station, and a restaurant to cater to the Highway 66 traveler, as he felt that the future would be the Highway traffic. He also built a new carrot shed nearby to pack carrots in the new cellophane bags. The shed was built away from the railroad, as refrigerated trucks were being used to haul the carrots and ice was no longer needed. (Courtesy of the Milan family.)

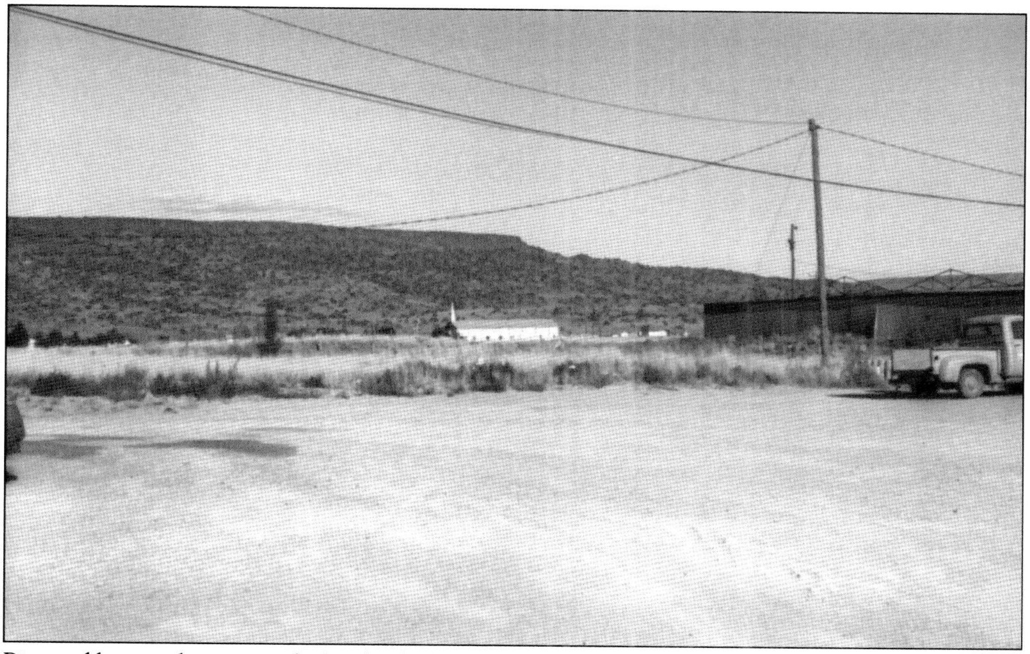

Pictured here is the west end of Milan before any development in the area, around 1956. (Courtesy of the Milan family.)

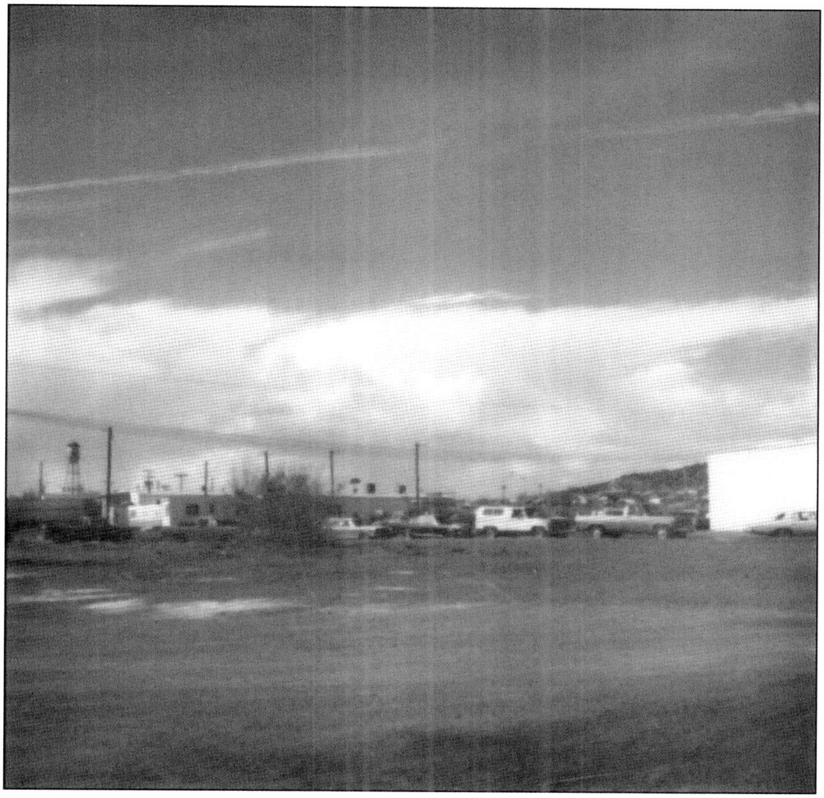

This building in the village of Milan housed the US Post Office, the Save-on Drugstore, and the Milan branch of the Grants State Bank in the early 1960s. (Courtesy of the Milan family.)

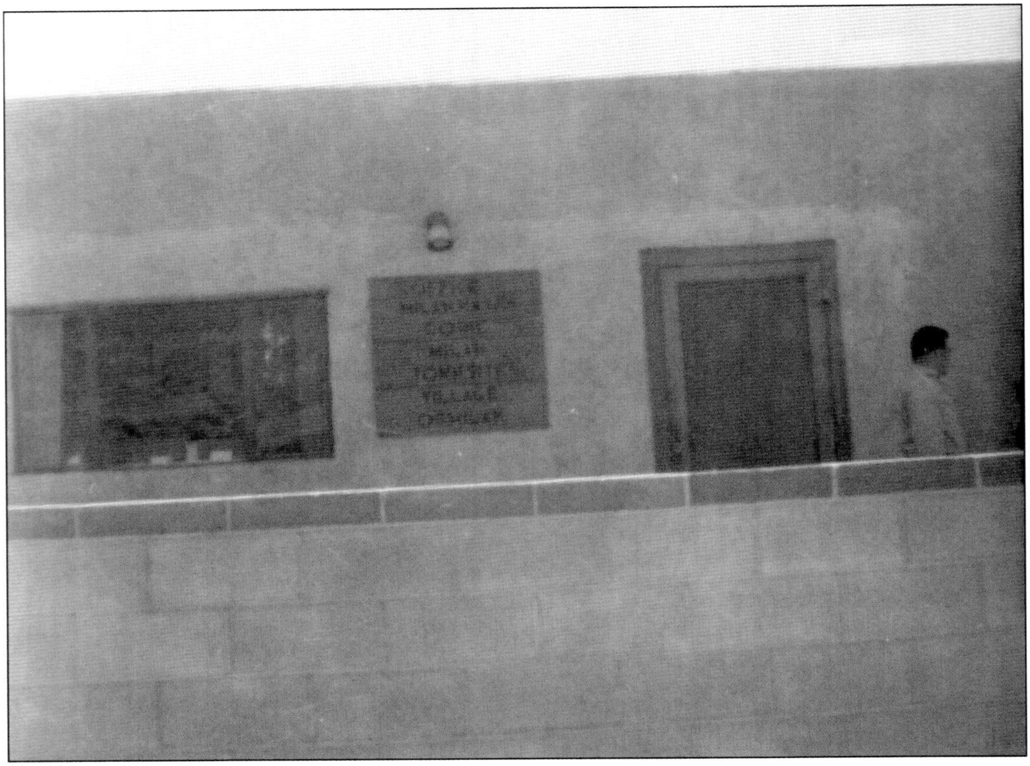

Since the village did not have a budget to build or rent a city hall, the mayor converted his garage into one. As the village expanded services, the mayor built a three-car garage in the back of the city hall, which housed the fire department, the water department, and the village maintenance department. The fire siren pole is still in the yard of the home that belonged to the mayor. During that time, the mayor's telephone number was used for the village fire department and all of the municipal services. The mayor built a post office next to the city hall, and it was eventually used as the municipal judge's office once the present post office was constructed. The village city hall was moved to its present location when the early-1960s uranium bust occurred and the offices that the Atomic Energy Commission abandoned were put up for sale for a small percentage of their value. (Courtesy of the Milan family.)

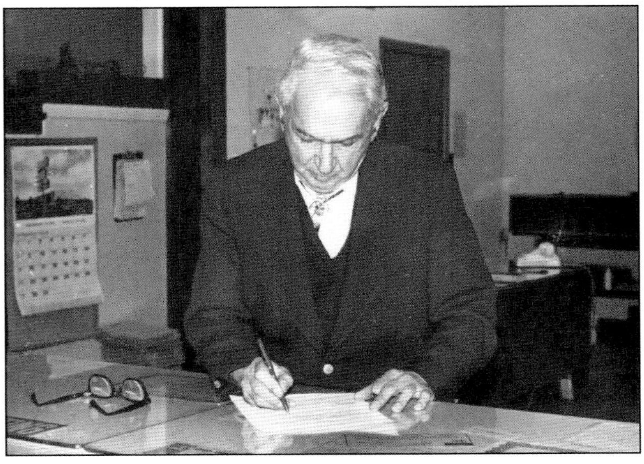

Mayor Salvador Milan signs his oath of office following his last election. The *Albuquerque Journal* described Milan as the "dean" of New Mexico mayors, having served from 1957 to 1979, longer than any other mayor in New Mexico at the time of his death. (Courtesy of the Milan family.)

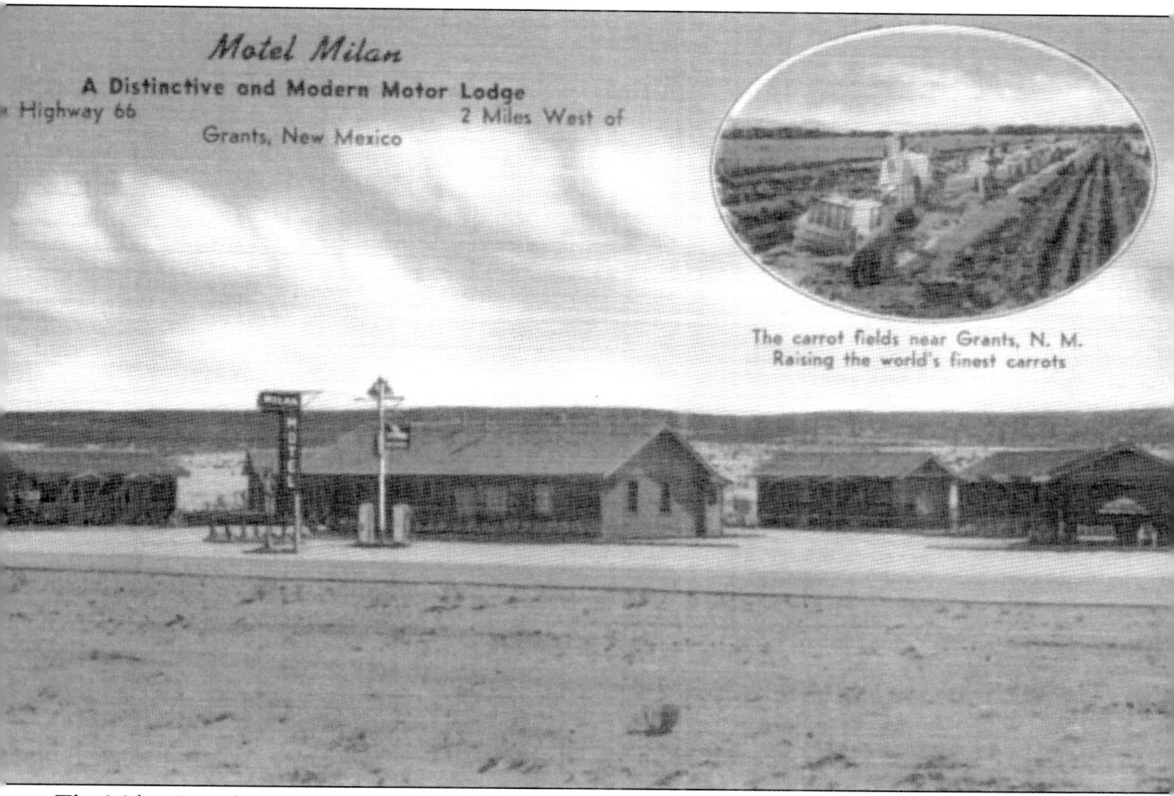

The Milan Motel was built by Salvador Milan in 1947 in response to the increased tourist traffic on Highway 66 after World War II. It was the second business built in what was to become the village of Milan to cater to tourists. The first building was the Cobra Gardens, which became a huge attraction and led to the belief that the strip was to be a main tourist stopover. The uranium boom changed the focus of the area in the 1950s, and the interstate highway moved the traffic to the interchange. There were six motels in what is now the village of Milan, and there is only one left today. (Courtesy of the Milan family.)

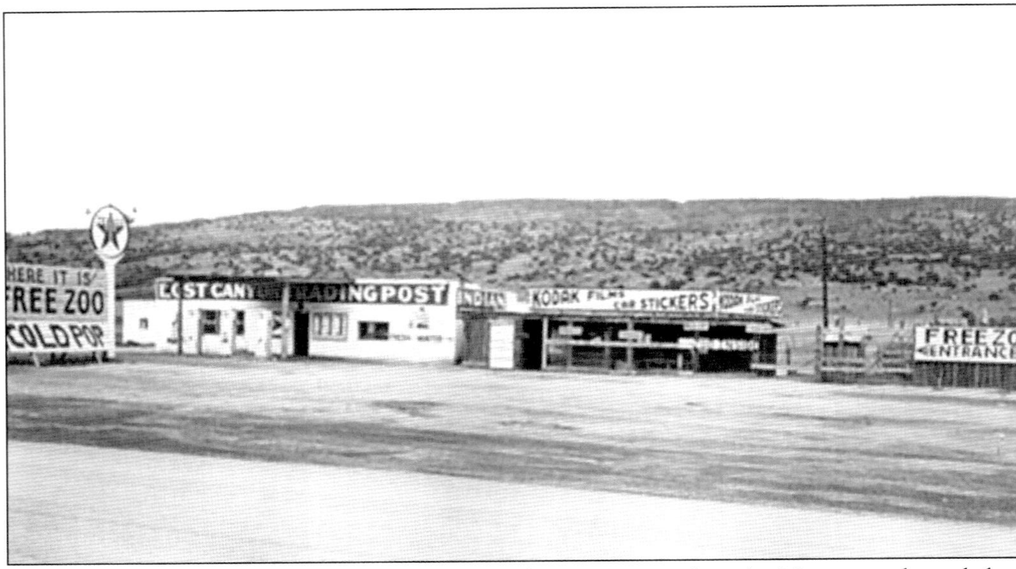

West of Milan, this typical trading post on Highway 66 catered to the Navajo trade and then developed attractions to lure the tourists to stop and shop. (Courtesy of Aurelio Apodaca.)

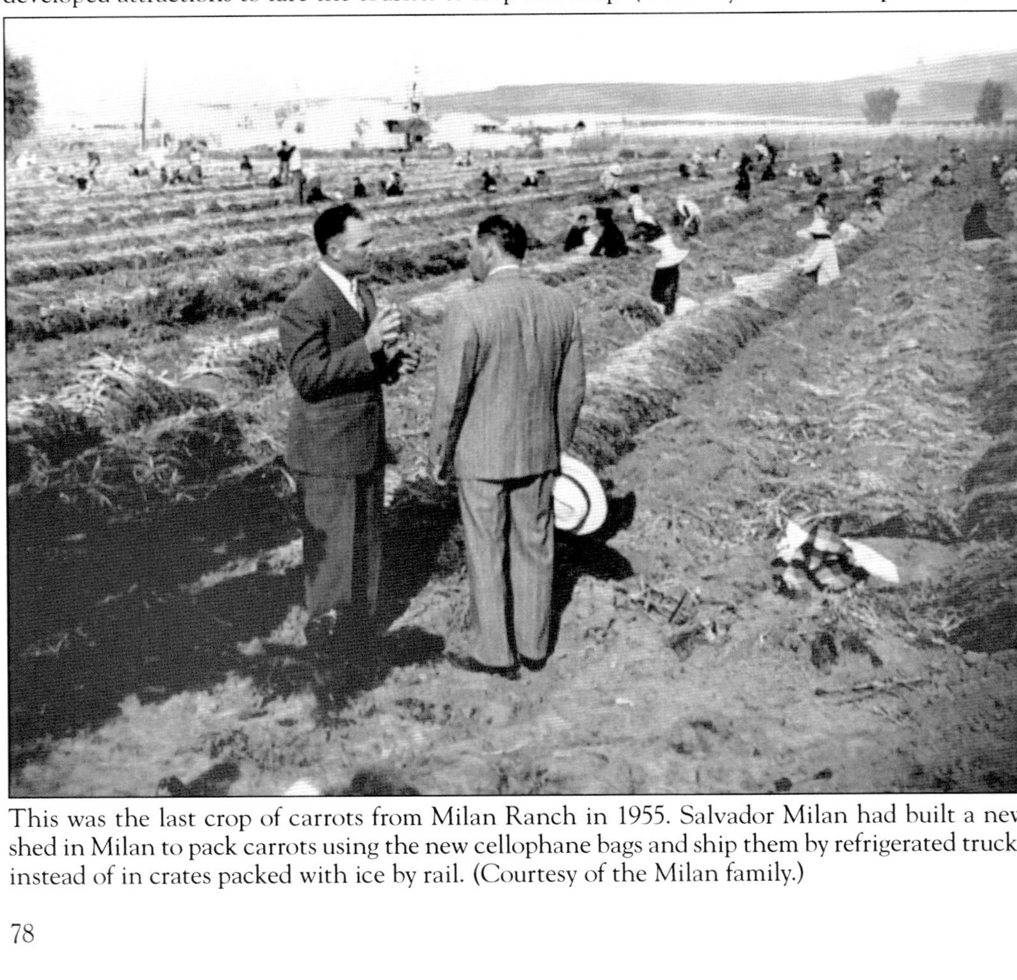

This was the last crop of carrots from Milan Ranch in 1955. Salvador Milan had built a new shed in Milan to pack carrots using the new cellophane bags and ship them by refrigerated trucks instead of in crates packed with ice by rail. (Courtesy of the Milan family.)

Four

RANCHING, FARMING, MINING, AND AVIATION

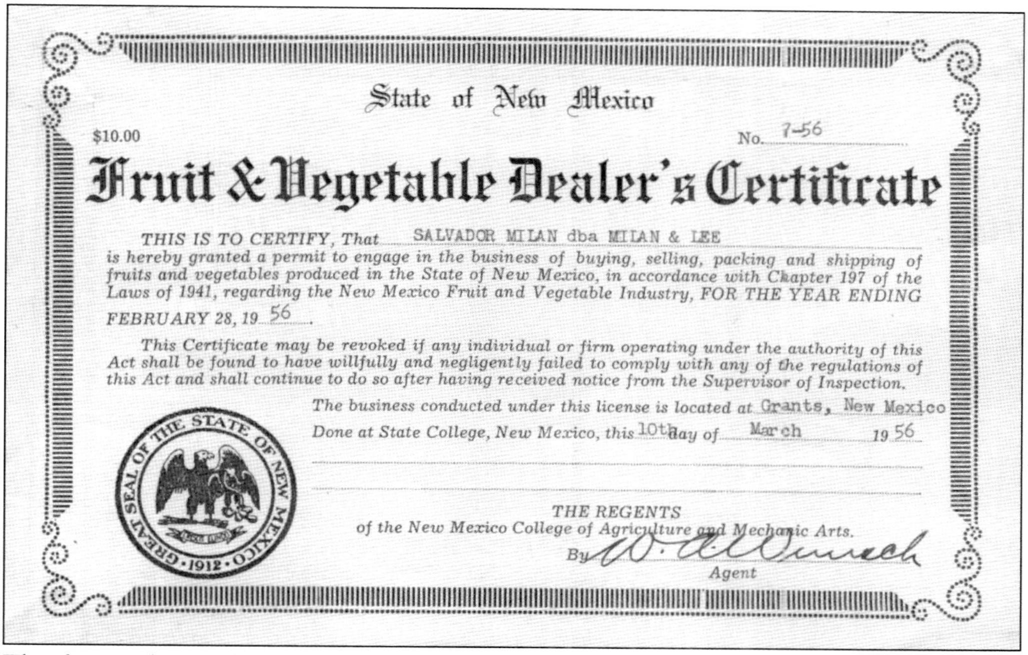

State of New Mexico

$10.00 No. 7-56

Fruit & Vegetable Dealer's Certificate

THIS IS TO CERTIFY, That SALVADOR MILAN dba MILAN & LEE is hereby granted a permit to engage in the business of buying, selling, packing and shipping of fruits and vegetables produced in the State of New Mexico, in accordance with Chapter 197 of the Laws of 1941, regarding the New Mexico Fruit and Vegetable Industry, FOR THE YEAR ENDING FEBRUARY 28, 19 56.

This Certificate may be revoked if any individual or firm operating under the authority of this Act shall be found to have willfully and negligently failed to comply with any of the regulations of this Act and shall continue to do so after having received notice from the Supervisor of Inspection.

The business conducted under this license is located at Grants, New Mexico

Done at State College, New Mexico, this 10th day of March 19 56

THE REGENTS
of the New Mexico College of Agriculture and Mechanic Arts.

By [signature]
Agent

GREAT SEAL OF THE STATE OF NEW MEXICO · 1912 ·

This fruit and vegetable certificate was issued to the Milan and Lee partnership farms. Mr. S. Lee, a Japanese immigrant, was allowed to live in the Bluewater area during World War II instead of a Japanese internment camp because of the influence of the late Capt. W.C. Reid. Captain Reid had connections in Washington and was able to bring a number of Japanese families to the Bluewater valley to help manage the farms. Lee, a mining engineer, was able to acquire heavy farming equipment that he engaged in custom work for the farmers. After the war, he approached Salvador Milan with the prospect of setting up a partnership with his equipment and his knowledge of vegetable farming that he acquired at the farms during the war. Milan was to provide the land, water, financing, and marketing, and Lee would provide the equipment and farming ability. This successful partnership lasted until Lee's death in 1953. (Courtesy of the Milan family.)

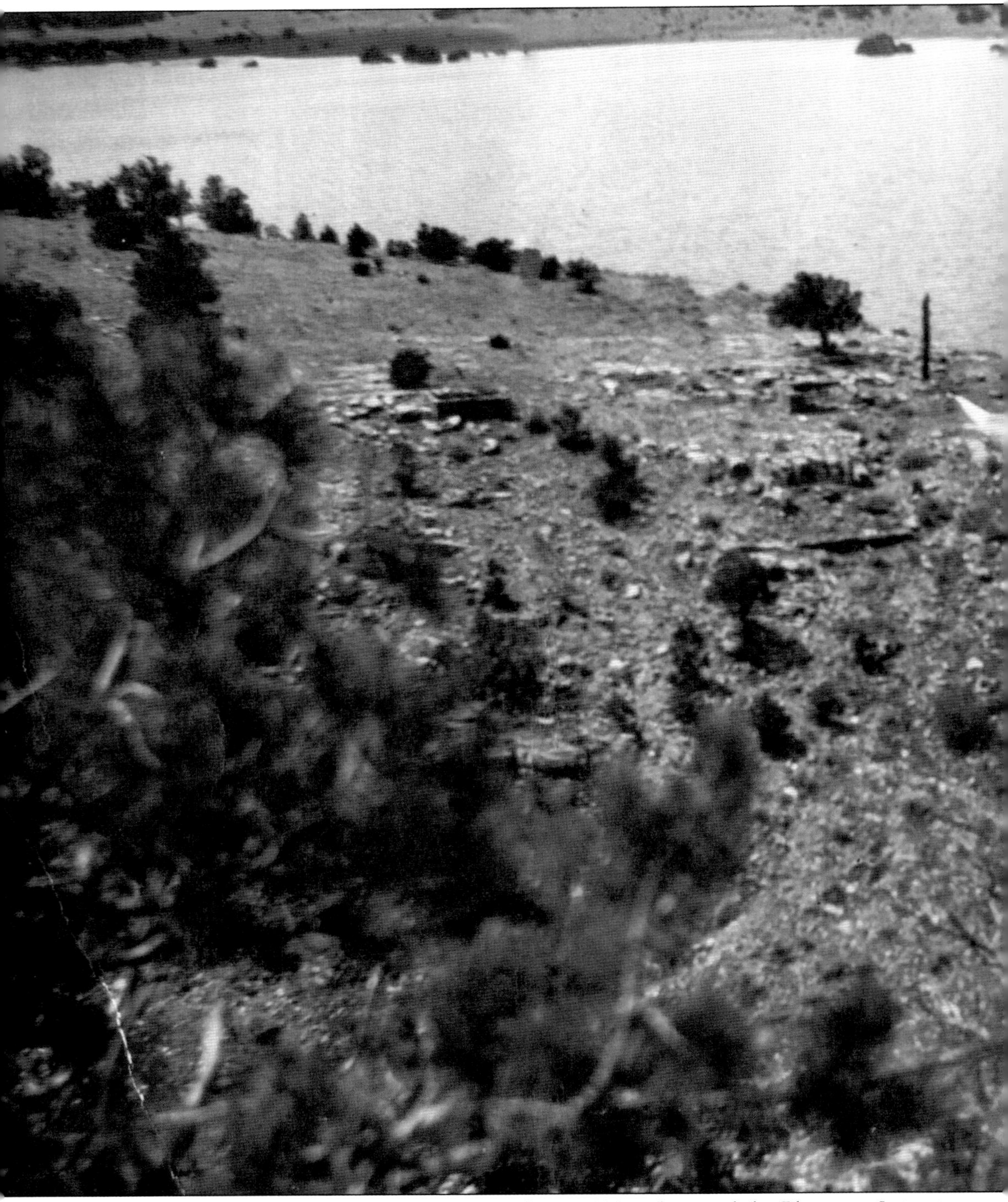

Bluewater Dam was completed at Bluewater Lake in 1928 and created the Bluewater Irrigation District, which gave birth to the local vegetable truck farming industry, which led to Grants becoming known as the Carrot Capital of the World. In 1939, the first shipment of carrots reached an eastern market, and it attracted much attention because of color, size, and quality of the

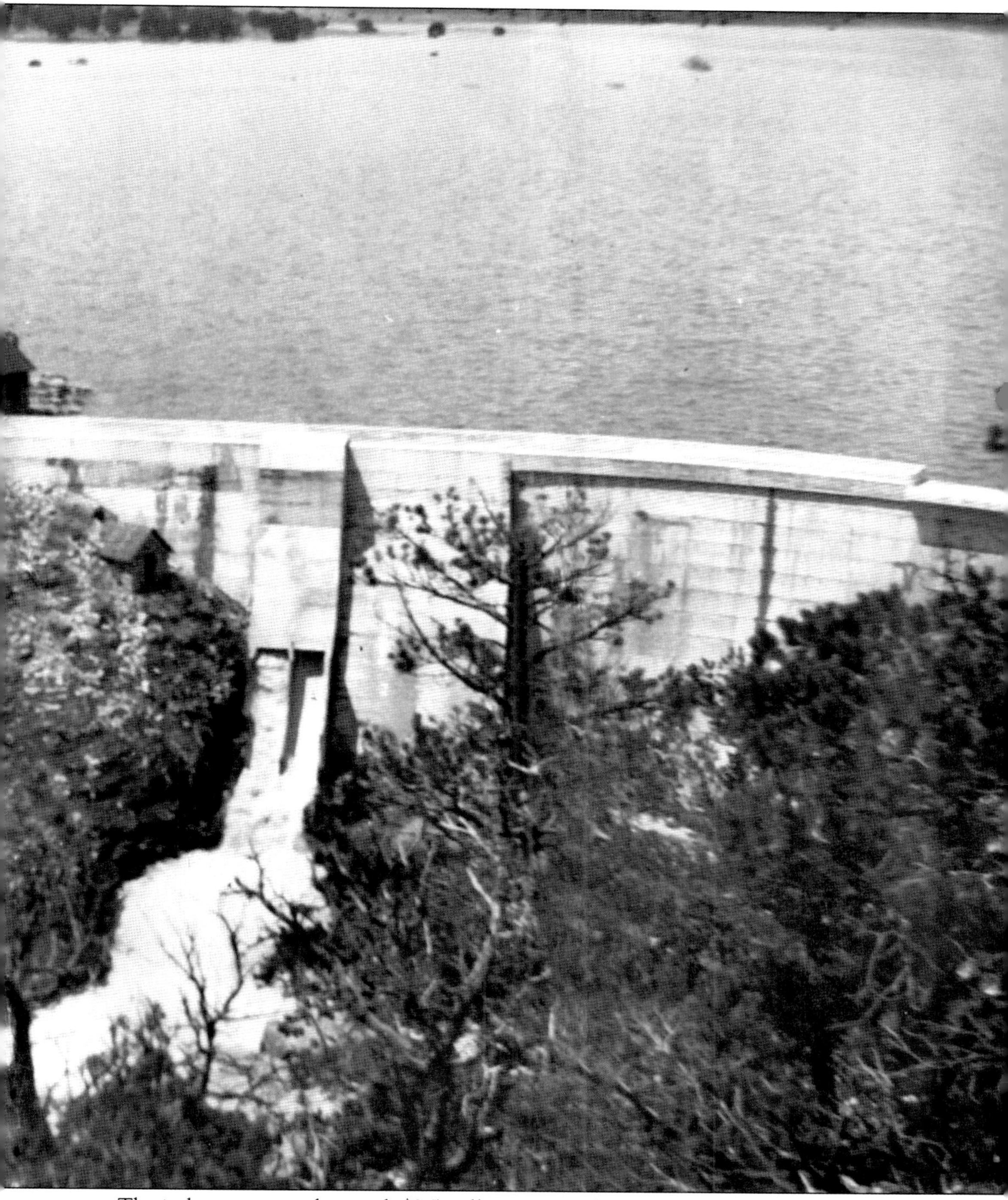

carrots. The industry grew to be worth $2.5 million in a single year, with 2,000 carloads shipped from 2,000 acres. The valley produced many types of vegetables, including lettuce, peas, cabbage, potatoes, and onions, but carrots led as the chief of produce. (Courtesy of Jack Freas.)

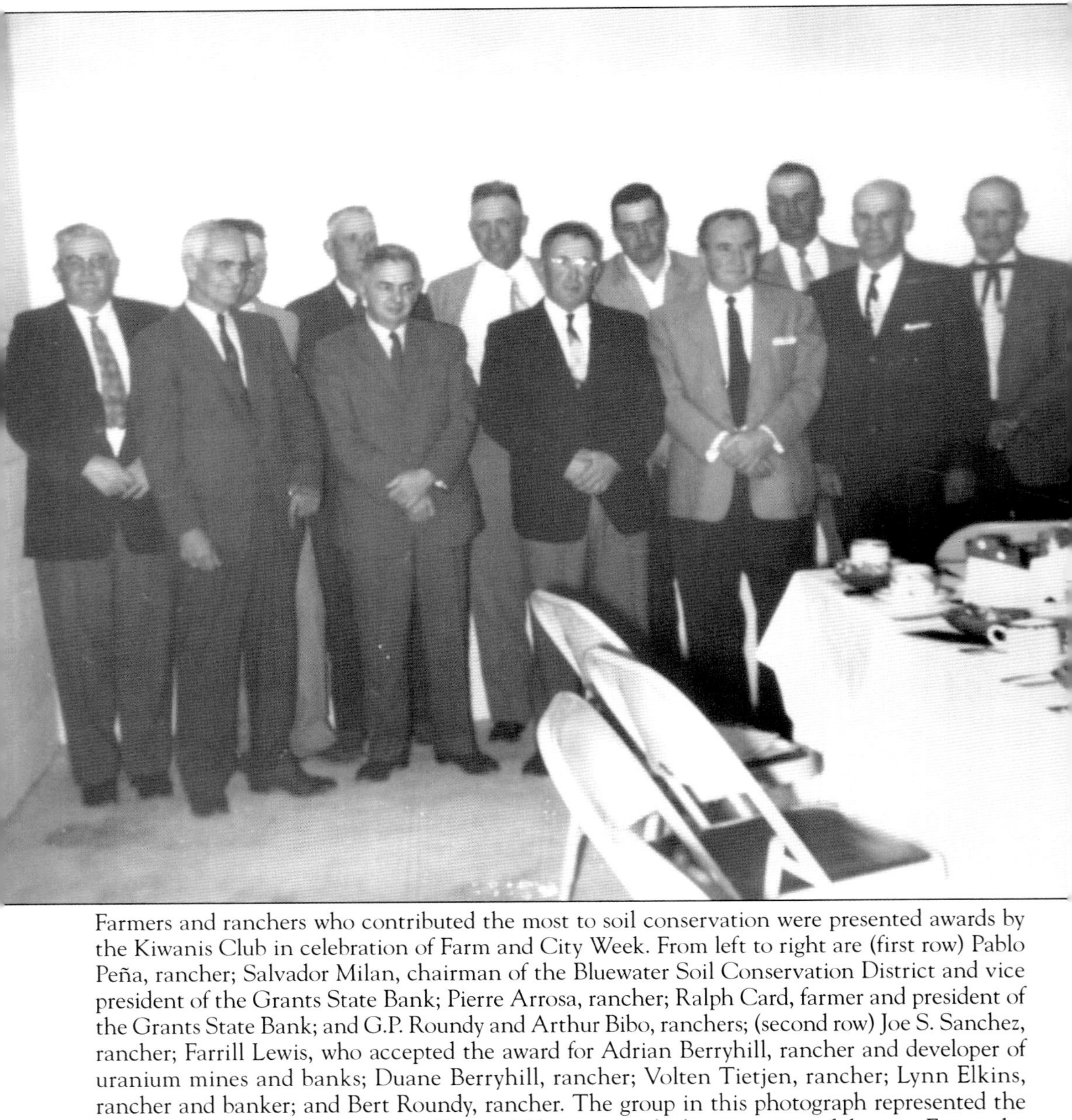

Farmers and ranchers who contributed the most to soil conservation were presented awards by the Kiwanis Club in celebration of Farm and City Week. From left to right are (first row) Pablo Peña, rancher; Salvador Milan, chairman of the Bluewater Soil Conservation District and vice president of the Grants State Bank; Pierre Arrosa, rancher; Ralph Card, farmer and president of the Grants State Bank; and G.P. Roundy and Arthur Bibo, ranchers; (second row) Joe S. Sanchez, rancher; Farrill Lewis, who accepted the award for Adrian Berryhill, rancher and developer of uranium mines and banks; Duane Berryhill, rancher; Volten Tietjen, rancher; Lynn Elkins, rancher and banker; and Bert Roundy, rancher. The group in this photograph represented the majority of the landowners in the Grants-Milan area with the exception of the vast Fernandez Ranch owned by the Lee family. (Courtesy of the Milan family.)

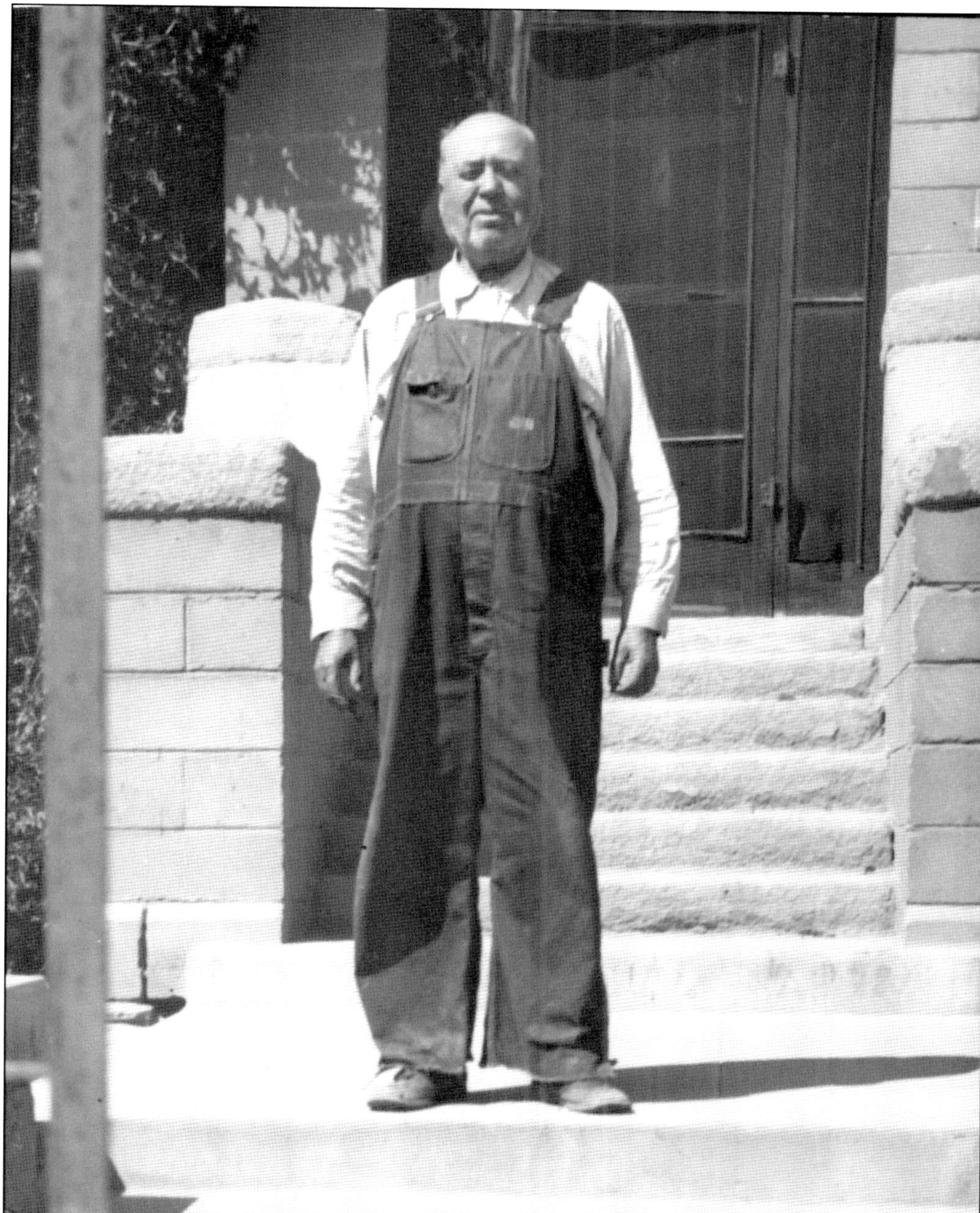

This is the last photograph taken of Silvestre Mirabal, pictured in front of his home in San Rafael, New Mexico. He was a rancher of both sheep and cattle, a banker, a politician, and Cowboy Hall of Fame honoree. Silvestre was the son of Monico Mirabal and Juana Maria Sanchez de Mirabal and was born in Seboyeta, Valencia County (now Cibola County), on May 10, 1864. Silvestre enjoyed working with his cowboys and sheepherders, teasing, and playing pranks, and he roamed around the area dressed as a sheepherder as if incognito. Silvestre had accumulated ranch land estimated at 384,000 acres at the time of his death. His biggest purchase was from the Breese Lumber Company in 1919 of 170,000 acres. (Courtesy of the Milan family.)

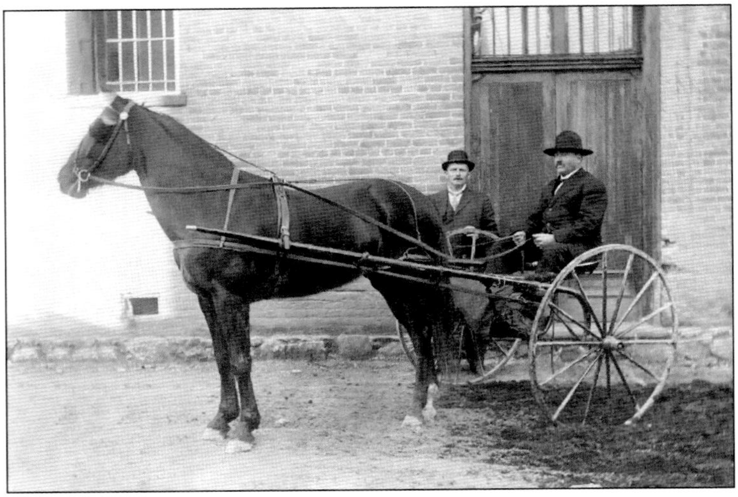

Silvestre Mirabal is pictured here with his favorite buggy horse, Trixie, which he won in a raffle. Silvestre was a person of many facets and enjoyed doing whatever caught his fancy. Trixie was a very intelligent horse and could be gentle unless she did not like a person, and then she would chase after them like a mad dog. (Courtesy of the Milan family.)

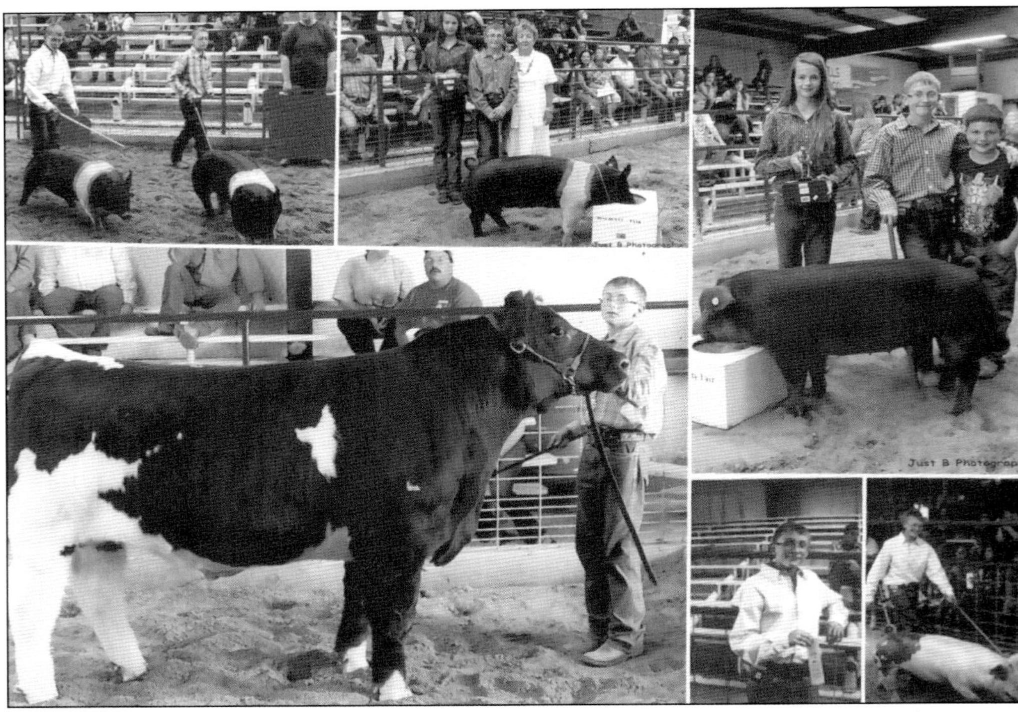

In 1981, Valencia County was split in half, and the western part was designated Cibola County, with Grants named the county seat. The new county negotiated with McKinley County to the west to establish a bi-county fair, especially since many of the ranches overlapped the two counties. Because Cibola County went as far as the Arizona line, it was reasonable that the Bi-County Fair be held close to Grants and Gallup, which were the population hubs of the two counties. The fair has been very influential for 4-H clubs, whose members are able to show and sell their animal projects for college funds. (Courtesy of the Grants State Bank.)

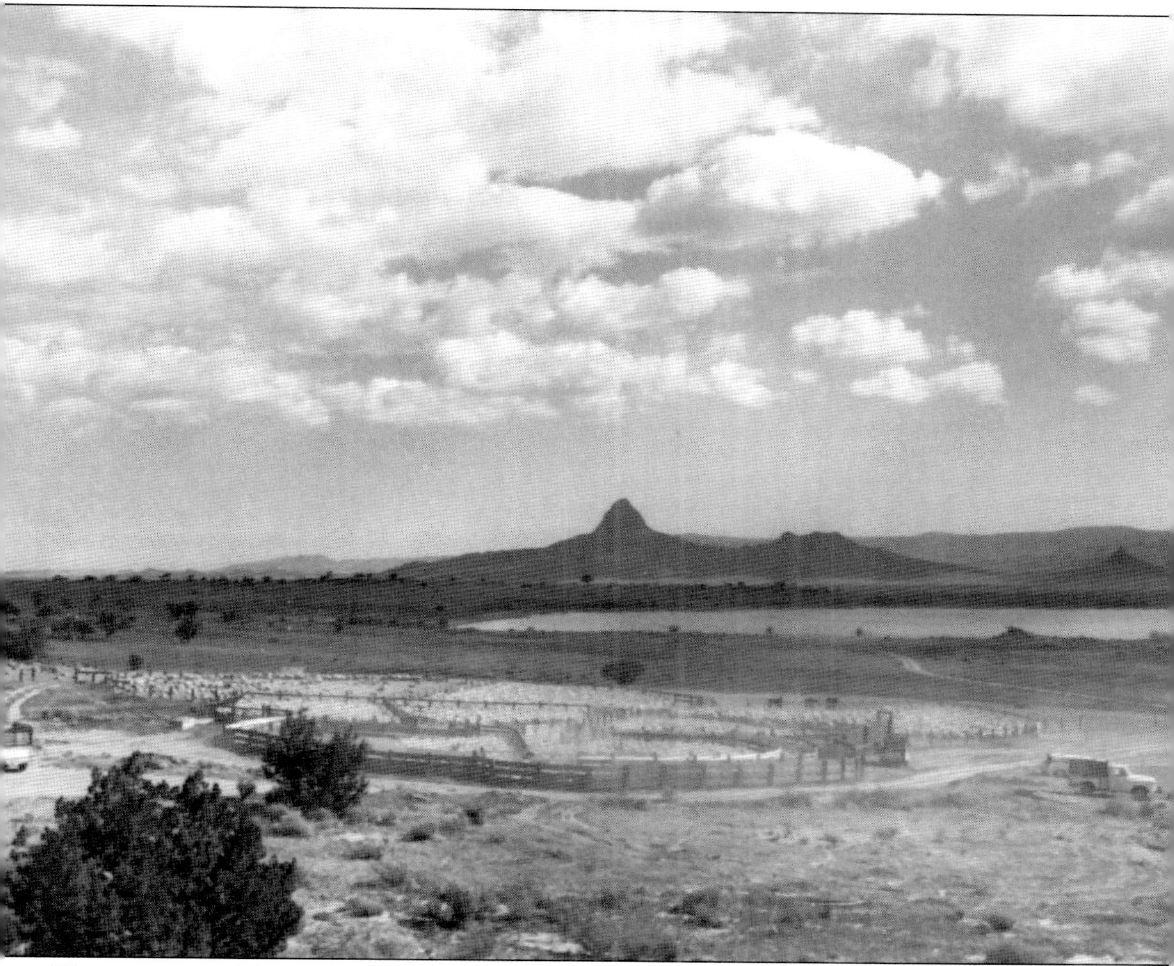

This is a scene of the huge Fernandez sheep and cattle ranch owned and operated by the Floyd Lee family. According to Sherry Robinson's book *El Malpais, Mt. Taylor, and the Zuni Mountains*, the Fernandez Ranch is one of New Mexico's oldest and biggest surviving cattle companies, and at one time, it covered 300,000 acres. The Lees also accumulated land by buying sections from the railroad and homesteaders. (Courtesy of the New Mexico State Library Archive.)

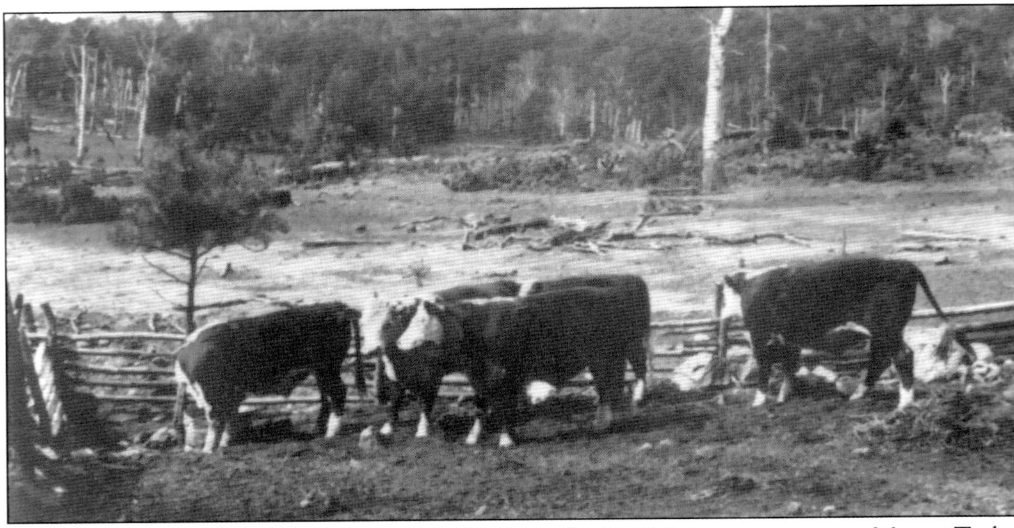

This is a scene from the Elkins Ranch, probably at the family's summer camp at Mount Taylor. The Elkins family came from Texas and homesteaded in the area. Three brothers, Mark, Tom, and Henry, developed large cattle ranches in the area, and their descendants have played an important part in local politics, banking, and business. (Courtesy of the Elkins family.)

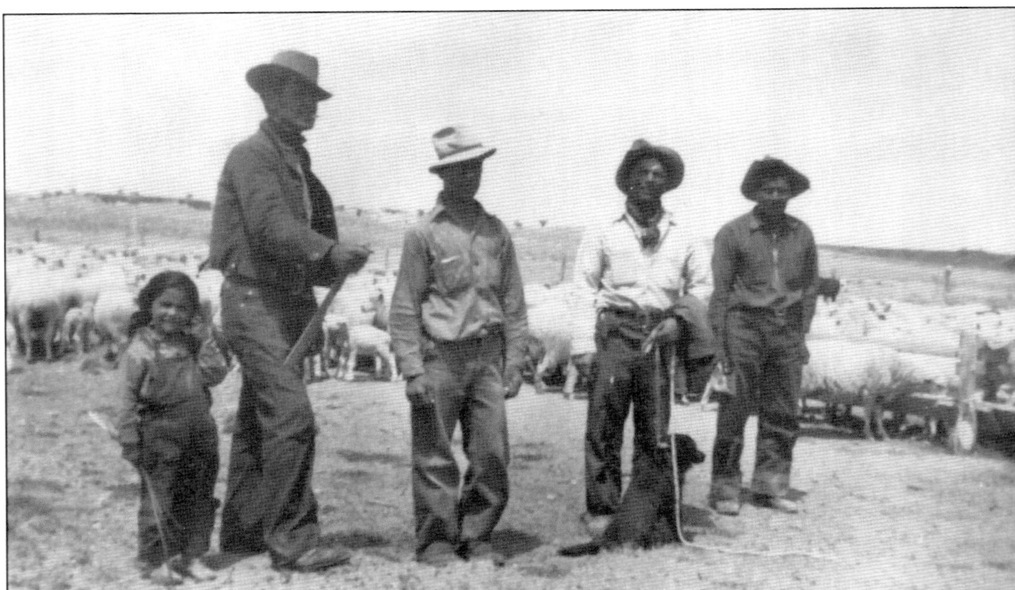

The Peña sheep ranch is up around San Mateo, one of the Spanish villages in the surrounding area of Grants-Milan. Pablo Peña is pictured with his daughter Lydia and three sheepherders overlooking a herd of sheep at the Peña Ranch. Lydia was educated at the Lorreta's Catholic School for girls in Santa Fe and enjoyed a career as a Catholic nun traveling all over the world. Pablo and children have been involved in ranching, politics, banking, government, education, and several businesses in the Grants-Milan area for more than a three quarters of a century. (Courtesy of the New Mexico State Library Archive.)

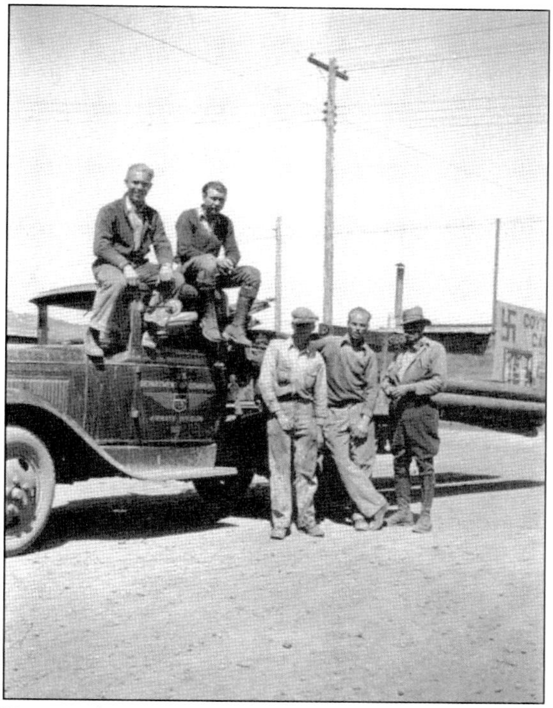

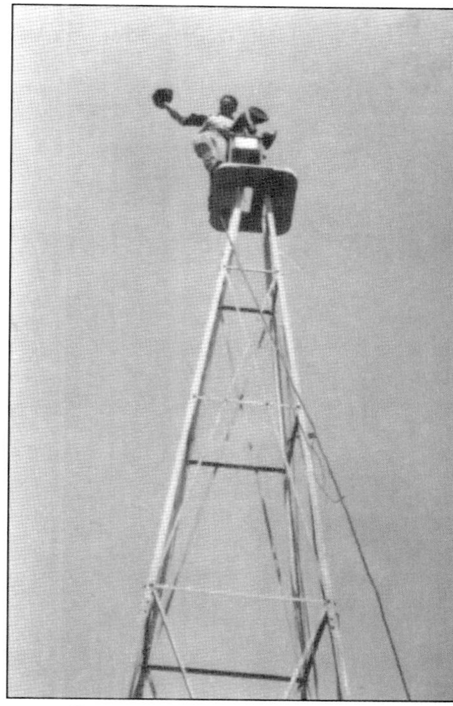

During the 1930s, the Department of Commerce Airways Division crews installed power lines across New Mexico to install beacon signals. The power lines connecting the beacon towers and generator sheds in the small towns were usually located on high ground for maximum signal strength and visibility. (Both, photographs by Jack Bell; courtesy of Bill Bell.)

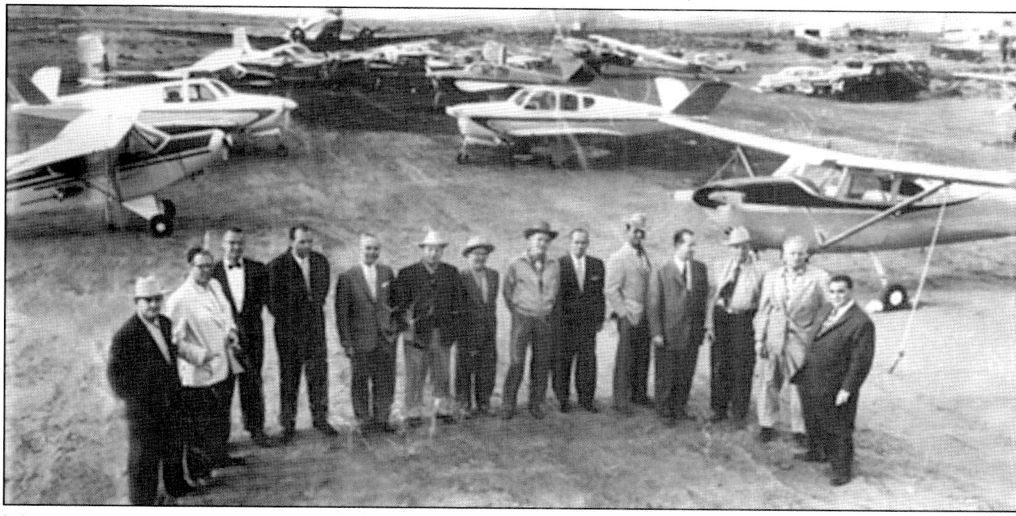

Mining executives represented all of the companies that established mines and mills in the area. It was unusual to get all of these high-ranking officials together at the same time, as they flew in from many parts of the country and represented the giants of the energy corporations. The Grants airport was built on the Milan Ranch before the village was incorporated and is now a joint venture between the two entities called the Grants-Milan Airport. (Courtesy of the *Cibola Beacon*.)

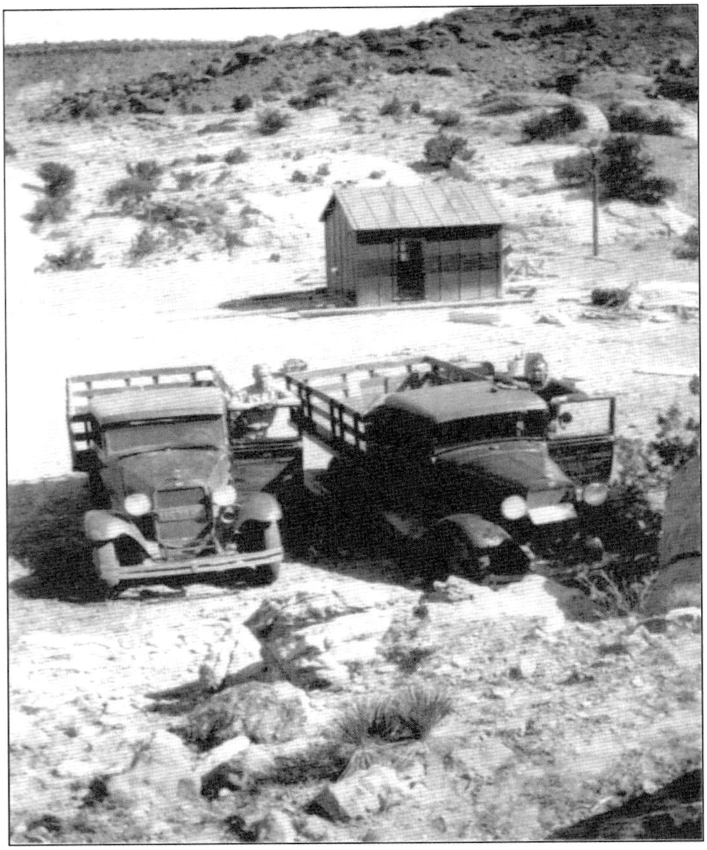

The Airway crews often worked in rough terrains and with minimal equipment. The old Ford flatbed trucks hauled the necessary tools up winding, dirt roads and were often traveling with the heavy loads for several miles. The towers were abandoned in the 1950s, and now many of them are becoming historical markers. (Both, photographs by Jack Bell; courtesy of Bill Bell.)

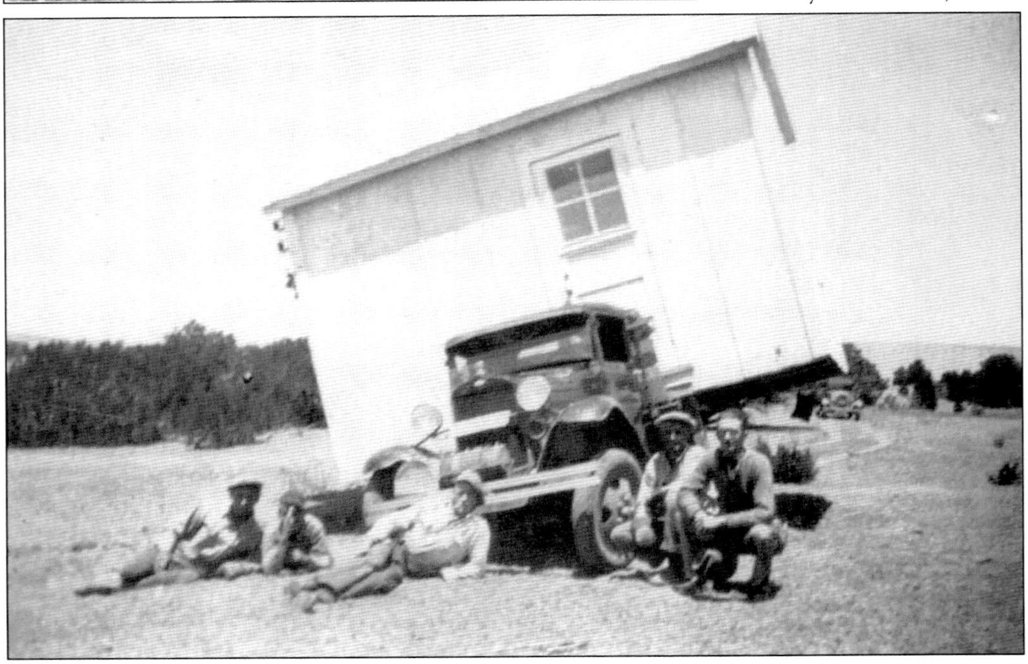

Pictured here is H.C. Elkins, an original pioneer of the area. (Courtesy of the Elkins family.)

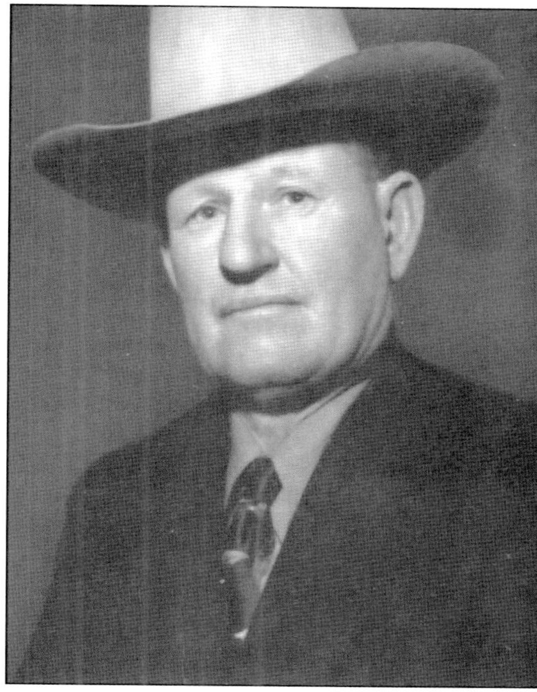

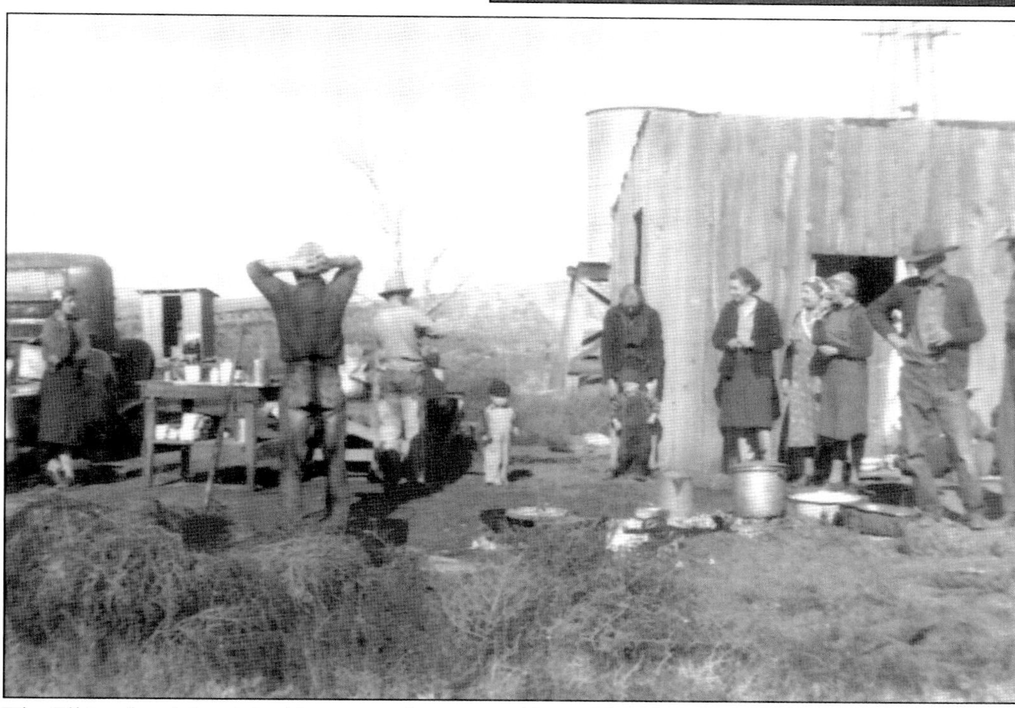

The Elkins family's original homestead is pictured here. They have established themselves as four generations of cattle ranchers, expanding their original homestead into large ranch holdings, and they have been involved in banking, school development, trading posts, and a variety of businesses. (Courtesy of the Elkins family.)

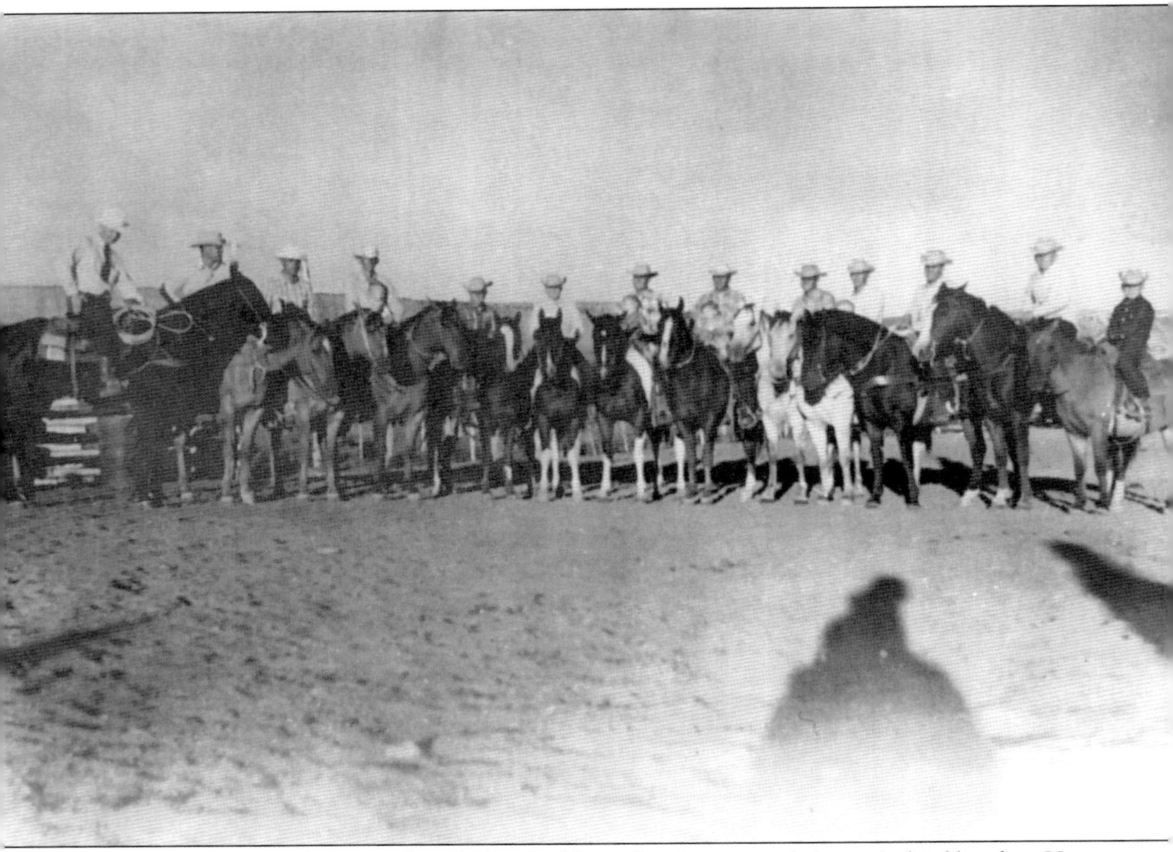

The two Elkins brothers, Mark and Tom, had large families—mostly boys. A third brother, Henry, did not have any children, although he raised two Native American boys. It is evident by this picture that the Elkins brothers supplied the two families with an adequate number of cowboys as well as athletes for the schools. The photograph shows 13 boys, and there were also three girls between the two families. (Courtesy of the Elkins family.)

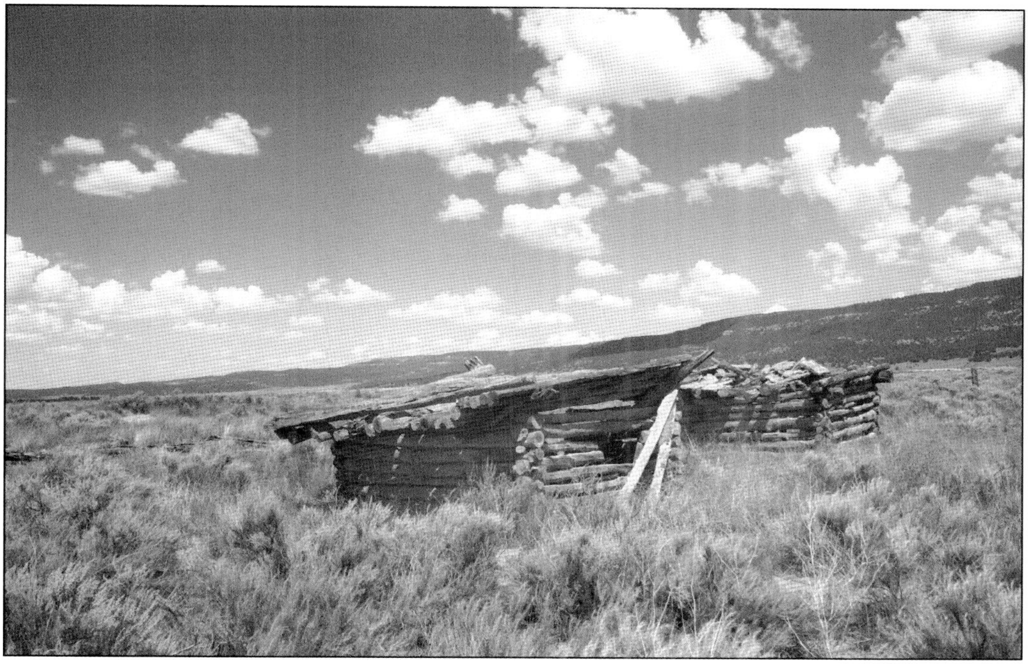

The ruins of one of the many homesteads that dotted the area are pictured here. Homesteads like this one led to the development of ranching and farming in the area, and during the logging boom, they supplied loggers. As other booms developed in the area, many homesteaders moved to Grants for high-paying jobs and sold their ranches and farms to the large ranch owners. (Courtesy of the US Forest Service.)

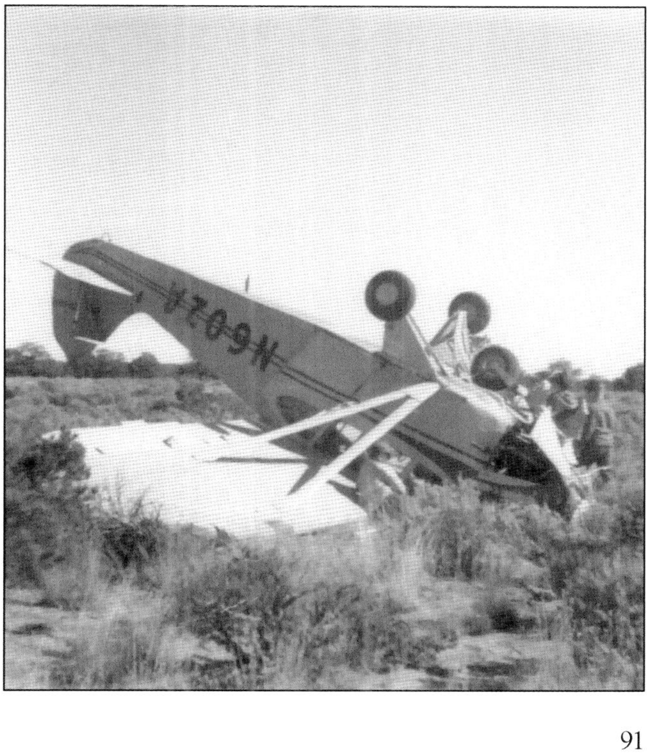

During the early 1950s, the Mark Elkins family established ranches in Mexico and utilized airplanes to fly back and forth. Some of the Elkins family learned to fly, but unfortunately the sudden winds in the area have their hazards. Jim is the younger son of Mark Elkins and is still ranching. (Courtesy of the Elkins family.)

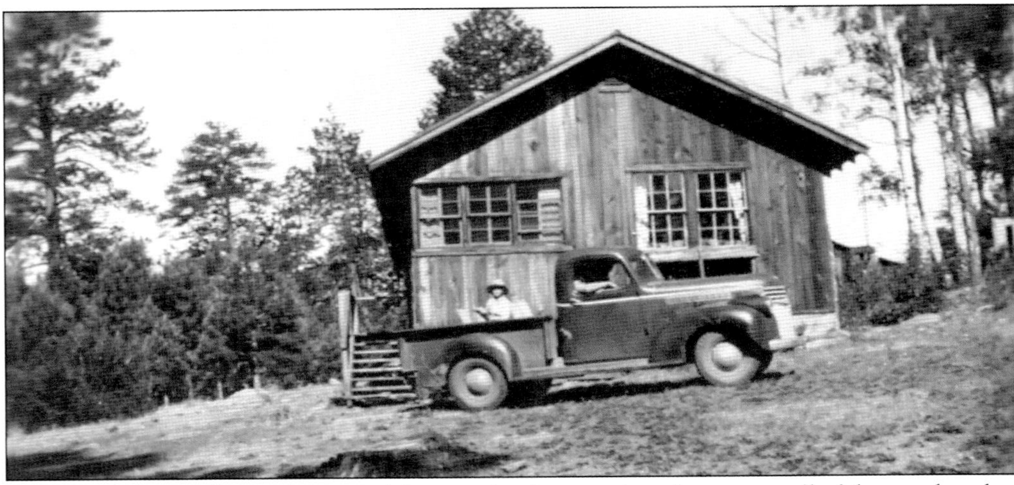

Because of the weather and the need for grass for sheep and cattle, most or all of the ranchers had pastures in the valleys and summer camps up on the mountains. Grants-Milan is located between Mount Taylor and the Zuni Mountains, and the semidesert-like valley can change to pine trees or grassy country in less than 20 miles. (Courtesy of the Elkins family.)

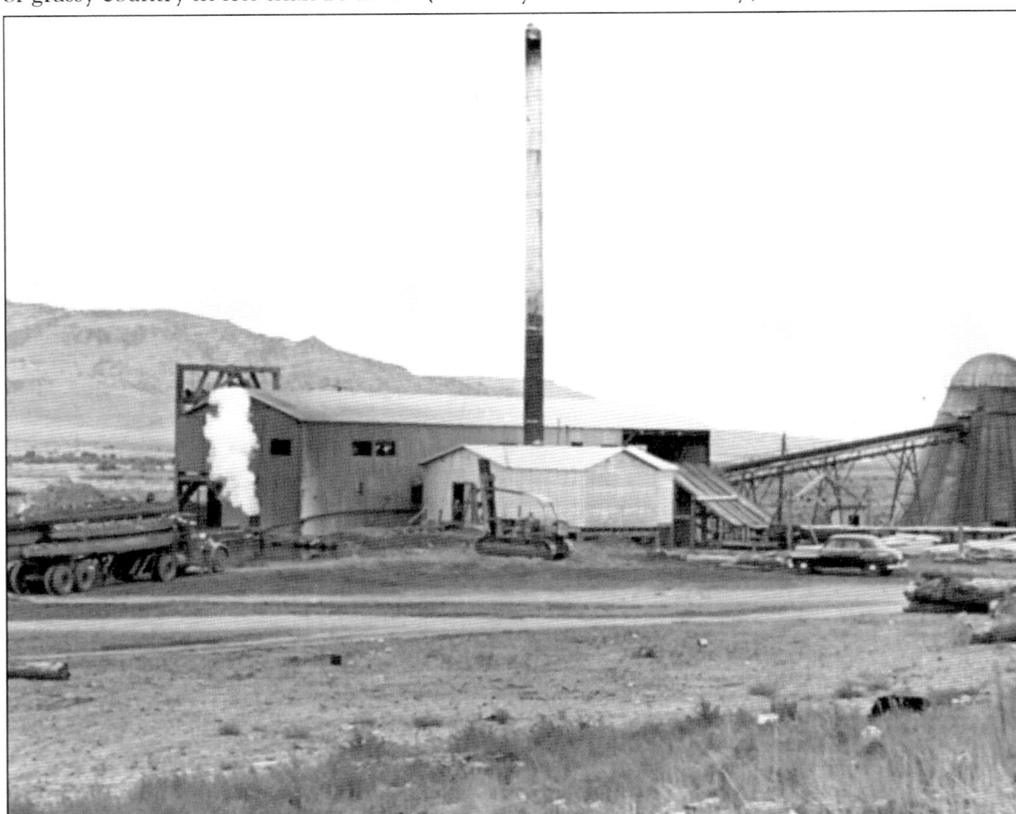

A typical lumber sawmill of the area, this one was located in Breece Town, adjoining Grants. Others included the Blevins Sawmill, about a mile west of Milan, and the Hawkinson Sawmill north of Grants. None of the sawmills are still operating today. (Courtesy of E.B. Dawson.)

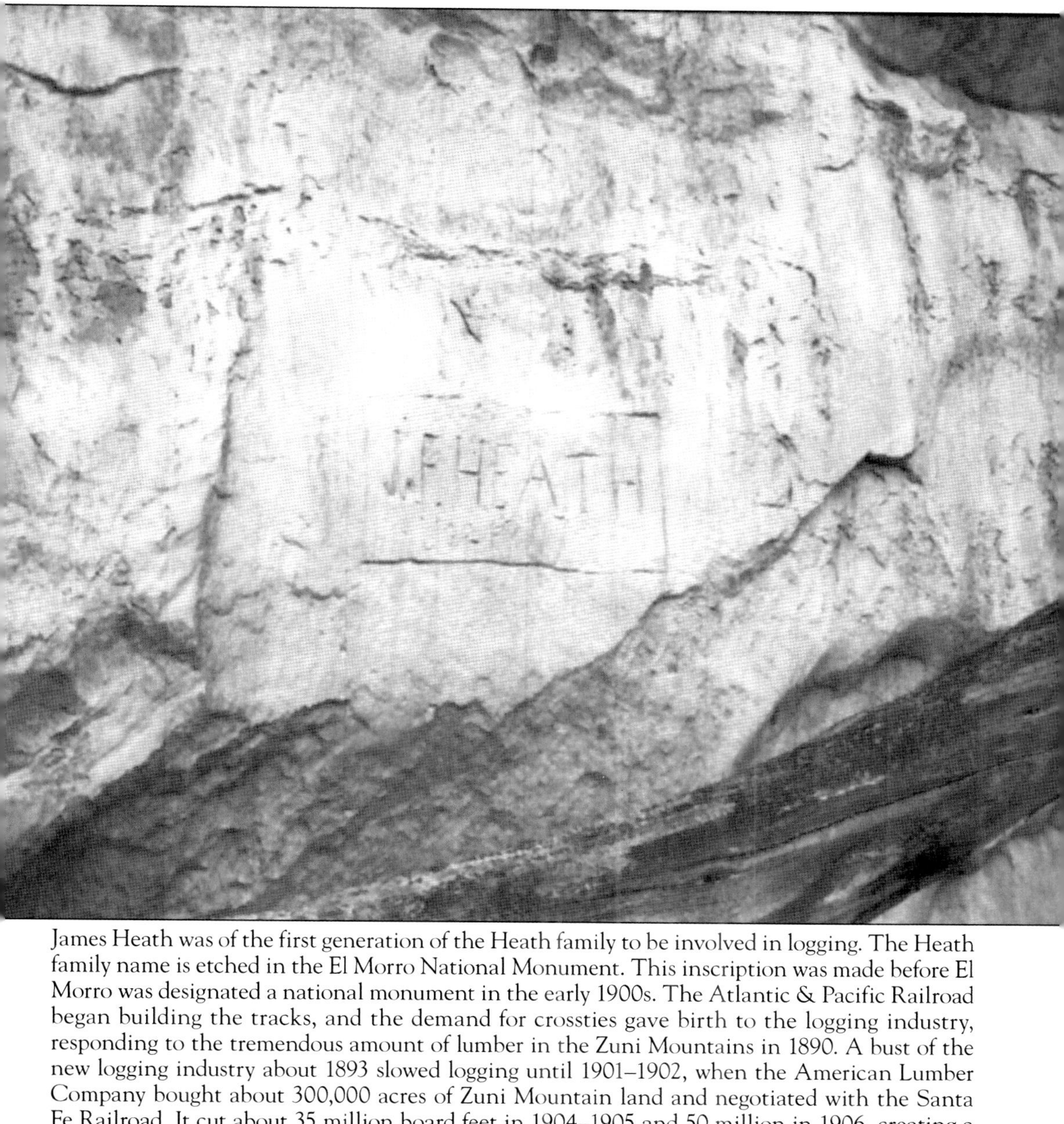

James Heath was of the first generation of the Heath family to be involved in logging. The Heath family name is etched in the El Morro National Monument. This inscription was made before El Morro was designated a national monument in the early 1900s. The Atlantic & Pacific Railroad began building the tracks, and the demand for crossties gave birth to the logging industry, responding to the tremendous amount of lumber in the Zuni Mountains in 1890. A bust of the new logging industry about 1893 slowed logging until 1901–1902, when the American Lumber Company bought about 300,000 acres of Zuni Mountain land and negotiated with the Santa Fe Railroad. It cut about 35 million board feet in 1904–1905 and 50 million in 1906, creating a new logging boom. According to Sherry Robinson, at its peak, in 1910, the American Lumber Company produced 60 million board feet of lumber, employed 700 loggers, and shipped 100 carloads a day. The logging industry headquarters moved around the area, with railroad tracks built to different locations by the lumber companies, and in 1922 the rising freight rates turned Grants into a boomtown. (Courtesy of the Heath family.)

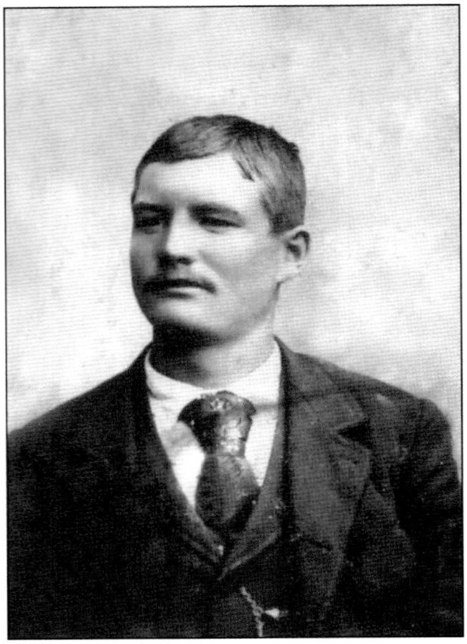

In 1926, a new railroad was constructed from Grants to the Zuni Mountains by George Breece. By 1931, Breece sold his operation to Grants businessmen Carl Seligman and M.R. Prestridge. In 1941, locomotives hauled their last load of timber about the time that commercial timber ran out. The railroad tracks were removed before World War II, and it was said that the Japanese bought all of the metal. Individual loggers like the Heaths continued to log in the area, as did the Blevins, Cecil Moore, and Hawkinson families. (Courtesy of the Heath family.)

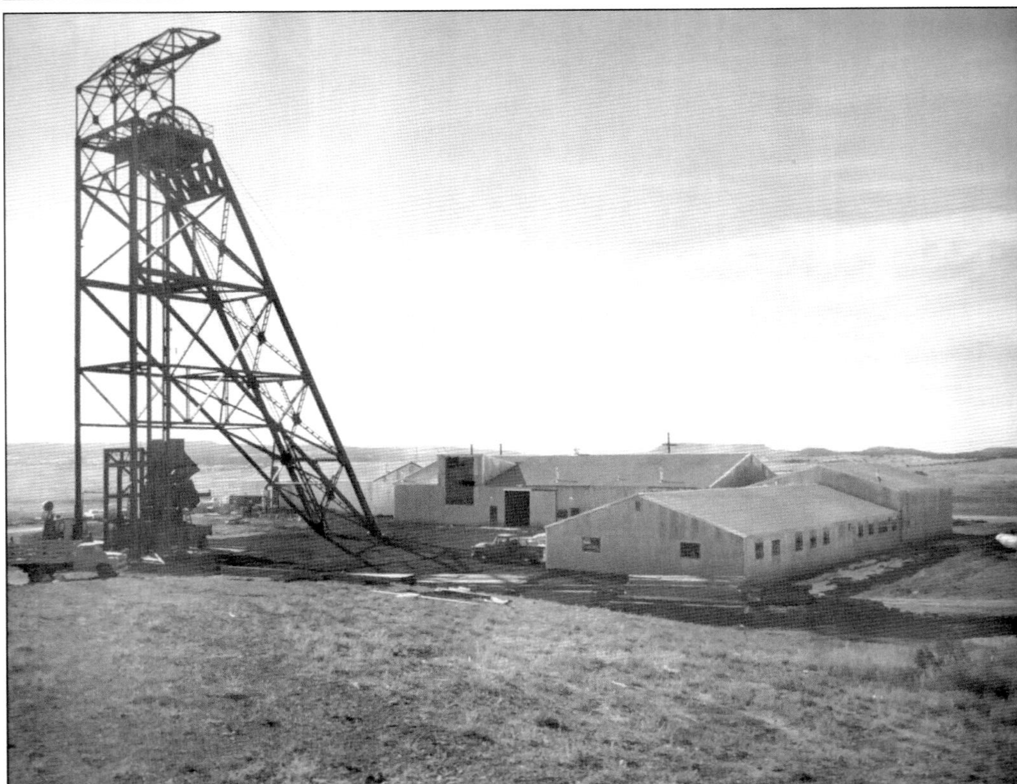

During the spring of 1950, at Haystack Mountain near Grants, Navajo Paddy Martinez picked up a piece of yellow rock that proved to be high-grade uranium ore. These are uranium mining rigs that were used to haul the ore from underground mines in the Ambrosia Lake area. (Courtesy of the Uranium Mining Museum.)

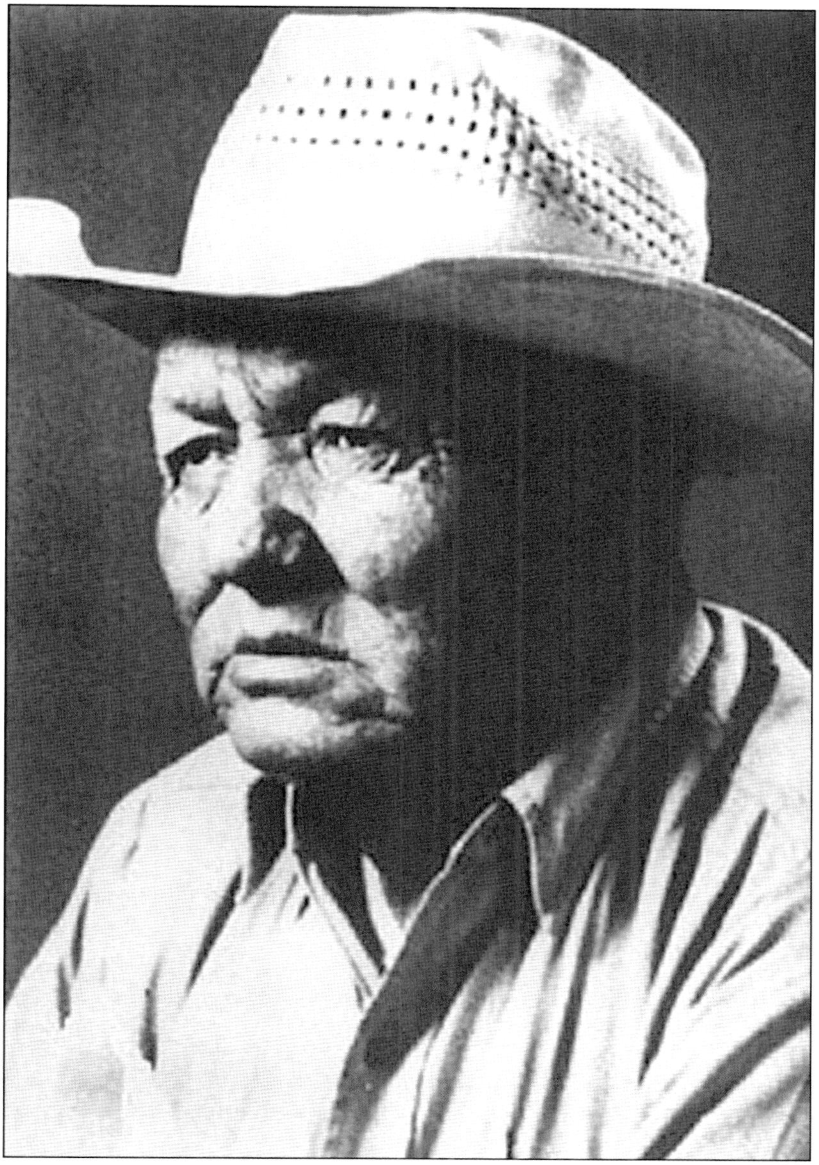

Paddy Martinez (pictured) was a Navajo sheep rancher who was credited for the discovery of uranium around Grants. Paddy took the yellow rock to Carrol Gunderson at his mercantile store, and Mr. Gunderson sent the sample to the Colorado School of Mines. There it was verified to be uranium. This find was on Santa Fe Railroad land, and the company immediately sent a geologist to the site for possible production. The government was the only entity legally allowed to buy uranium, and the Atomic Energy Commission was set up in the area to negotiate purchase, leading to the race for uranium mines and the uranium boom. The word was that a reward of $10,000 was offered for the discovery of uranium, and Paddy was rewarded by the railroad company with non-working employment. Paddy was a man of many facets; he had his ranch and many relatives. If someone needed a wire fence, he would assemble a crew immediately, and if someone needed workers for the farm, he would get them immediately, and he did this with a great sense of humor. (Courtesy of Leona Plaineagle.)

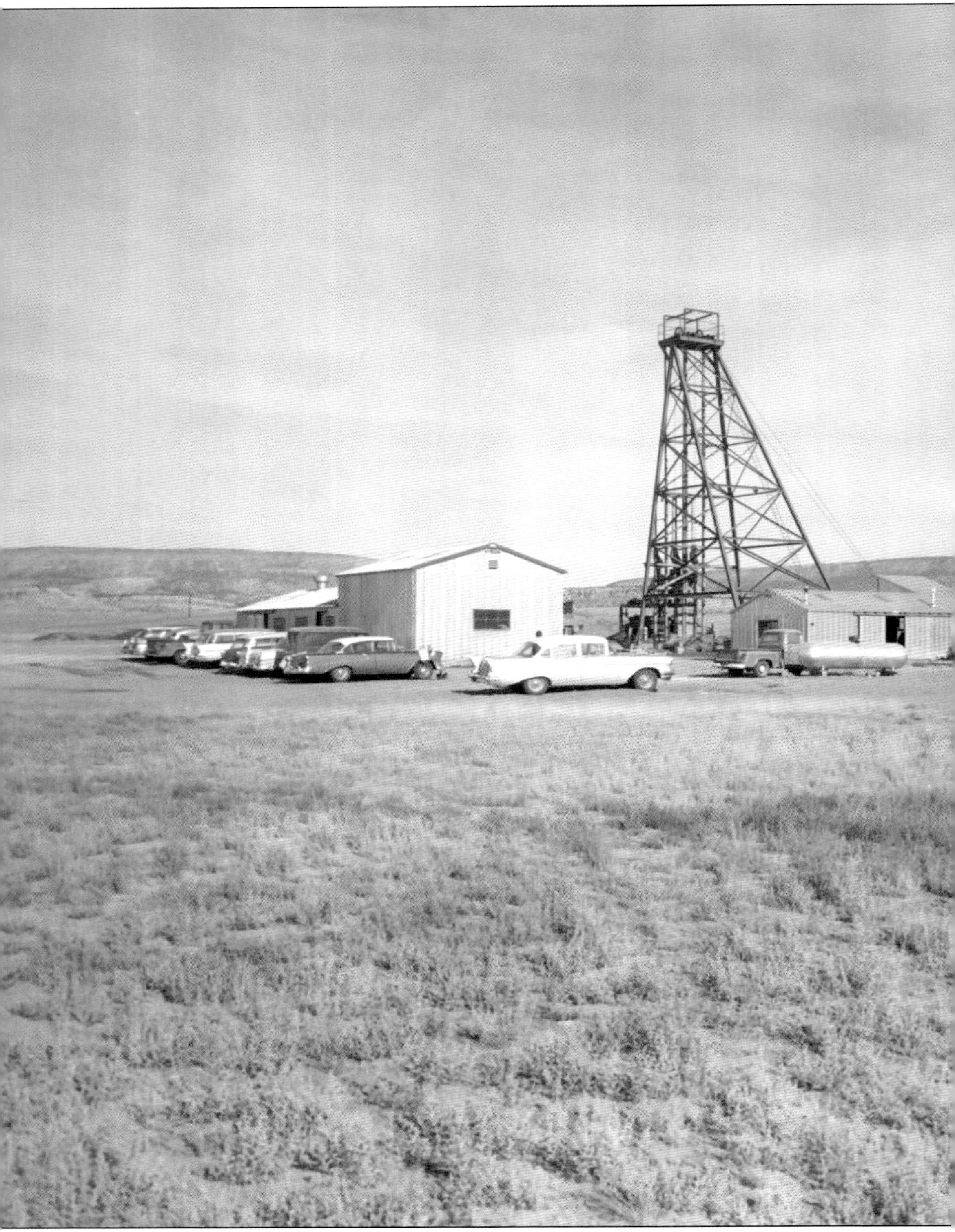

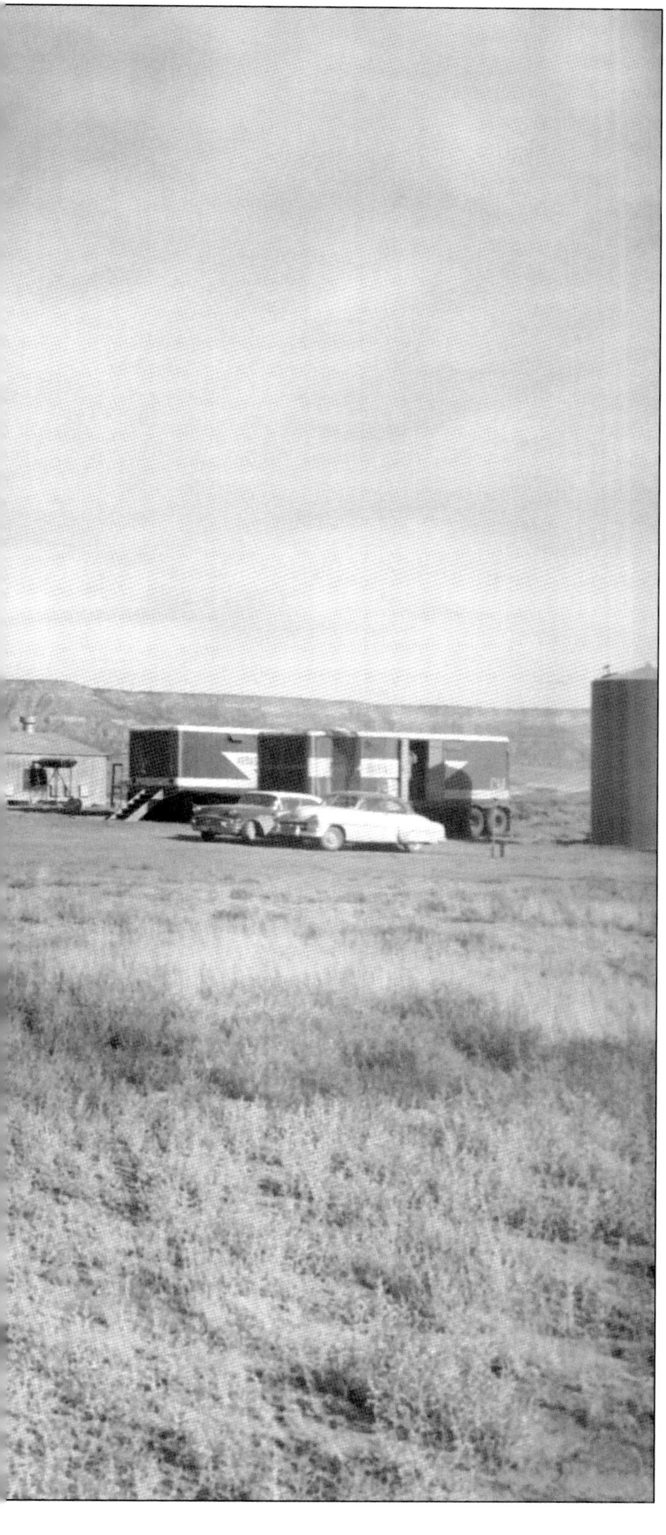

In 1950, the Santa Fe Railway began its first exploratory study of uranium deposits. The great uranium hunt was on! Grants became the west's new frontier. In the early 1960s, the Atomic Energy Commission was the only entity that could buy uranium, and its stockpile was over capacity, so a deal was forged to extend the contract at a lower capacity until commercial use was available. This caused the uranium companies to slow down production, causing an economic bust for the area. Beginning in the early 1970s, commercial use of uranium began as nuclear plants were built worldwide. (Courtesy of the Uranium Mining Museum.)

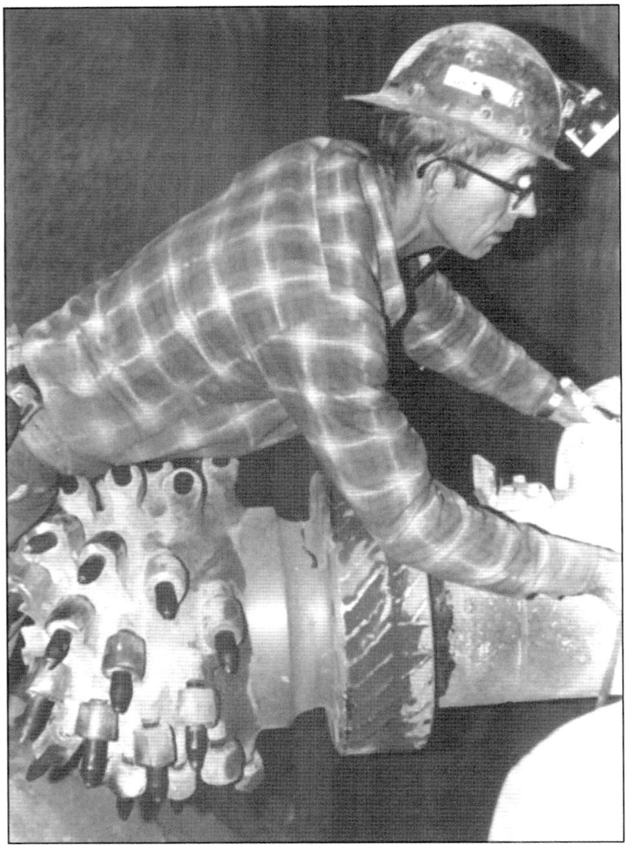

This is an underground uranium miner during the uranium boom in the 1970s. The miner is working with a drilling bit. At that time, the uranium price was at a level that the expense was not a factor, even though there was some competition from surface mining, which was much cheaper. One of the factors that helped create a bust was that the price of uranium had dropped, and underground mining could not compete with surface mining from other countries, especially Canada and Australia. (Courtesy of Sherry Robinson.)

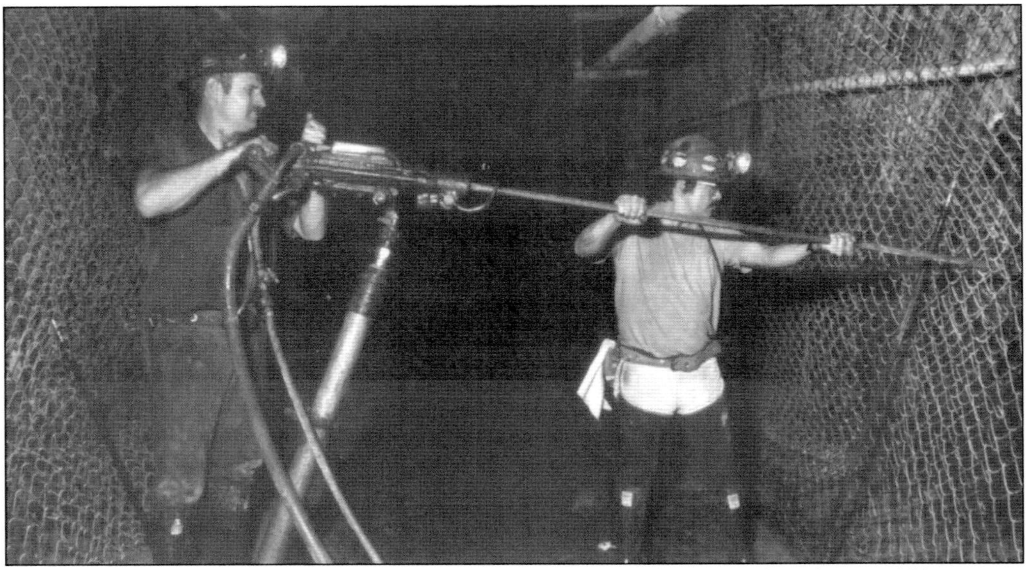

Two uranium miners work underground. According to some who remember, they could be setting the area up for dynamiting. Since uranium was not hard-rock mining like coal, apparently the wire mesh was a safety precaution. (Courtesy of Sherry Robinson.)

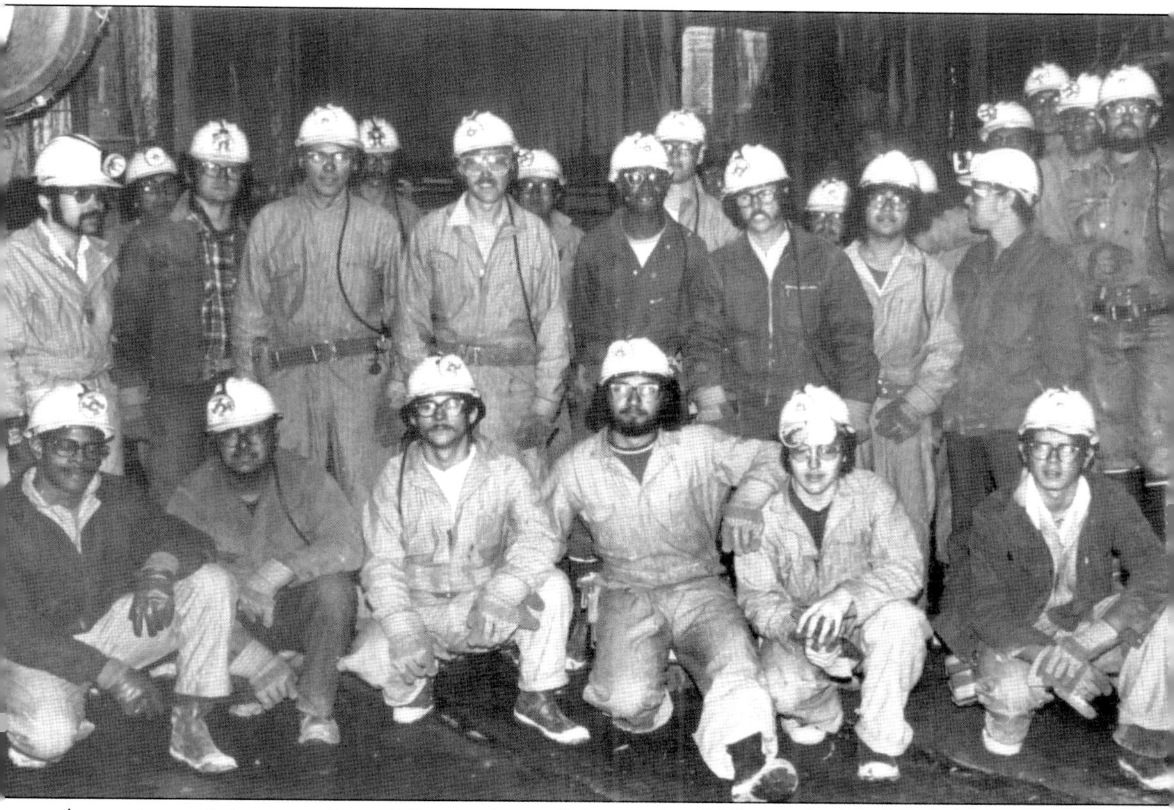

A uranium mining crew in training is pictured during the 1970s, at the height of the uranium boom. During this time, experienced miners were hired from all over the world. There were French Canadians, Hungarian, Germans, and miners from all over the United States. There were so many coal miners from West Virginia that there was a "Logan County Day" celebration. Many of the companies had mining facilities in many parts of the world, and some of their personnel transferred to the Grants-Milan area. As uranium production grew, the mines set up training programs to utilize local personnel. There was even a problem with young boys leaving high school before graduation because they could learn to become miners and were highly paid for that time. (Courtesy of Sherry Robinson.)

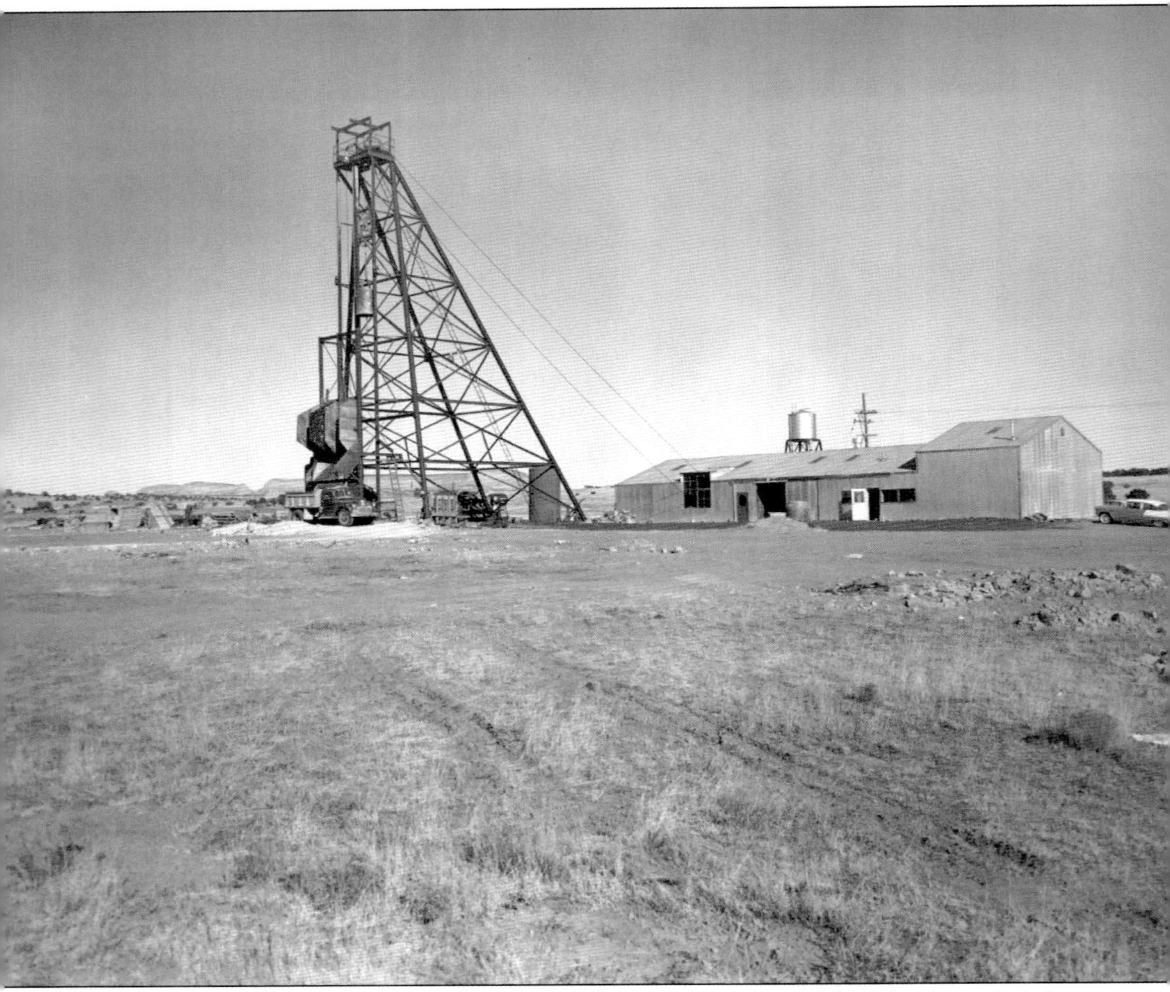

The 1970s were prosperous times locally until the disaster on Three Mile Island scuttled plans to build a large series of nuclear plants. Also, existing plants were able to buy cheaper uranium from Canada and Australia, where surface mining was practiced at a much lower cost. This resulted in the biggest bust ever from the 1980s until now. (Courtesy of the Uranium Mining Museum.)

Five

EVENTS

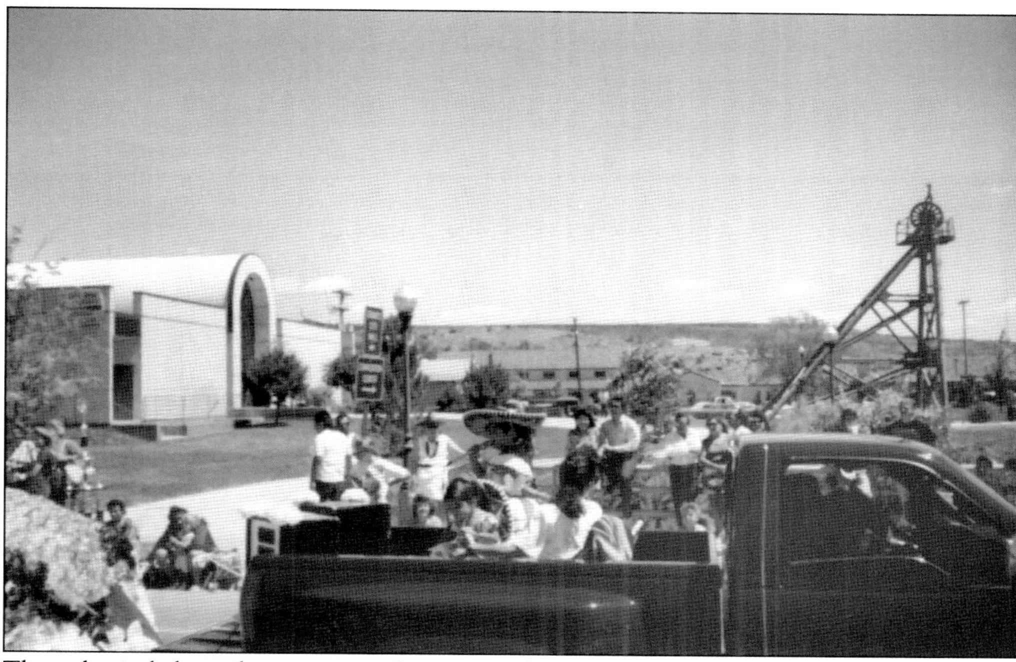

The rodeo is dedicated to amateurs who were working cowboys and cowgirls. Here is an example of the many parades that were held over a number of years with participants from many walks of life. Besides the rodeo and parade, the residents and guest enjoyed barbecue, art, and rodeo dances. Premier entertainment has always been part of the rodeo. (Courtesy of the Grants Rodeo Association.)

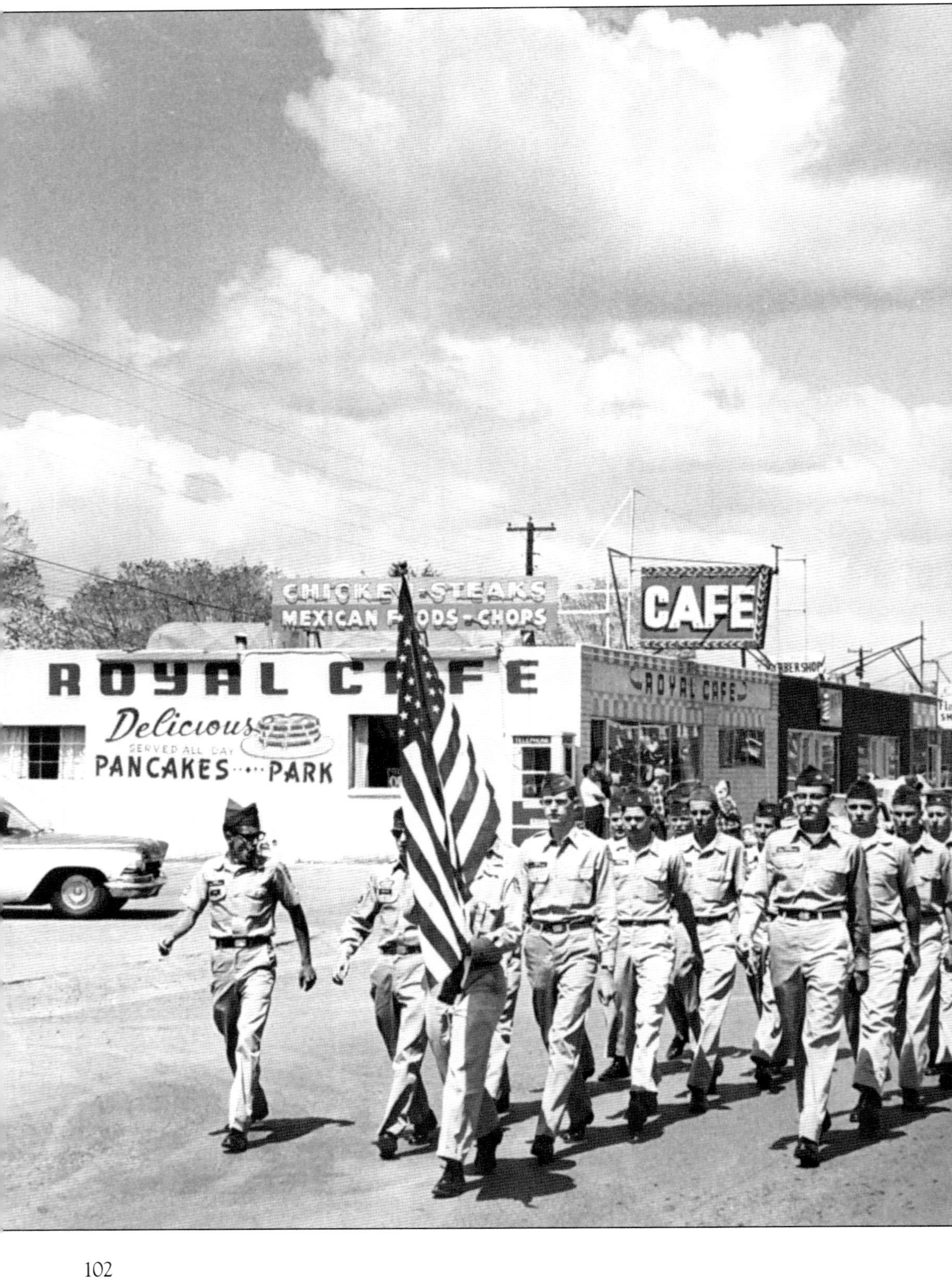
CAFE
Delicious
SERVED ALL DAY
PANCAKES
PARK
ROYAL CAFE

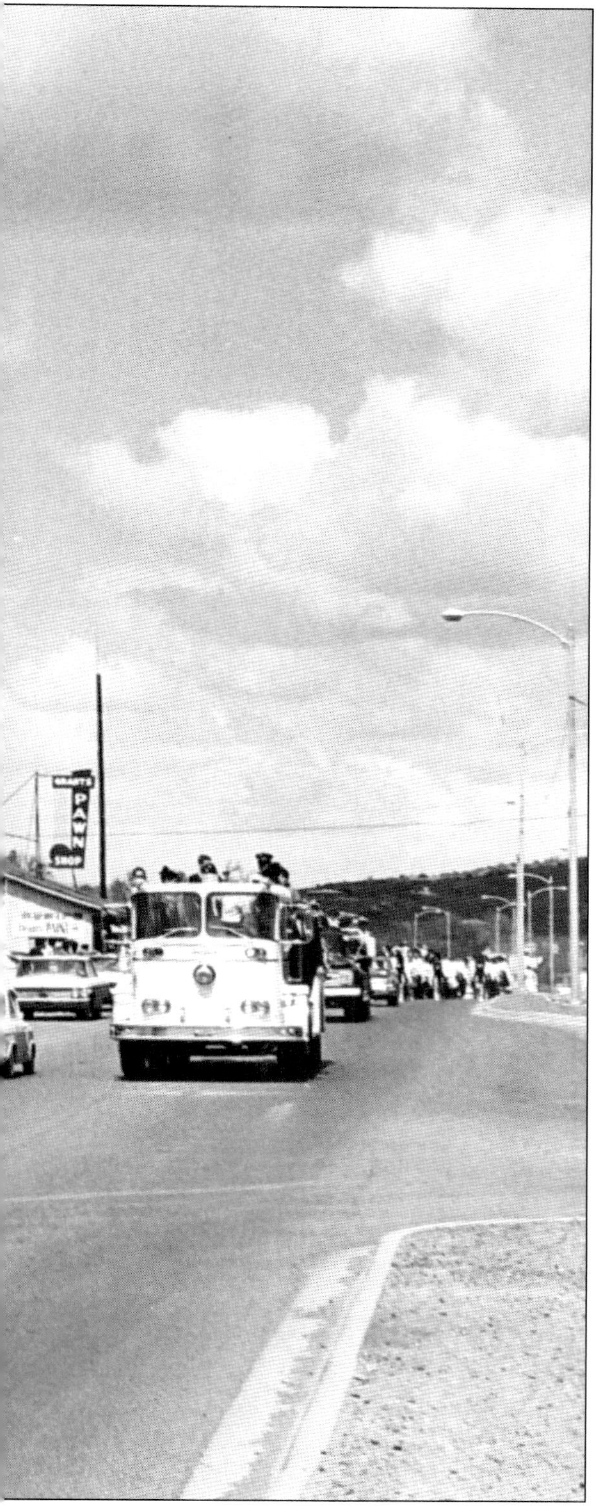

The Fourth of July Parade and Rodeo has been continuous since 1928 in Grants and is one of the highlight events of the area. (Courtesy of the Grants Rodeo Association.)

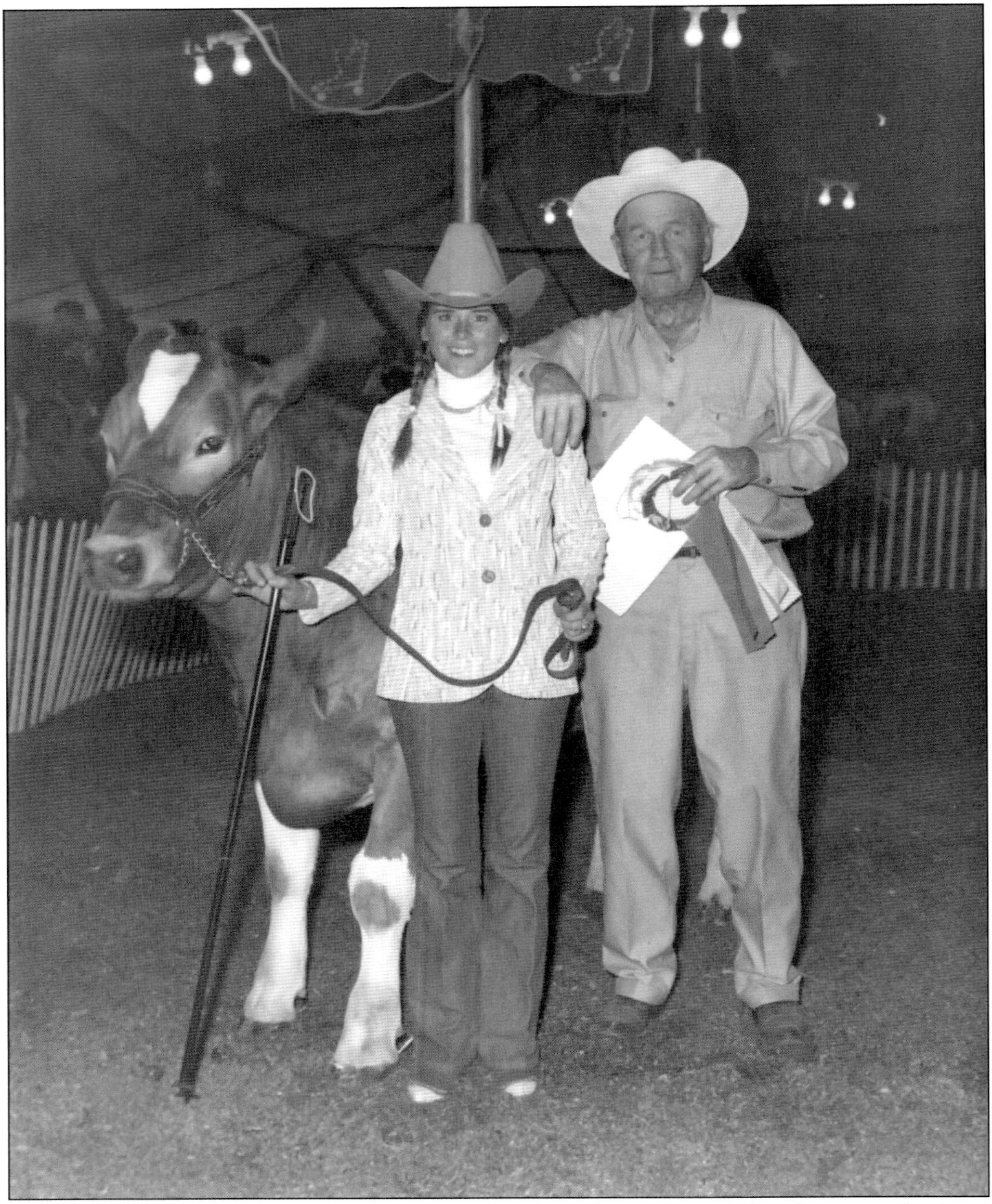

This is a photograph of the purchase of a 4-H calf at the Bi-County Fair by a popular local businessman, O.H. "Hawk" Hawkins. (Courtesy of Grants State Bank.)

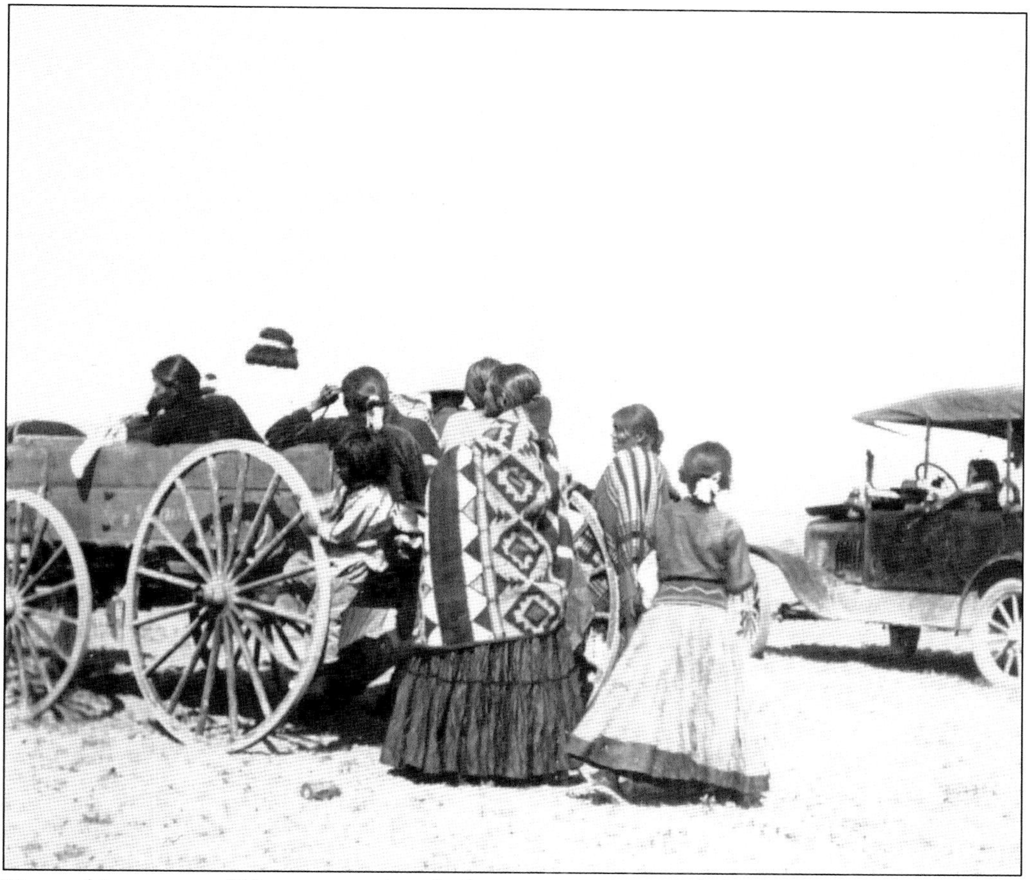

Pictured is a group of Navajos traveling by horse wagon to attend the Annual Laguna Fiesta as part of their peace treaty. Some would travel up to 100 miles one way for the celebration. (Both, courtesy of the Elkins family.)

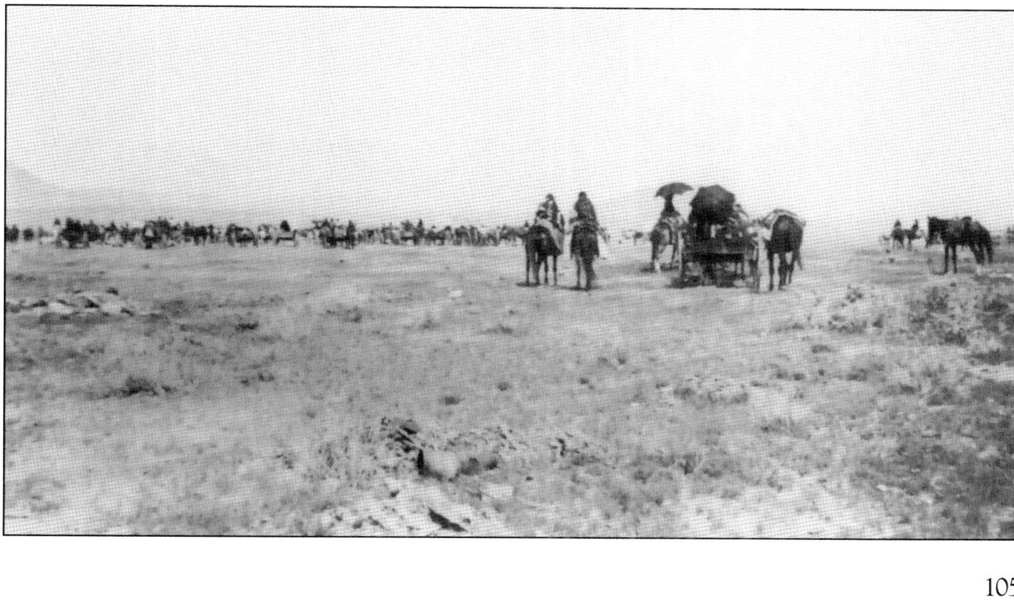

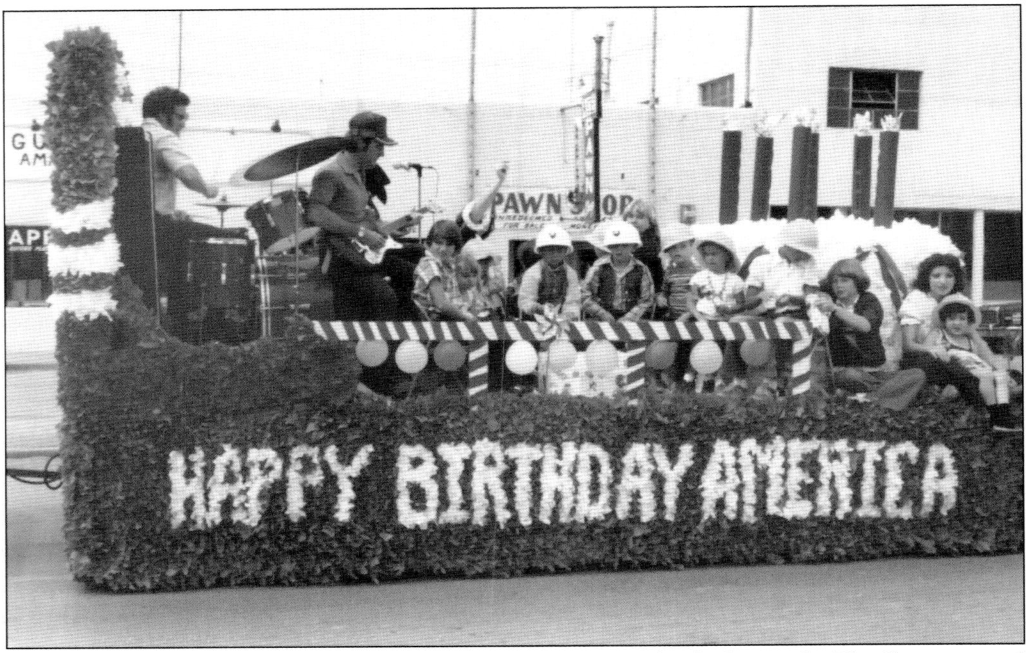

Patriotism is always on display in abundance during the Fourth of July parade. The float pictured below features live music. Note the man on the drums and another playing an electric guitar on this "Happy Birthday America" float. (Both, courtesy of the Grants Rodeo Association.)

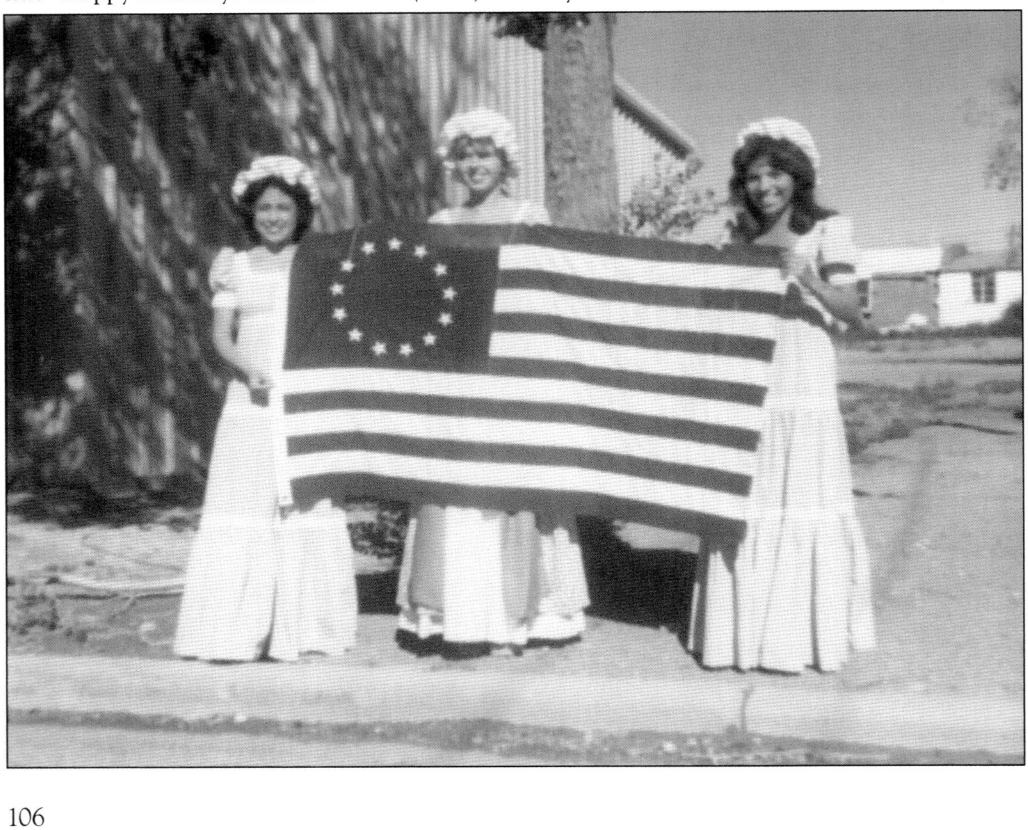

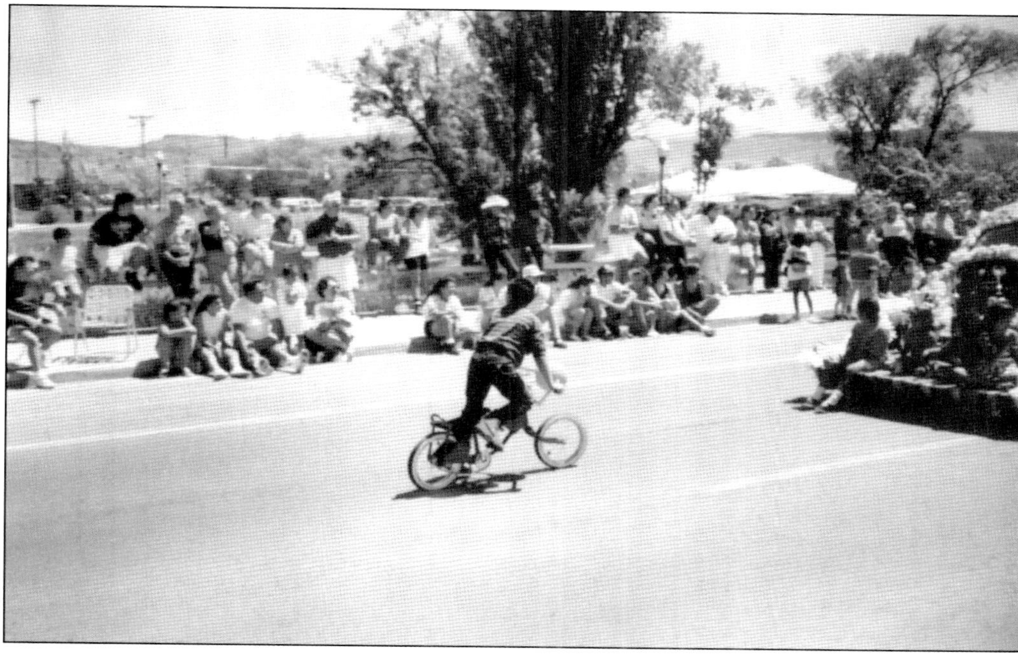

Children riding bicycles (above) and costumed adults on horseback (below) have been common sites at the parades over the years. (Both, courtesy of the Grants Rodeo Association.)

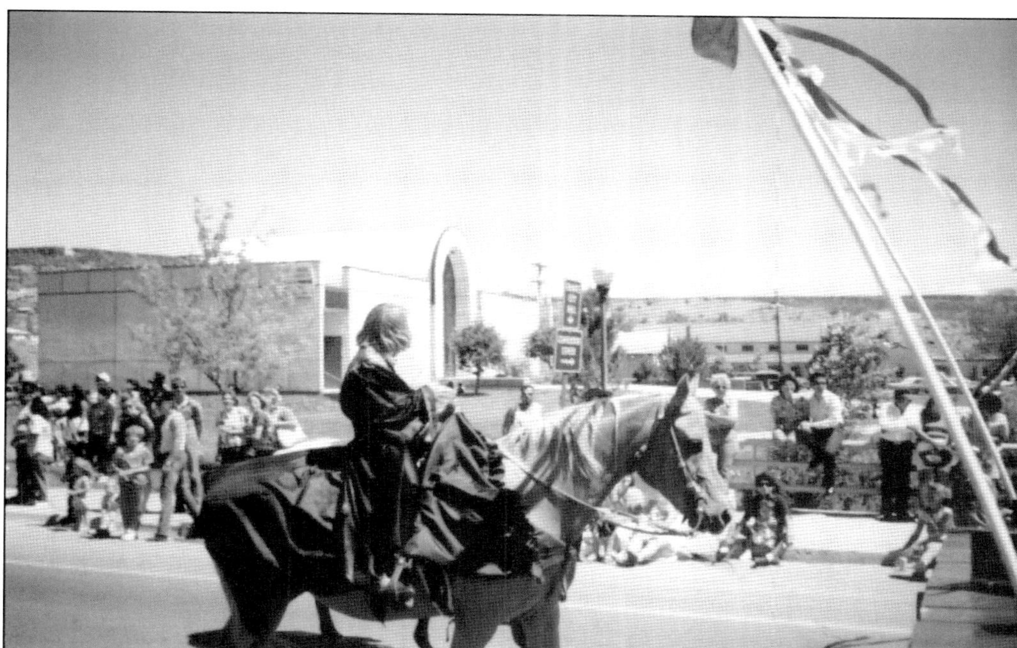

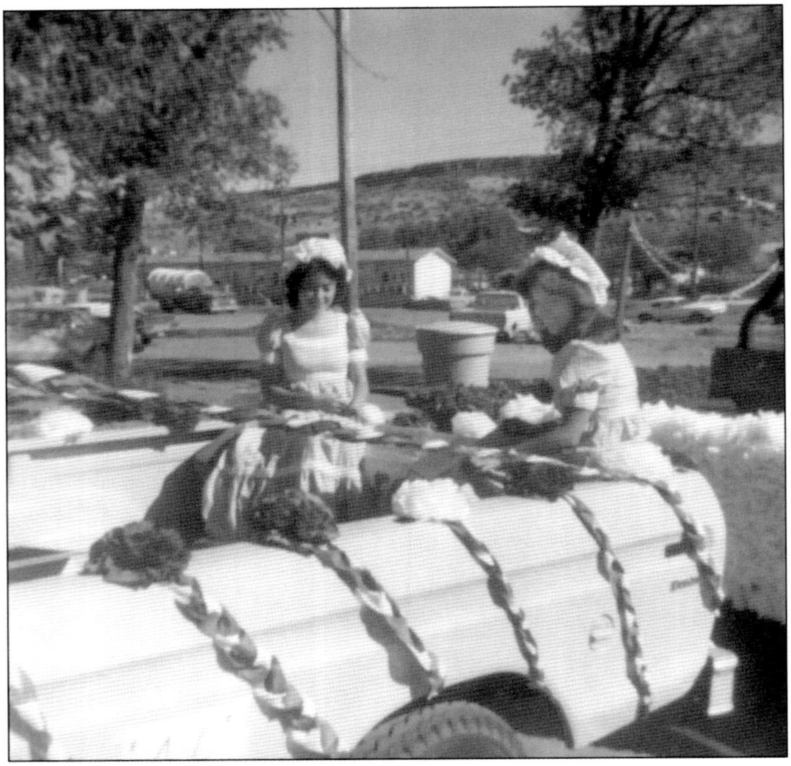

These floats at the Fourth of July parade include one decorated by Cub Scouts in the late 1940s. The Yucca Hotel and the Caradine Drugstore are in the background on the south side of Highway 66 on the west end of Grants. (Both, courtesy of the Grants Rodeo Association.)

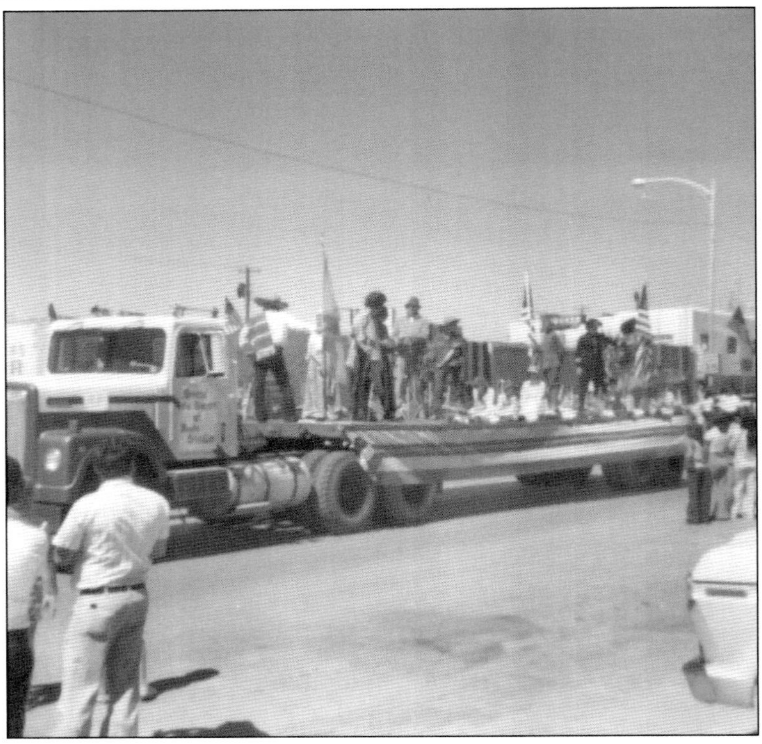

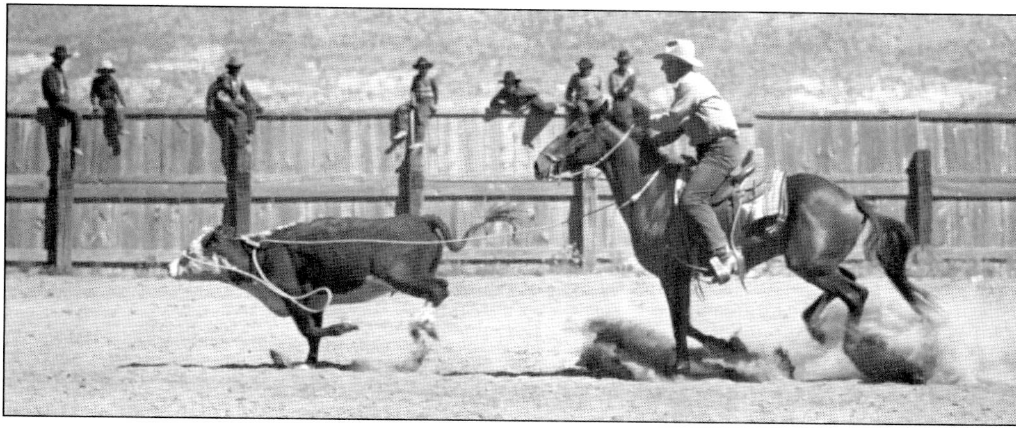

The Wild West Days rodeo began in 1924 and is still a proud tradition of the locals. The rodeo has always brought a good crowd to the Grants-Milan area to watch the many events, such as saddle bronc, bareback riding, bull riding, and team roping. (Both, courtesy of the Elkins family.)

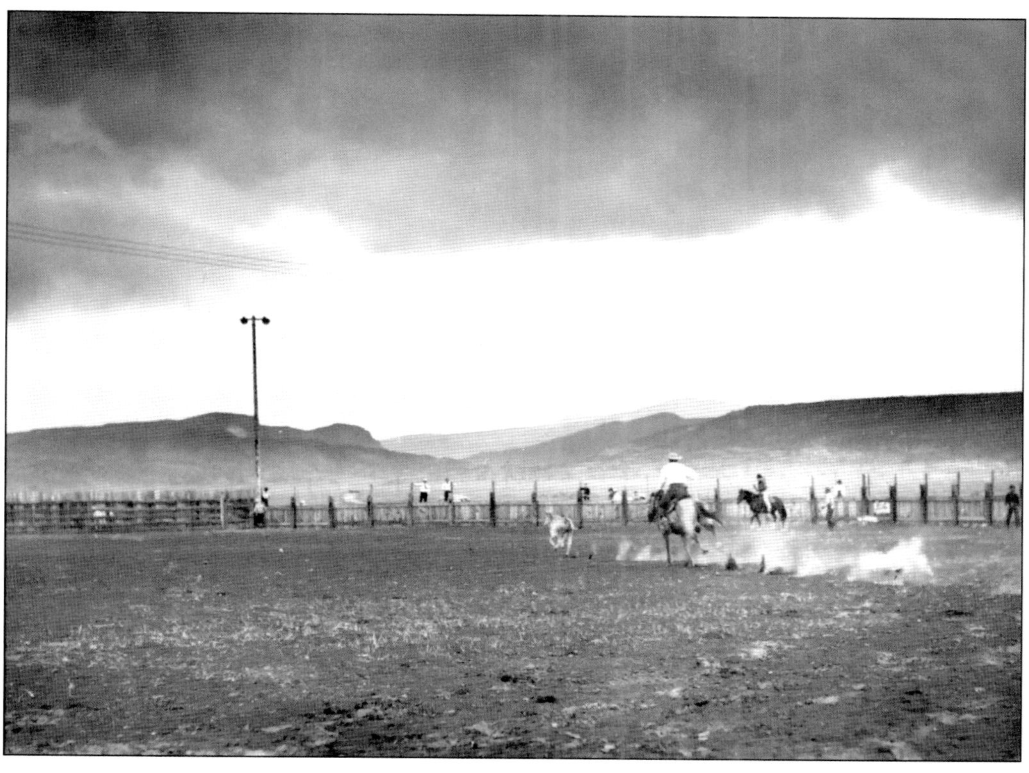

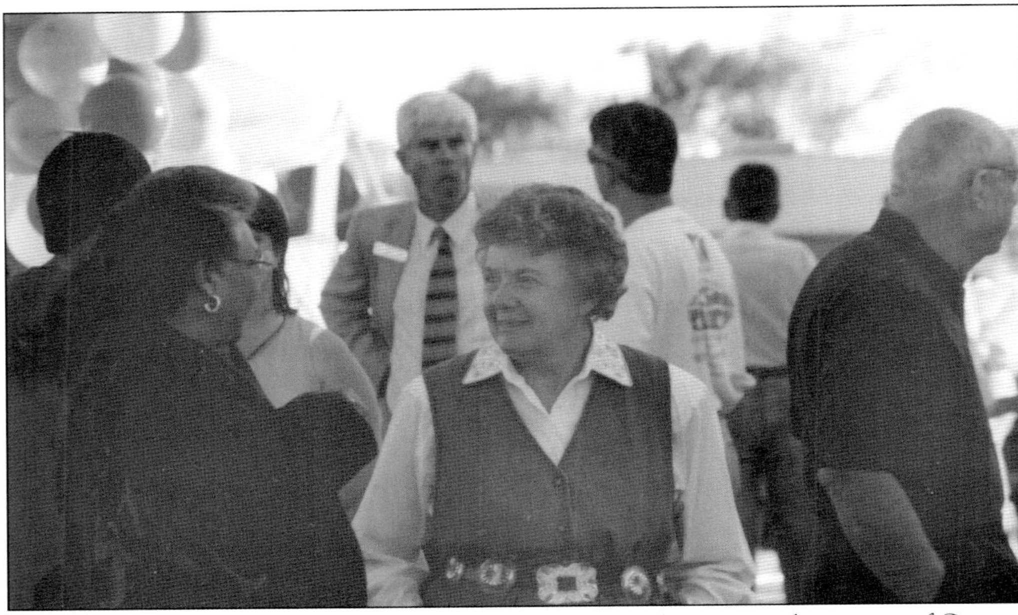

The Grants State Bank commemorated its 50th anniversary by inviting the citizens of Grants and Milan to enjoy an old-fashioned picnic. In 1947, the bank celebrated its grand opening by inviting the area to a family picnic, and it was decided to celebrate the 50th anniversary in the same fashion. In 1997, the bank invited all of the citizens to participate with food, music, and entertainment. Board director Mitch Wells and his wife, Marie Wells, are greeting the participants. (Courtesy of the Grants State Bank.)

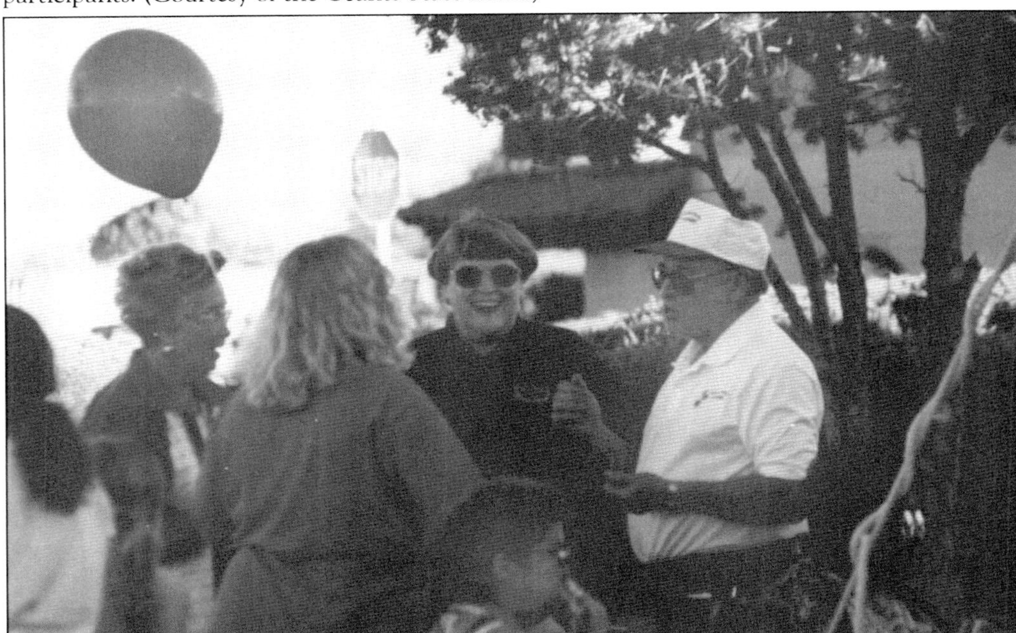

Board director Charles Harding, on the right, is entertaining guests with his humor and jokes at the Grants State Bank 50th-anniversary celebration. Some of the directors are third- and fourth-generation families of the area. (Courtesy of the Grants State Bank.)

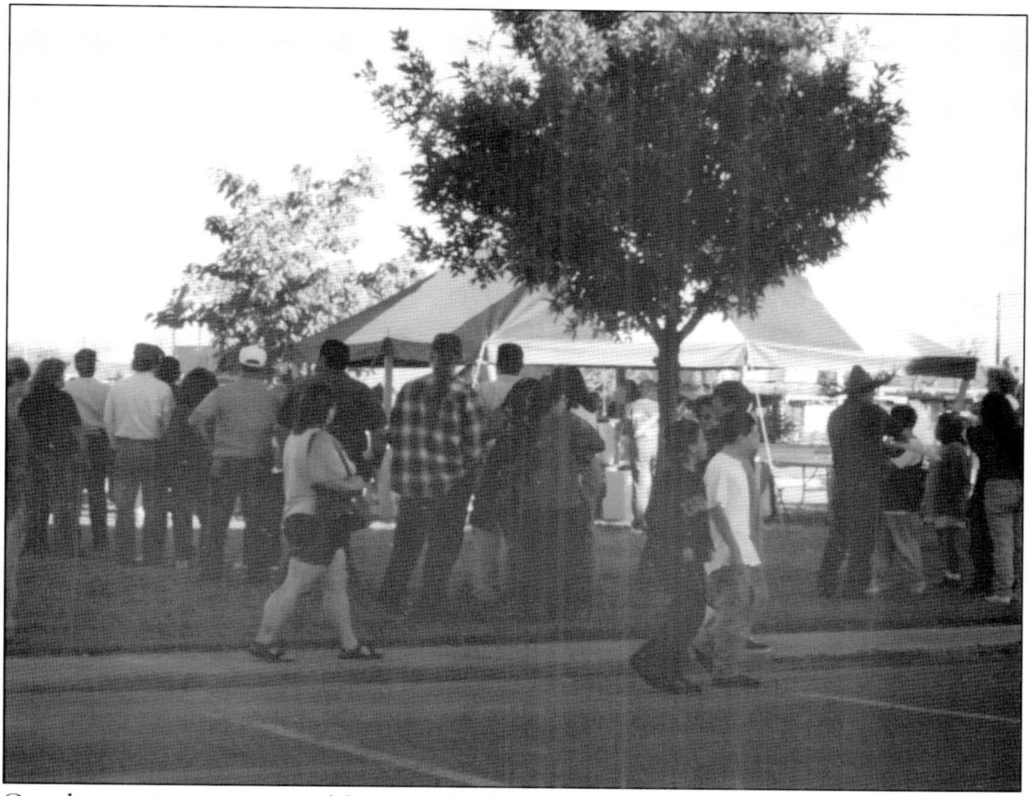

Crowds came in anticipation of the picnic for the citizens. The celebrants of the 50th anniversary of the Grants State Bank are lining up around the food tent to enjoy the variety of picnic goodies. (Courtesy of the Grants State Bank.)

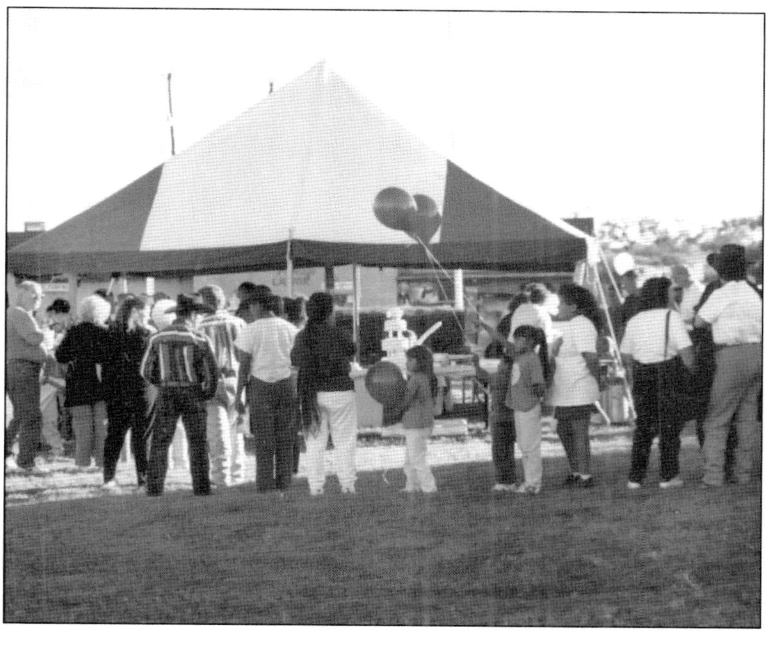

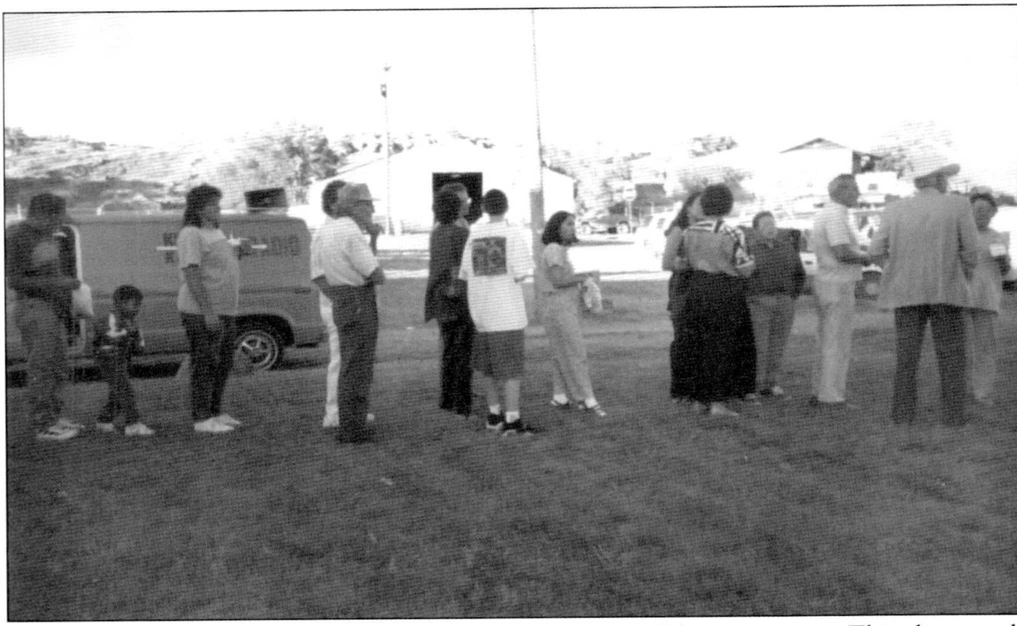

The variety of cakes was on display and for the consumption of the picnic-goers. This photograph was taken before the crowds lined up for dessert—not a crumb was left. Besides the main food tent, there were a number of other food stands, including cake, ice cream, popcorn, and soft drinks. (Courtesy of the Grants State Bank.)

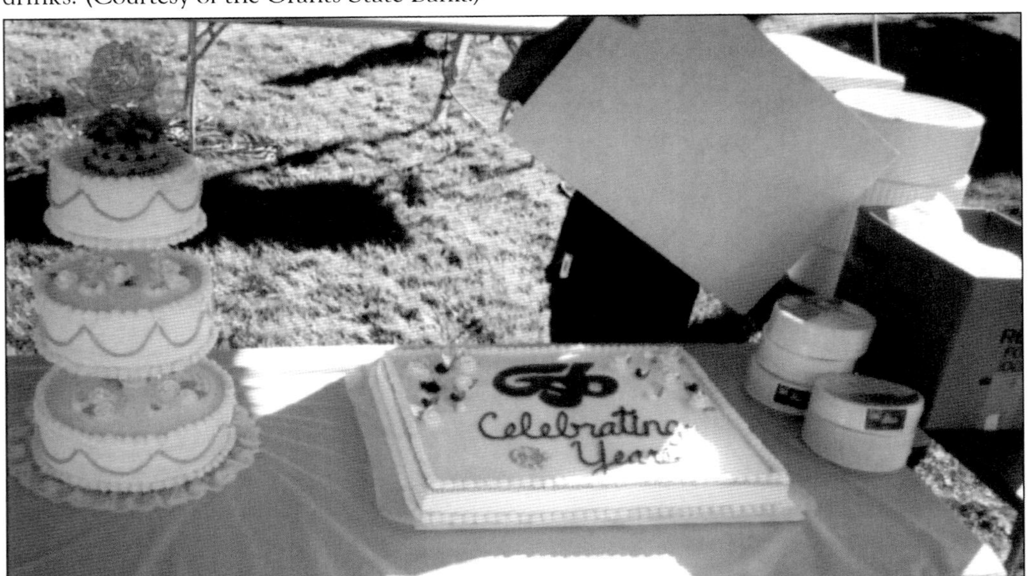

Another photograph shows the celebrants around the many food tents to help celebrate this one-time event. (Courtesy of the Grants State Bank.)

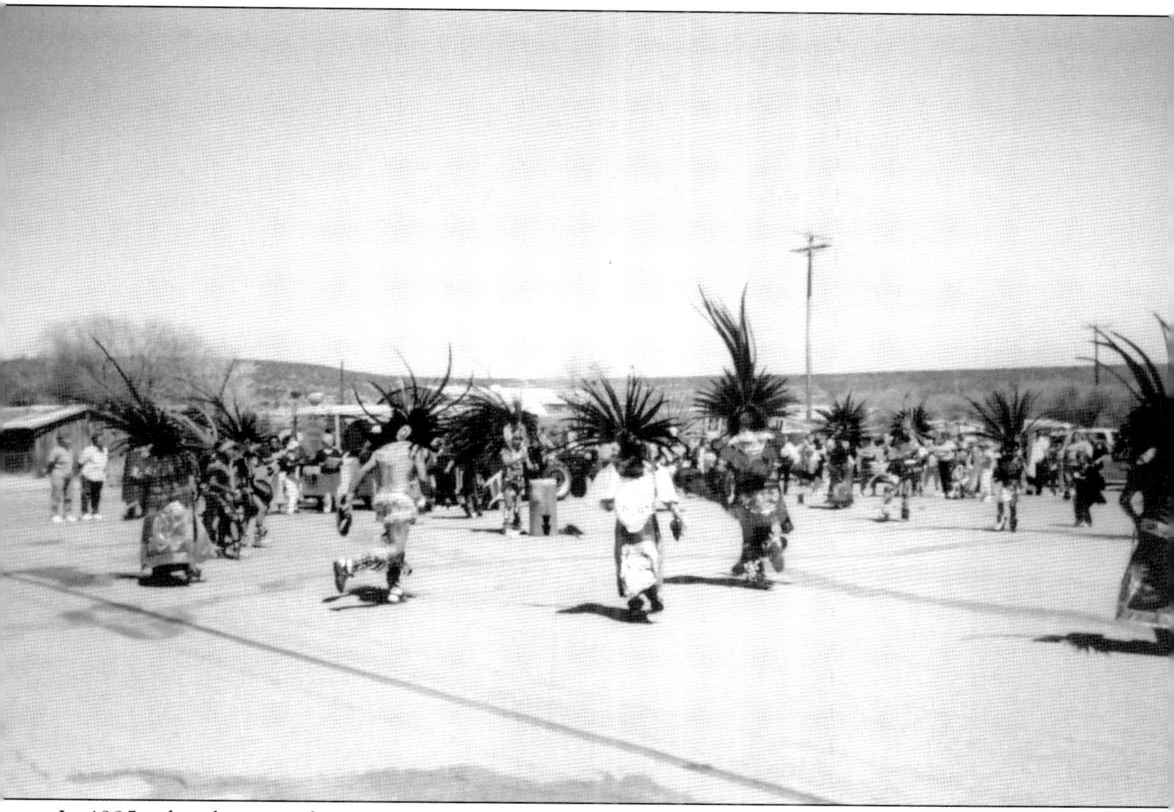

In 1995, a local group of Hispanic families realized that their children did not know much of the Hispanic culture and felt that it was up to them to provide programs that would depict their art and culture in a way that was entertaining and educational. La Fiesta de Colores is held the first weekend of May, not because of the Cinco de Mayo celebration but because it at the end of the spring semester of school and there were not many celebrations locally. In this photograph, Aztec dancers are leading a traditional procession. All of the churches are invited to carry their patron saint from the city park to the St. Teresa Park. There is an award for the best group and an award for the group that is dressed in traditional attire. (Courtesy of the Fiesta de Colores Committee.)

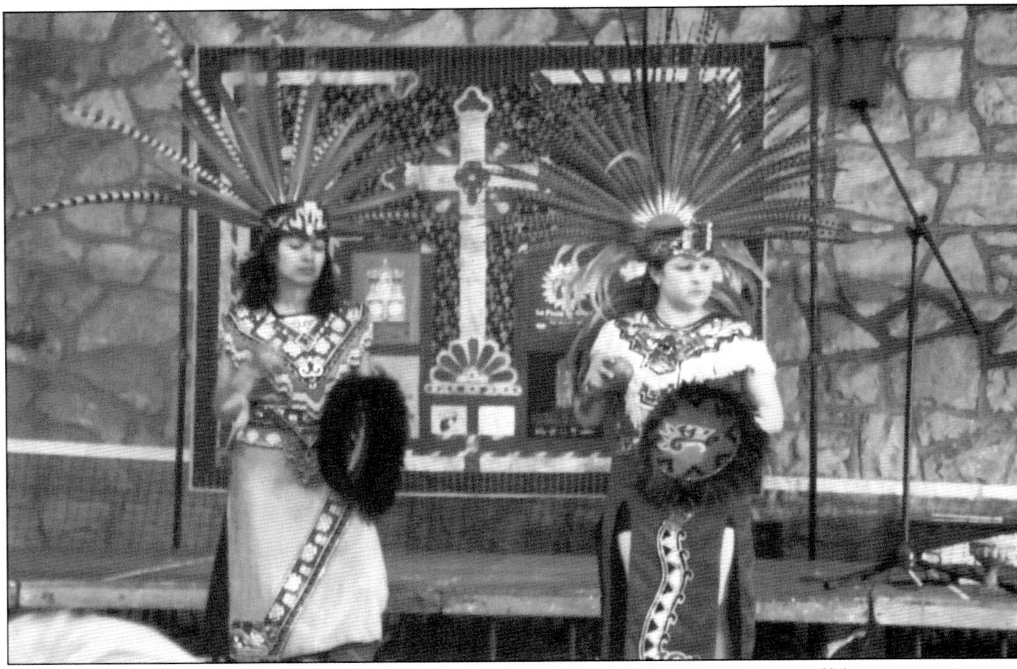

Aztec dancers are pictured in front of a quilt donated by Utha Russell, a well-known artist and quilter. The quilt features 10 T-shirts printed with best-of-show artwork from the first 10 years of the fiesta. The quilt is used to lead the traditional procession from the city park to the church park featuring the Aztec dancers. When the Spaniards came to New Mexico, they brought many Aztecs to work, and they introduced much of their food and culture to New Mexicans and the Native Americans. (Courtesy of the Fiesta de Colores Committee.)

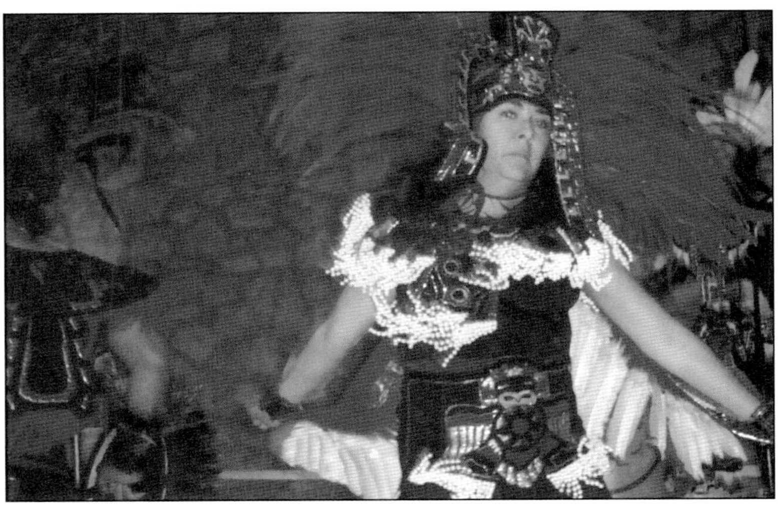

An artist displays her talents in one of 50 different types of traditional New Mexican arts and crafts at the fiesta. The artists are available for three days, and all demonstrate their particular techniques and share with the youth. (Courtesy of the Fiesta de Colores Committee.)

This display of unique art is by a New Mexican artist. There is a variety of art media on exhibit, including tin, wooden furniture, sculptures, animal horns, tapestry, *retablos* (paintings on decorated and carved frames), straw art (which is tedious), and jewelry, plus many more. Most of the artists are famous throughout the county, and some have art displayed at national museums. (Courtesy of the Fiesta de Colores Committee.)

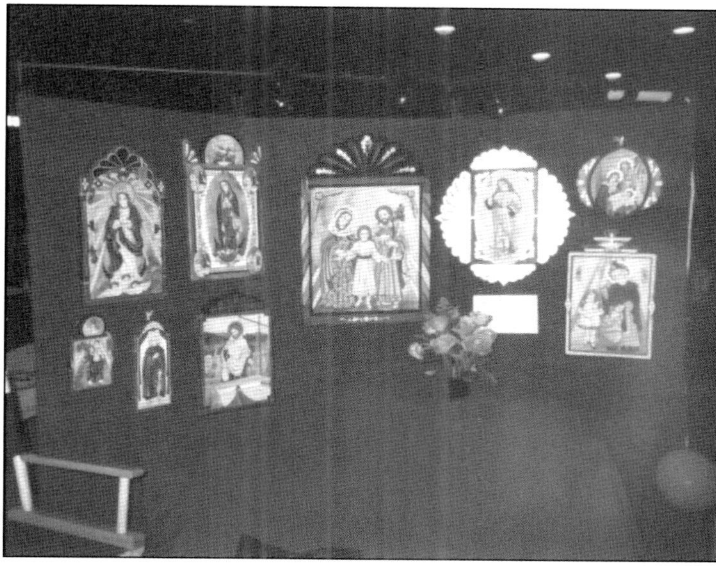

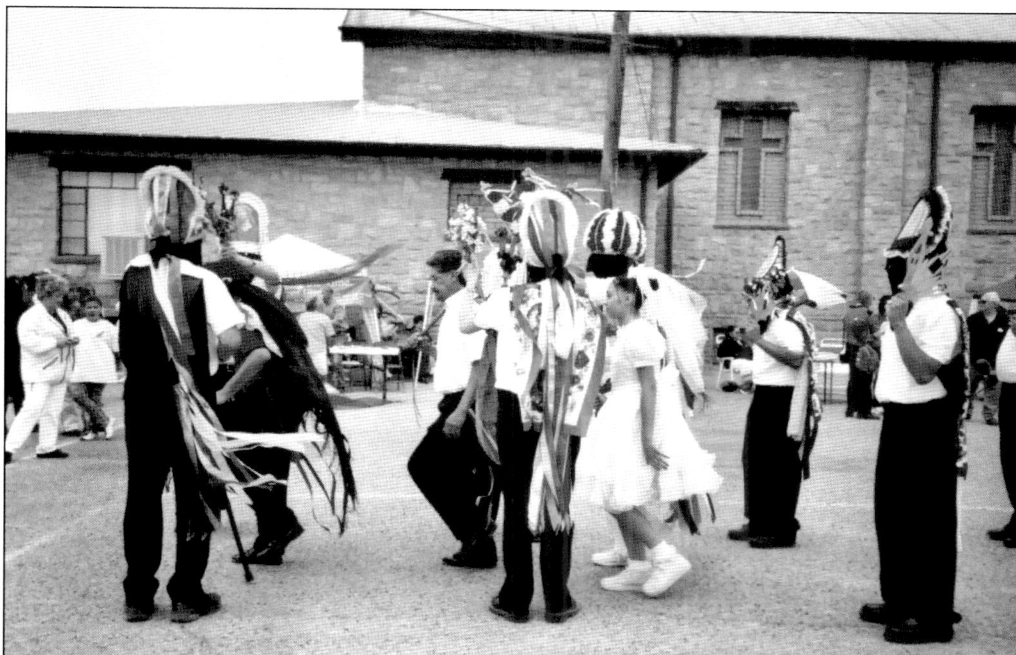

Matachines dancers are groups that can be found in many of the Hispanic villages and Indian pueblos. The dance was brought from Mexico by the native entourage that came with the Spaniards. The music and dance is unique and features a young girl called "Malinche," named for the Aztec maiden who interpreted for Cortez. The dance depicts good triumphing over evil—the young girl dressed in white as Malinche represents good, and usually an older man representing evil is masked with a bull with horns. The dance evolves with the bull being killed at its conclusion. The Spaniards found that the Indians were very visual learners, and so stories were taught by dance and music rather than the written word. (Courtesy of the Fiesta de Colores Committee.)

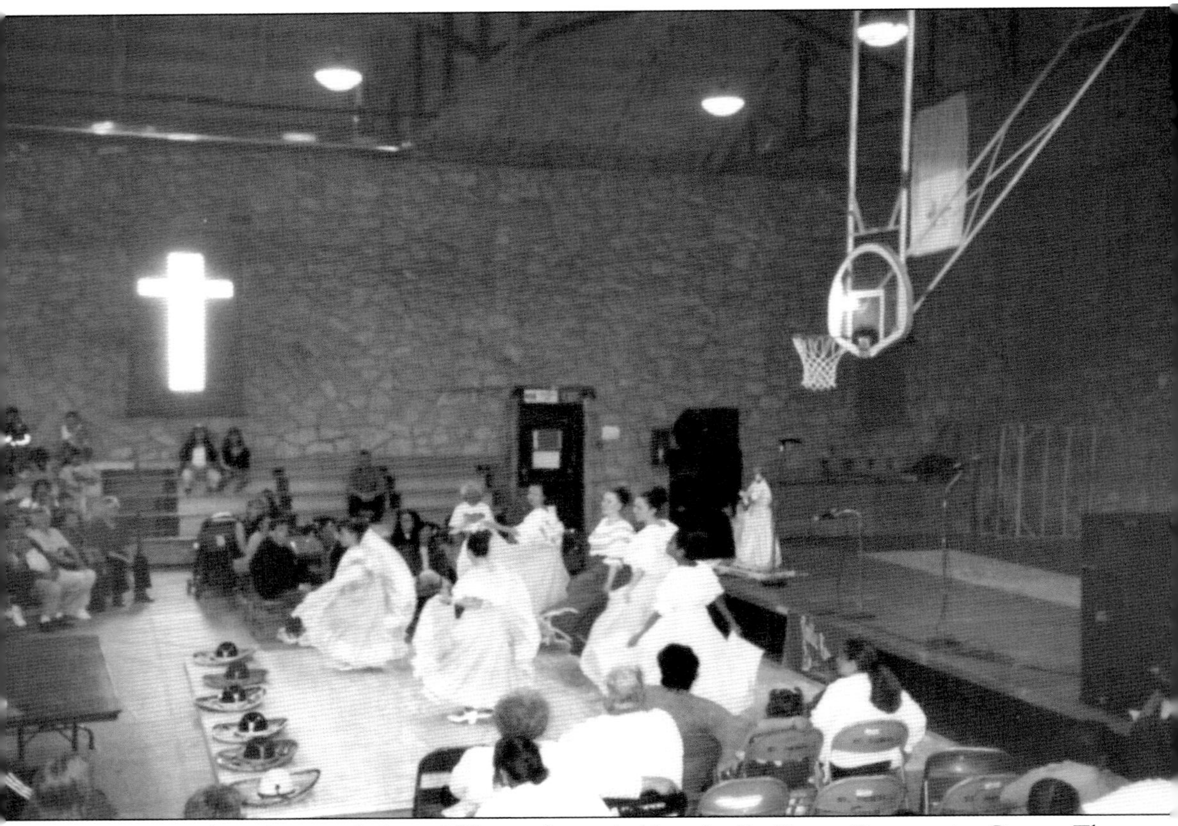

La Fiesta de Colores includes a *folklorico* dance, held at the St. Teresa Community Center. The fiesta features Spanish flamenco, Mexican folklorico, Aztec dancers, salsa, mariachi music, and Spanish guitar music. There is a matinee for children and a night show for everybody. The fiesta is free and non-alcoholic. (Courtesy of the Fiesta de Colores Committee.)

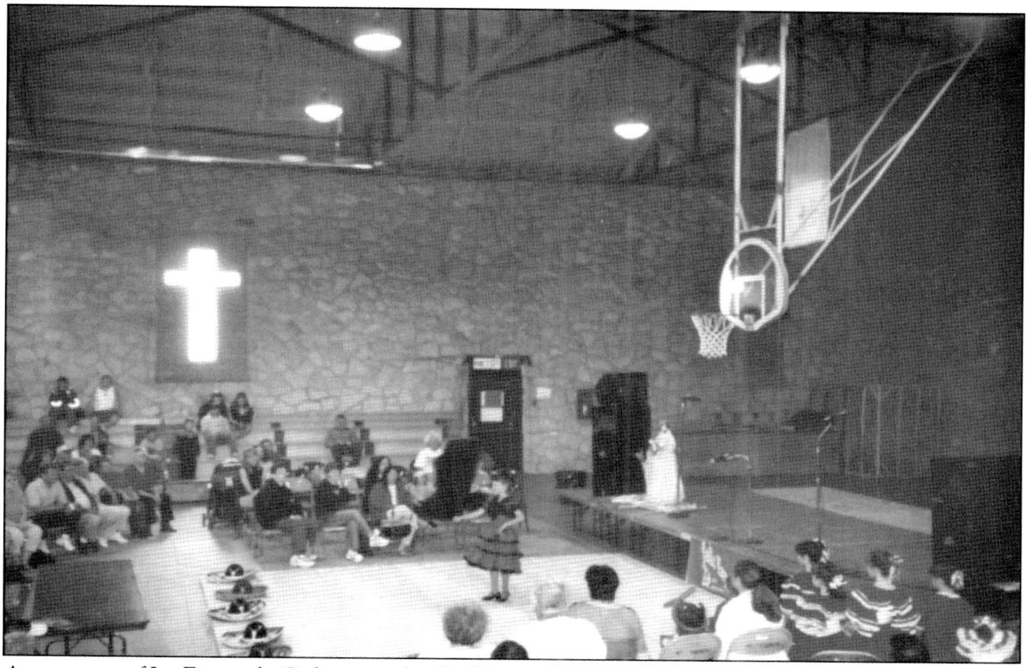

A program of La Fiesta de Colores at the St. Teresa Community Center features one of the many dance groups. The matinee for the children usually features children dancers when available. (Courtesy of the Fiesta de Colores Committee.)

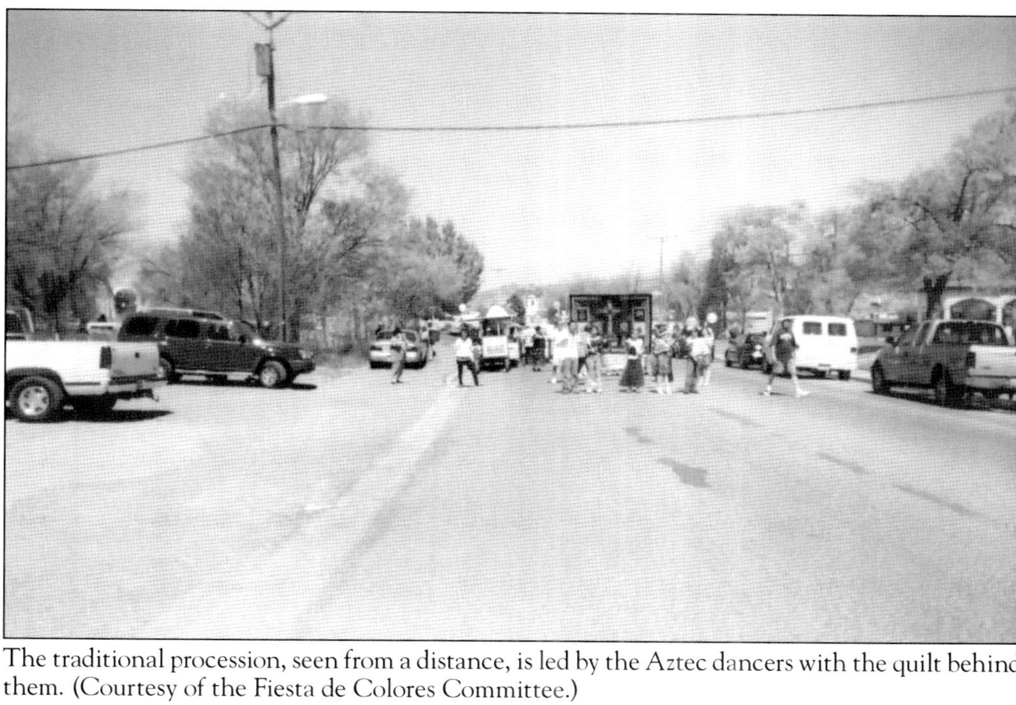

The traditional procession, seen from a distance, is led by the Aztec dancers with the quilt behind them. (Courtesy of the Fiesta de Colores Committee.)

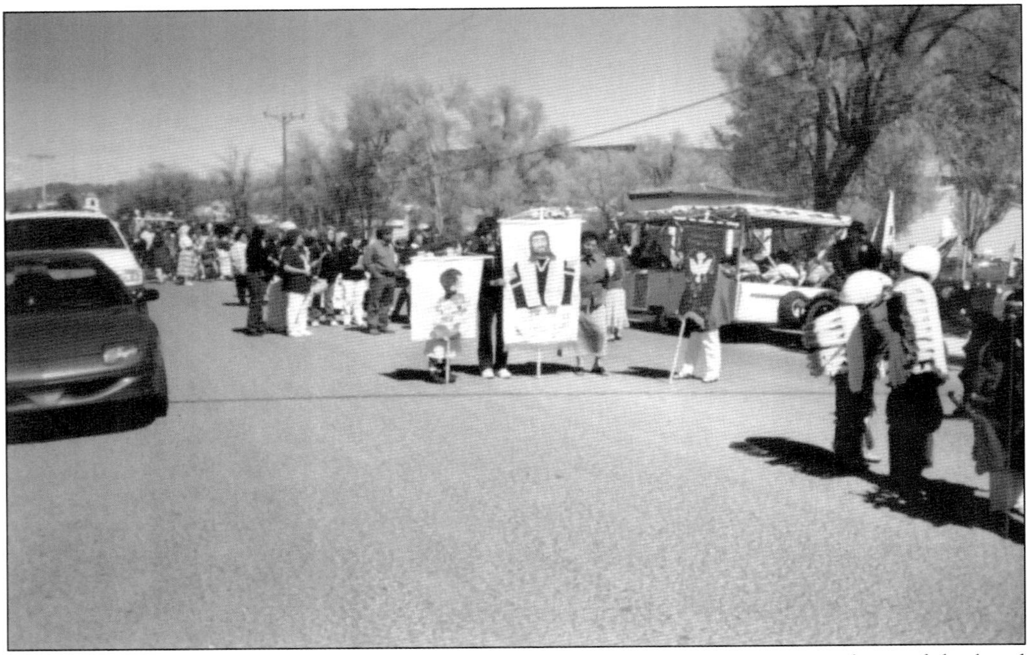

Part of the traditional procession is pictured here, with a banner representing of one of the local churches. (Courtesy of the Fiesta de Colores Committee.)

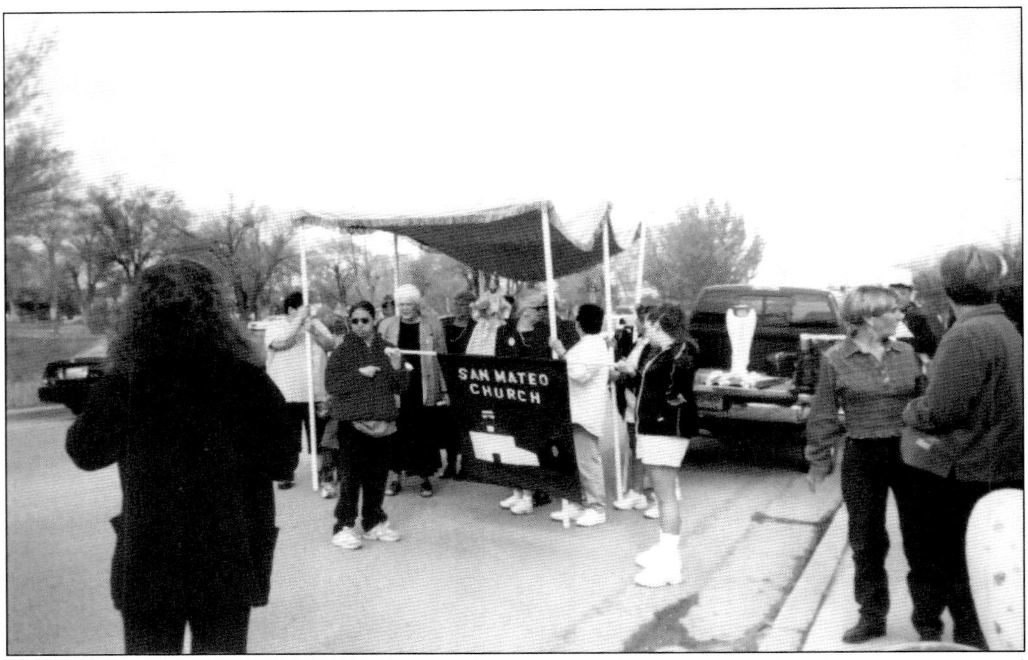

Another church displays its patron saint at the traditional procession. Churches are encouraged to bring musical groups to march and play at the procession. Pets are also invited to take part in the ceremony. (Courtesy of the Fiesta de Colores Committee.)

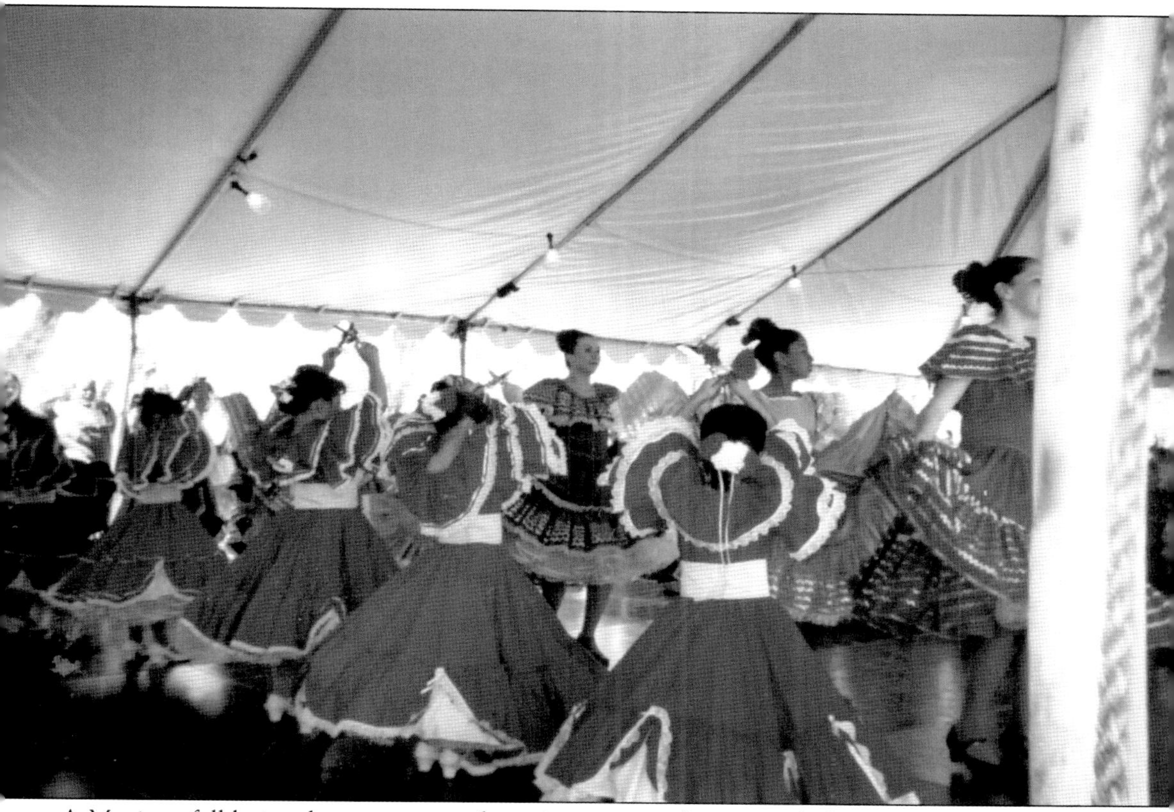

A Mexican folklorico dance group performs in a tent at the city park during the beginning of the fiesta, before moving to the St. Teresa Community Center. While the park was an excellent venue, the weather was too fickle to trust for such excellent entertainment. (Courtesy of the Fiesta de Colores Committee.)

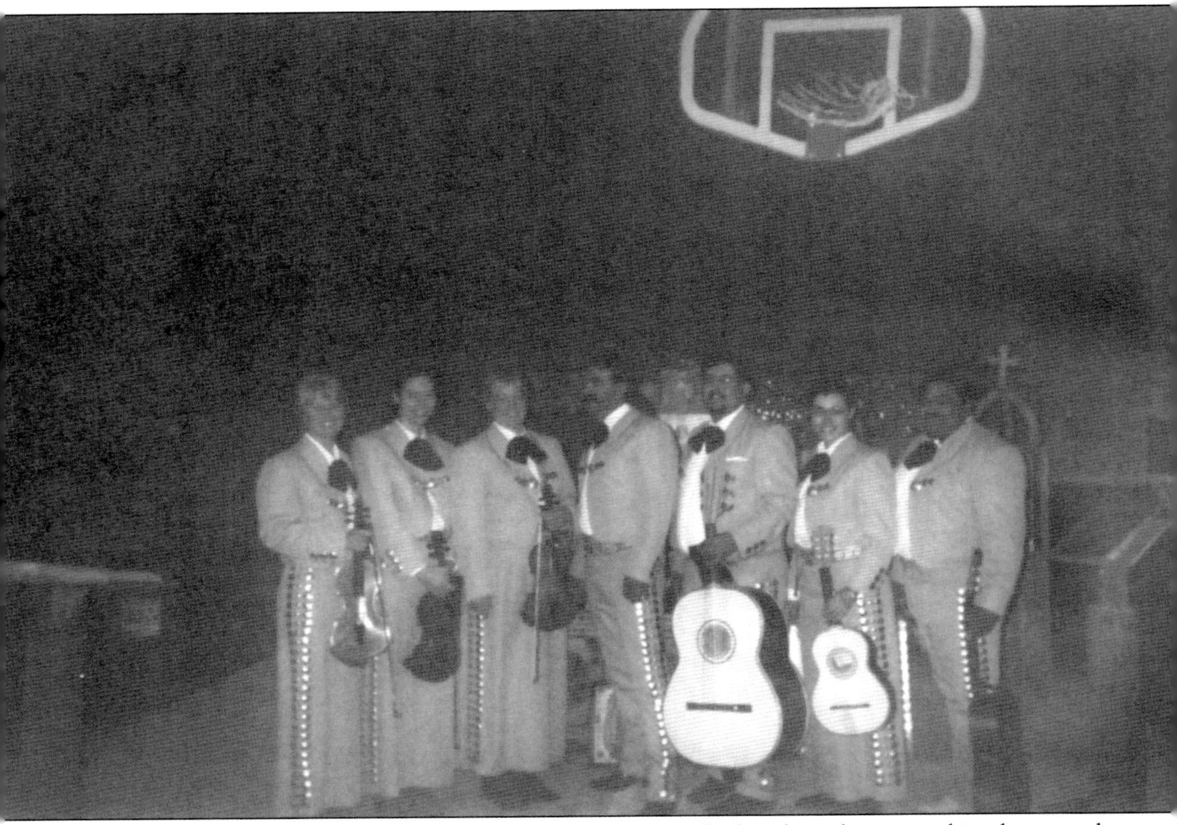

The fiesta ends with a mariachi mass featuring a mariachi band, as shown in this photograph. The local bishop has adopted the fiesta, and when available, he will officiate at the mariachi mass. He has also established a Bishop's Award for an outstanding artist juried by the bishop. (Courtesy of the Fiesta de Colores Committee.)

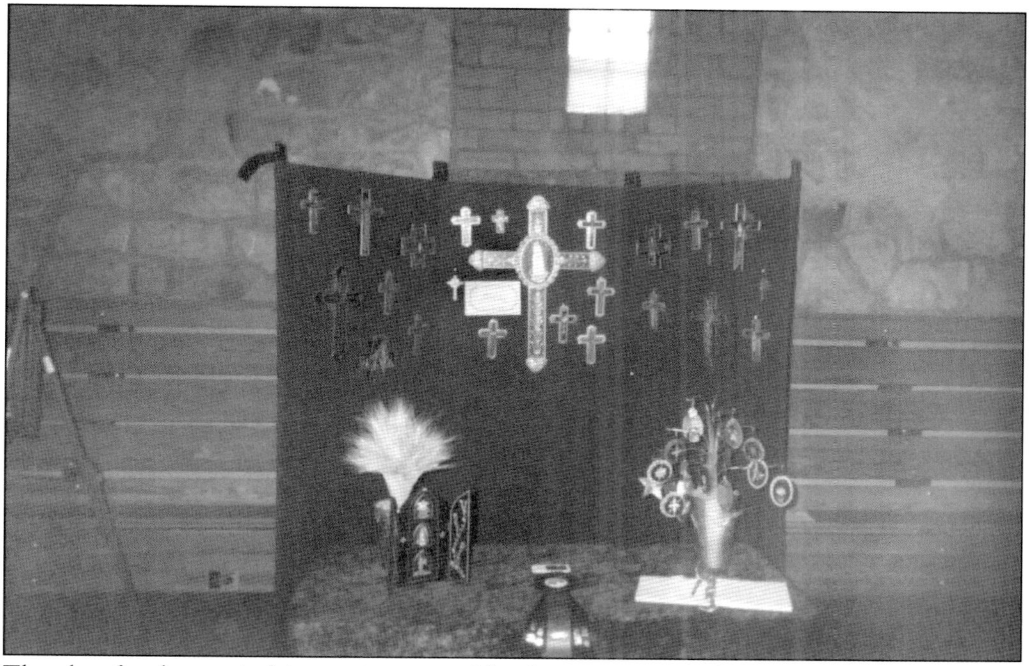

The altar for the mariachi mass is arranged by the artists using their art. Each of the 50-plus artists set up altar and, using the quilt as a backdrop, organize a different artistic altar every year. (Courtesy of the Fiesta de Colores Committee.)

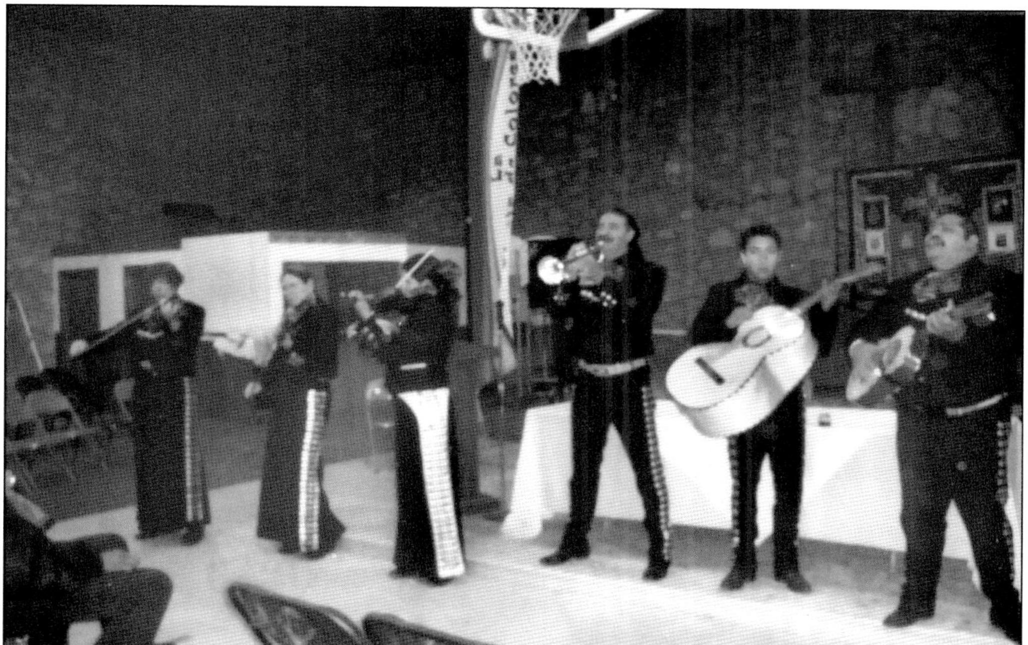

The mariachi band performs a concert after the mass has been completed. The community center reaches its capacity of local and visiting devotees. (Courtesy of the Fiesta de Colores Committee.)

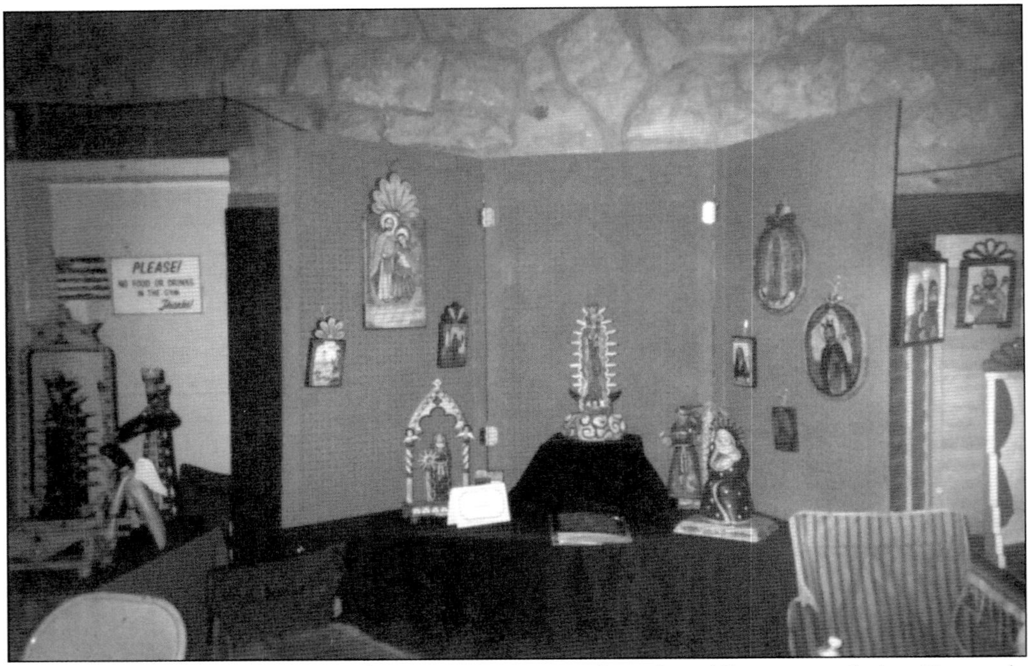

A display of Hispanic art utilizes many types of media. (Courtesy of the Fiesta de Colores Committee.)

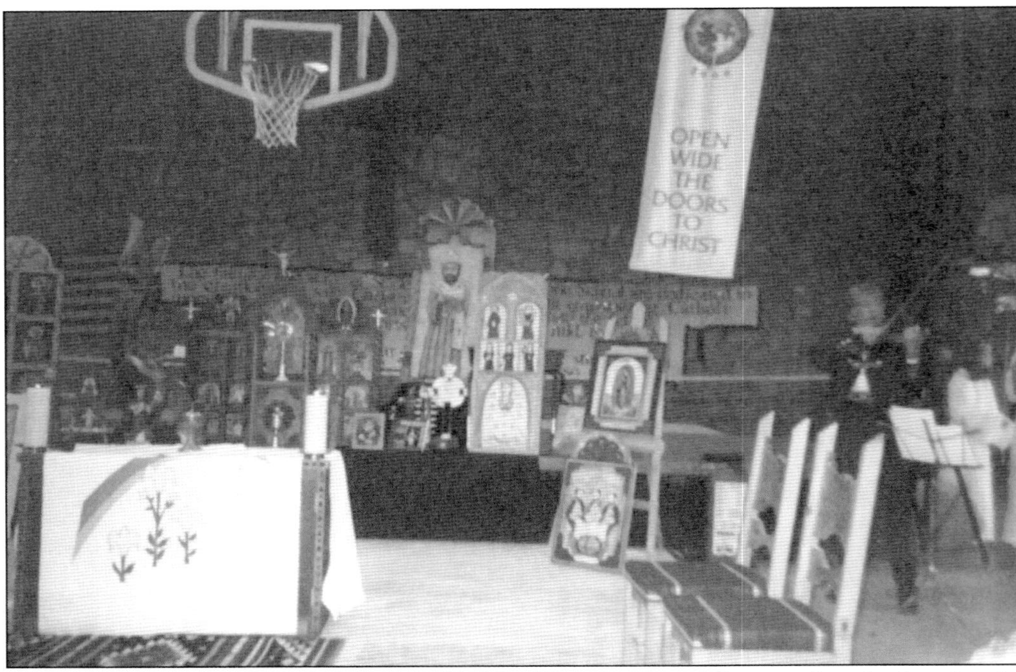

The altar is seen from the side. It is assembled by the artists using all types of art displayed at the Hispanic Art Show. (Courtesy of the Fiesta de Colores Committee.)

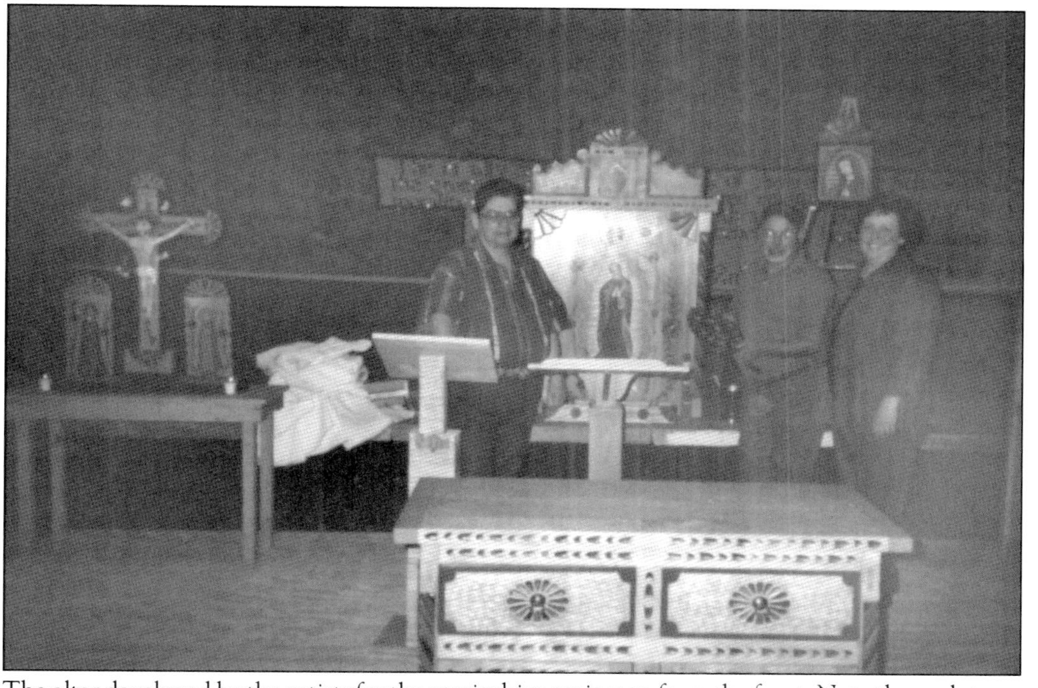
The altar developed by the artists for the mariachi mass is seen from the front. Note the sculptures decorating the altar. (Courtesy of the Fiesta de Colores Committee.)

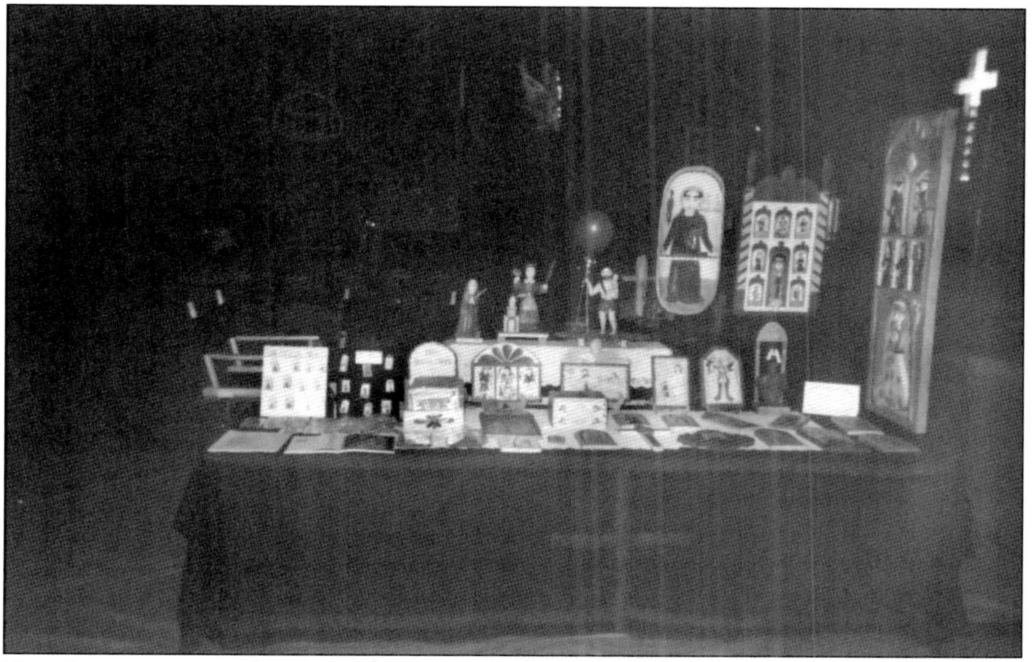
Note the unique types of art that make up the altar as if it was planned in advance. The altar is set up spontaneously an hour in advance of the mass. (Courtesy of the Fiesta de Colores Committee.)

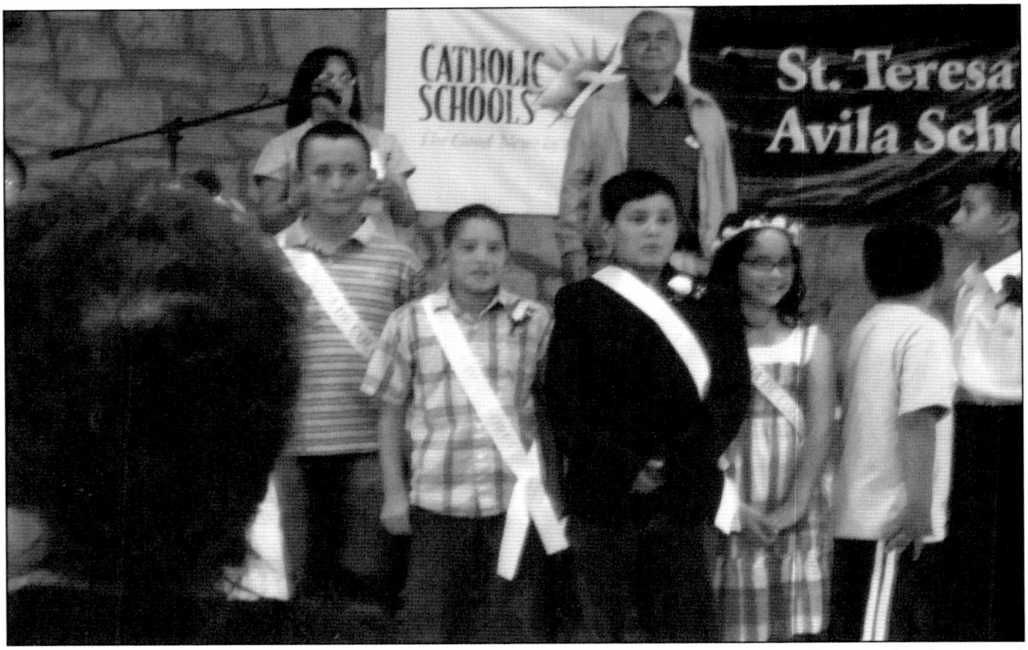

The king and queen contest is sponsored by the schools in honor of the fiesta. The king and queen are selected from essays or speeches that are based on some aspect of Hispanic culture. (Courtesy of the Fiesta de Colores Committee.)

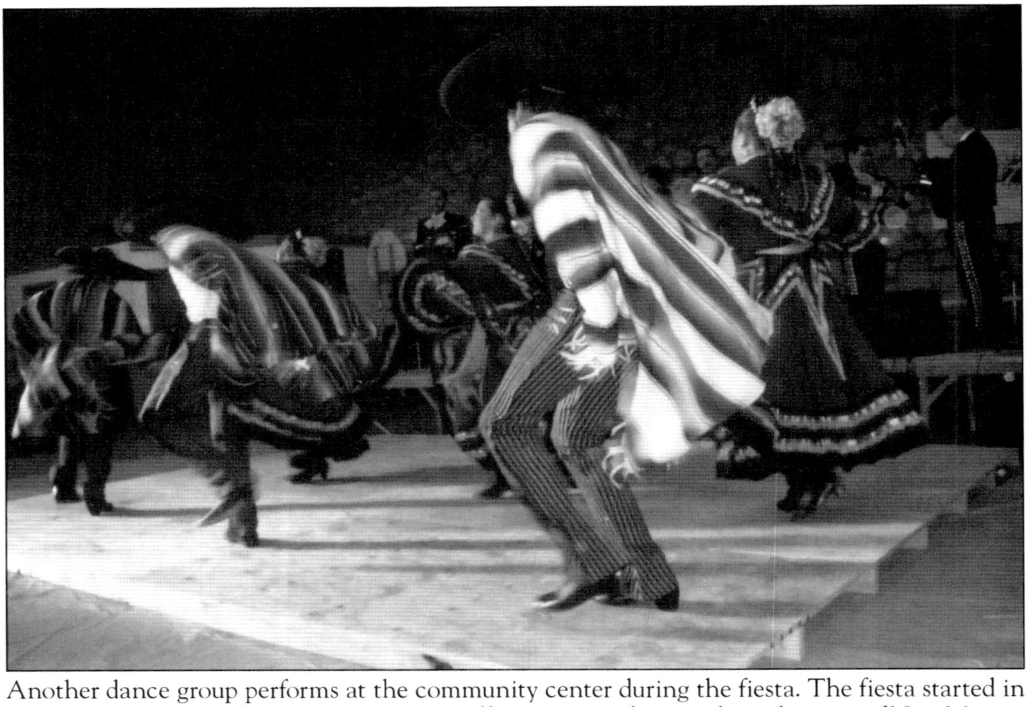

Another dance group performs at the community center during the fiesta. The fiesta started in 1995, and every year, there is an attempt to offer a variety of groups from the state of New Mexico and from Mexico. (Courtesy of the Fiesta de Colores Committee.)

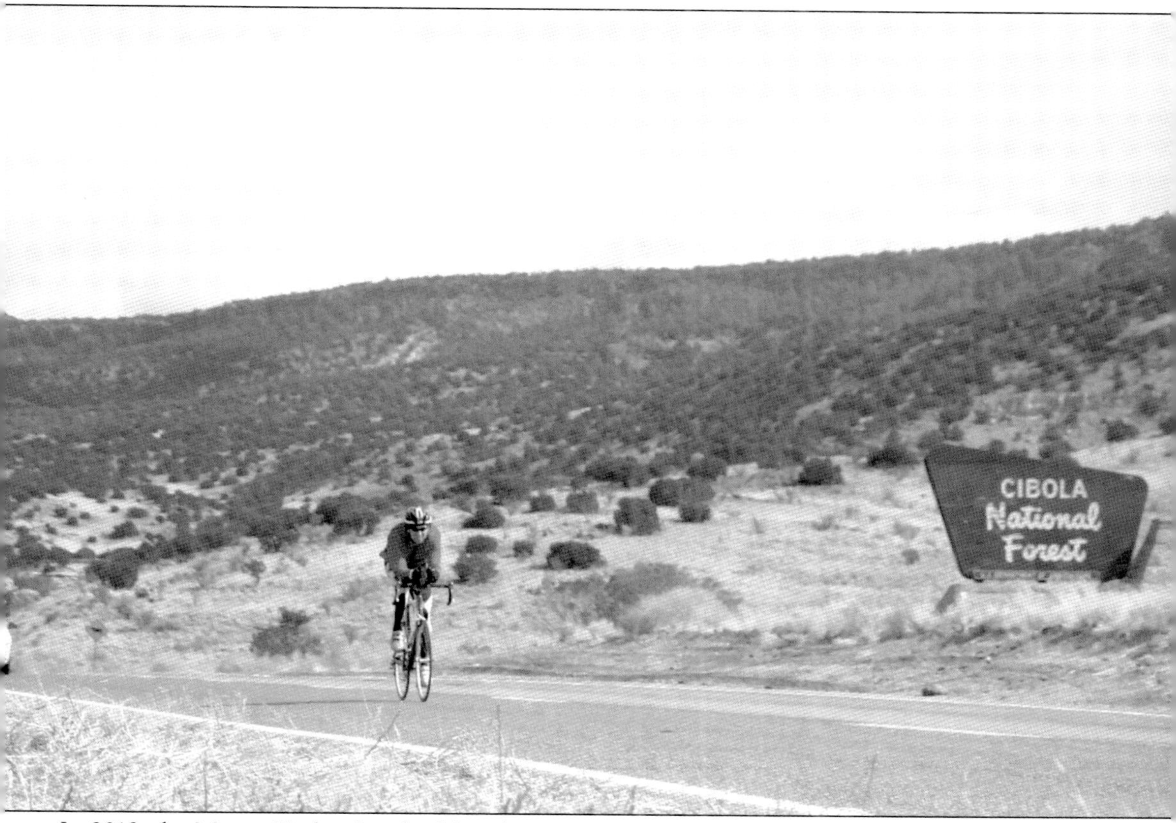

In 2013, the Mount Taylor Quadrathlon, known as the "Quad," celebrated its 30th anniversary. The Quad starts with a 13-mile bike ride from Grants City Hall at an elevation of 6,500 feet, followed by a five-mile run on a dirt road, then a two-mile, 1,200-foot cross-country ski climb, and finally a one-mile, 600-foot snowshoe slog to the top of an 11,301-foot peak before reversing it back to the city hall. This is a photograph of the first-place finisher. (Courtesy of the Mount Taylor Quadrathlon Committee, Terry Fletcher.)

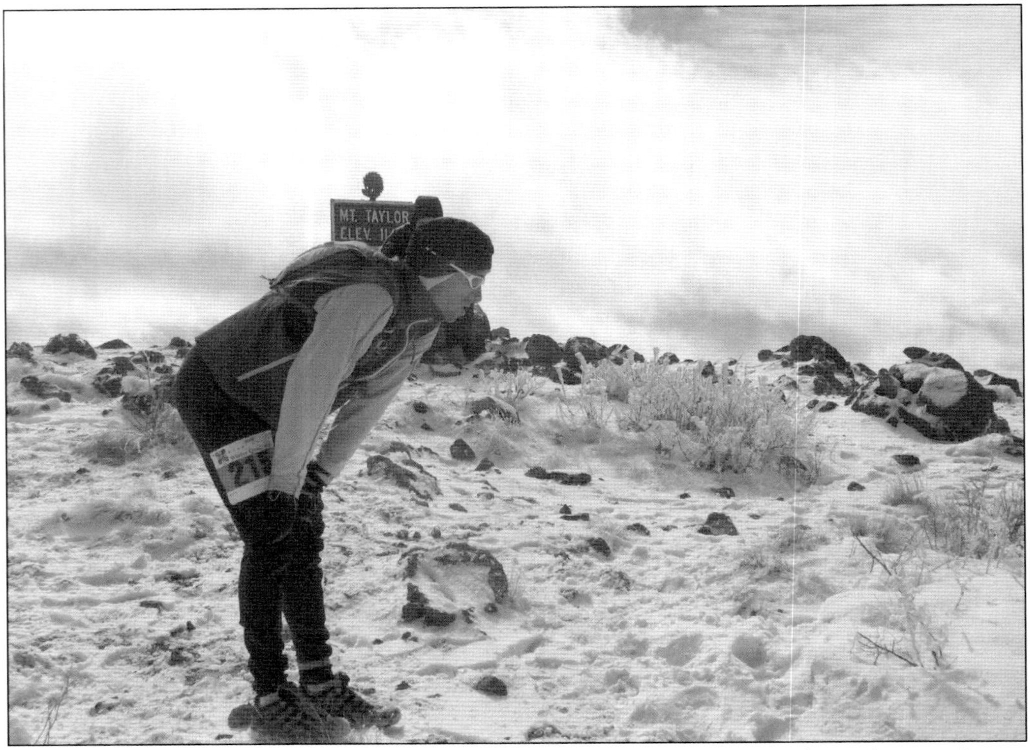

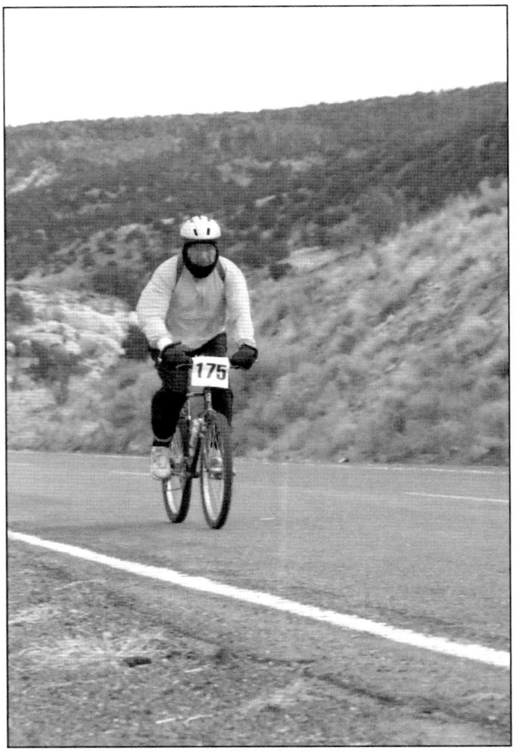

This is a contestant reaching the top of Mount Taylor. He is catching his breath after reaching the 11,301-foot height from the 6,500-foot start. (Courtesy of the Mount Taylor Quadrathlon Committee, Terry Fletcher.)

A contestant of the Quad pedals his bicycle on the first leg of the race, headed toward the top of Mount Taylor. The Quad originally included about 30 contestants and has had as many as 600 athletes at some of the events, with an average of 400. (Courtesy of the Mount Taylor Quadrathlon Committee, Terry Fletcher.)

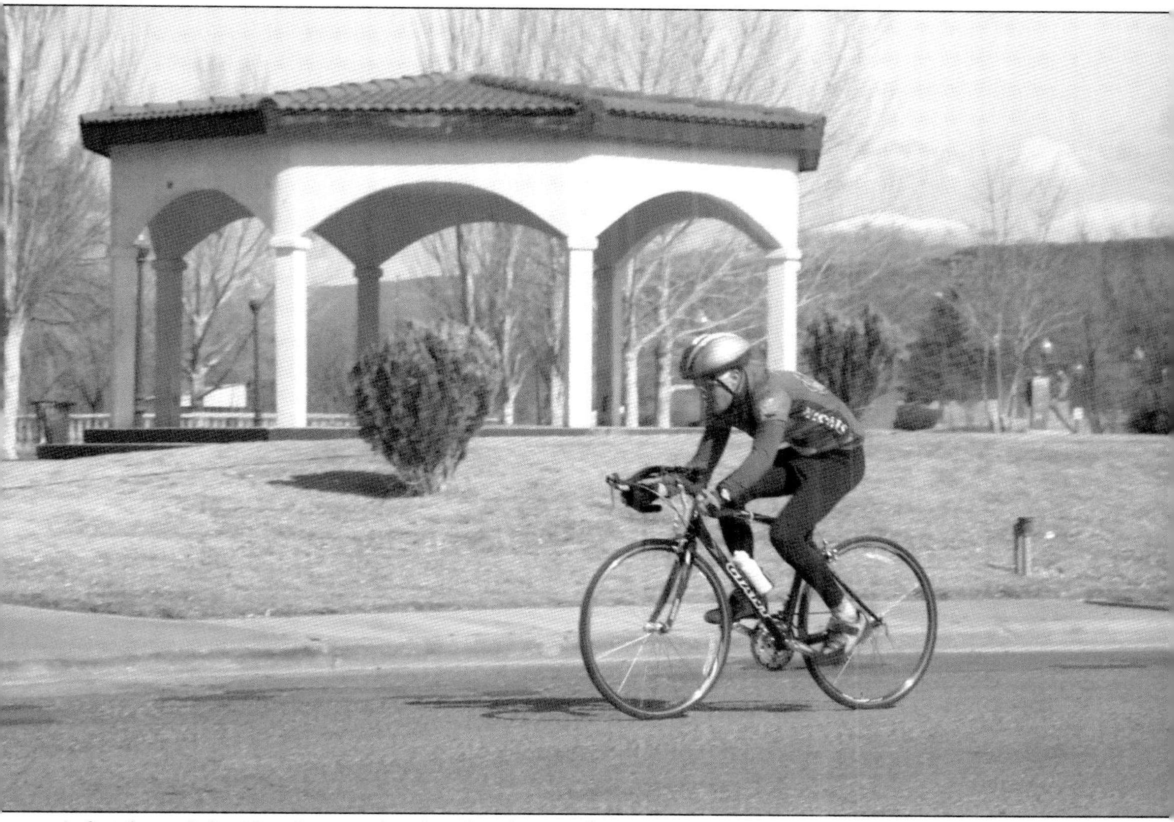

A finisher of the Quad passes by the Gazebo on the Riverside Park, a block away from the city hall and the finish line. Hundreds of athletes start the competition together, and they file back one by one following a lonely winner. (Courtesy of the Mount Taylor Quadrathlon Committee, Terry Fletcher.)

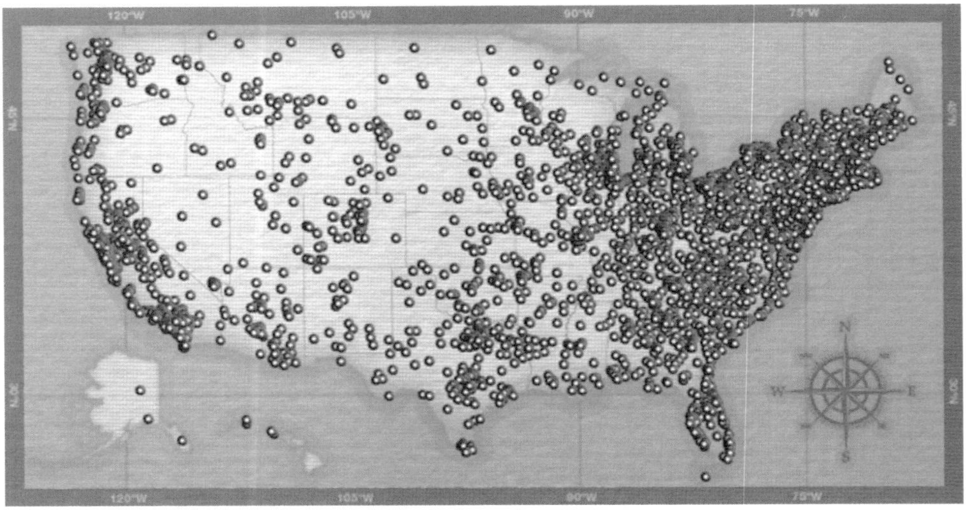